AEI'S AT THE POLLS STUDIES

The American Enterprise Institute
has initiated this series in order to promote
an understanding of the electoral process as it functions in
democracies around the world. The series will include studies
of at least two national elections in more than twenty countries
on five continents, by scholars from the United States and
abroad who are recognized as experts in their field.
More information on the titles in this series can
be found at the back of this book.

India
at the Polls,
1980

A Study of the
Parliamentary Elections

Myron Weiner

American Enterprise Institute for Public Policy Research
Washington and London

Myron Weiner is Ford Professor of Political Science and a senior staff member of the Center for International Studies at the Massachusetts Institute of Technology. Among his books are *India at the Polls: The Parliamentary Elections of 1977, Sons of the Soil: Migration and Ethnic Conflict in India,* and, with Mary Fainsod Katzenstein, *India's Preferential Policies: Migrants, the Middle Classes, and Ethnic Equality.*

Library of Congress Cataloging in Publication Data

Weiner, Myron.
    India at the polls, 1980.

    (AEI studies; 340)
    Includes index.
    1. Elections—India. 2. India—Politics and government—1947–   . I. Title. II. Series.
JQ292.W43   320.954'052   81-19064
ISBN 0-8447-3468-3   AACR2
ISBN 0-8447-3467-5 (pbk.)

AEI Studies 340

Printed in the United States of America

Contents

Acknowledgments

I am grateful to the American Enterprise Institute for funding my trip to India and for inviting me once again to write a volume on India's parliamentary elections; to many friends in Bombay, Calcutta, Patna, Lucknow, and Delhi who made local arrangements for me; to my research assistant in India, Aditya Bhattacharjea, for collecting materials for this study; to my research assistant in Cambridge, Roberta Ornstein, who helped prepare materials for the statistical analyses; to Professors Paul Brass, John O. Field, Harold Gould, Robert L. Hardgrave, Jr., and Paul Wallace for their editorial suggestions and thoughtful comments; to the Center for International Studies at M.I.T. for its administrative assistance; to the staff of DCM Data Products of New Delhi for providing computerized election data and some of the statistical tables; and to the staffs of the Press Information Bureau and the Election Commission of the Government of India for their cooperation.

M.W.

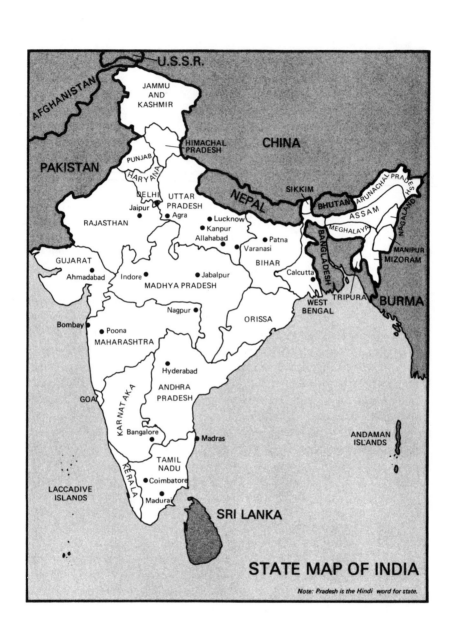

STATE MAP OF INDIA

Note: Pradesh is the Hindi word for state.

1

The Rise and Fall of the Janata Party

Introduction

The reelection of Indira Gandhi as India's prime minister in the parliamentary elections of January 1980, following her massive defeat by the Janata party in 1977, meant more than the electoral swings often experienced by democratic countries. For in the eyes of much of the world, Mrs. Gandhi's defeat in 1977 had represented a victory of democracy over authoritarianism when a majority of the electorate turned against a government that had declared a national emergency, censored the press, arrested opponents of the government, banned many political organizations, suspended elections, imposed compulsory sterilization, and demolished the homes of many urban slum dwellers. The victory in 1980 of Mrs. Gandhi's Congress party—with 84 million votes, nearly 20 million more than in 1977 and a whopping 46.7 million more than the Janata party—aroused concern both within and outside India that authoritarianism was on its way back. Many observers asked whether the Indian electorate in 1977 had really voted against authoritarianism or had simply protested against the "excesses" committed by the regime. The 1980 elections also raised the question whether the breakup of the Janata party would mean a weak opposition, unable to exercise any restraint upon a government that might be tempted once again to extend its authority.

Paradoxically, the victory of Mrs. Gandhi's Congress party also led many to wonder whether India would now have a stable government. The Congress party that won in 1980 was not the Congress party that had governed India in the 1950s and 1960s, or even the early 1970s. The party was organizationally weak and the electoral victory was primarily Mrs. Gandhi's rather than the party's. Moreover, with the death shortly after the elections of Mrs. Gandhi's

1

son, Sanjay Gandhi, whom many had regarded as her probable successor, India appeared to have a government excessively dependent on the well-being of a single person. Was it possible that even with nearly two-thirds of Parliament under its control, the Congress government might still prove unstable? Moreover, faced with an organizationally weak Congress party and perhaps weak Congress-run state governments, would Mrs. Gandhi attempt to centralize and consolidate her political power by enlarging the powers of the state apparatus?

The 1980 parliamentary elections also raised new questions about the Indian electorate. Was it as volatile as the election results seemed to suggest? There were, as we shall see, major shifts in the voting patterns of India's scheduled castes, tribals,[1] and Muslims. But perhaps the most dramatic finding, based upon a comparison of the 1980 election with three previous elections, is that even in a country as extraordinarily diverse as India, there are national trends in electoral shifts that cut across regions and social categories.

Are new forces at work? A more politicized peasantry? More demanding scheduled castes, tribes, Muslims, and other "minority" groups? Has partisan attachment diminished? Is the country more (or less) politicized, as indicated by changes in electoral participation? Or do we see instead substantial continuities in electoral behavior in a country in which it is the parties and political leaders who are floundering, not the electorate?

A close comparison of the 1980 parliamentary elections with earlier elections may suggest that, while there are shifts in the behavior of the electorate, there is in fact less electoral volatility than meets the eye. Perhaps it is the weakness of the parties, their organizational fragility, and above all the inability of India's political elite to forge reasonably enduring relationships that now threatens to erode the Indian political system.

This analysis, then, of the 1980 parliamentary elections focuses on the changing character of India's political parties as well as the electorate. The disarray of the one and the stability of the other are the subjects of this book.

---

[1] Ex-untouchables or harijans are officially called scheduled castes, and tribals are officially called scheduled tribes, "scheduled" because they are registered on a government list or schedule. Members of tribes and castes listed on the schedule are entitled to various government benefits, including quotas for admission to college and civil service jobs (known as reservations) and special representation in elective bodies.

The Two Phases of Congress, 1947–1969, 1969–1977

The story of the rise and fall of Janata must begin with an account of the Congress party and how it has changed. The Congress party that governed India from 1947 until its split in 1969 was a very different party from the one in power from 1969 until its defeat in 1977.

For thirty years the Congress party was the overwhelmingly dominant political force in Indian politics. It won each of the five successive national parliamentary elections and an overwhelming majority of the elections to the state governments. From the first general election of 1952 through the election of 1971 Congress won from 54 percent to 73 percent of the seats in the Lok Sabha, with 40.7 percent to 47.8 percent of the popular vote.[2]

Unlike most former nationalist movements, Congress played a critical role in sustaining a relatively open, democratic, participatory political system—and a stable government. While many other postindependence governments in the third world fell under the control of one-party authoritarian regimes, praetorian or patrimonial rulers, or under Communist domination, India continued to have a government chosen in free competitive elections. This was not because India differed from other developing countries in its level of development, its colonial experience, or its traditional social order, but because of the kind of party Congress was and its success in winning electoral support.

From the first election of 1952 through the mid-1960s, Congress successfully attracted support from a wide range of local political elites, who were able to get their voters to support Congress candidates. Congress could count among its supporters leaders of peasant-proprietor communities, much of the expanding urban middle classes, leaders of the ex-untouchable castes, the Muslims, the larger business community, and a variety of castes and tribal, linguistic, and religious groups who believed that their interests could best be served by working through the Congress party.

Old-fashioned patronage was an important incentive in attracting individuals and groups to the party. Contracts, licenses, permits, jobs, and, within the government, promotions and transfers were allocated by bureaucratic officials, and the various factions influencing

[2] India's constitution provides for a parliament with a popularly elected lower house (the Lok Sabha) and an upper house (the Rajya Sabha) elected by members of the state legislative assemblies. Under India's federal system there are twenty-two states, each with an elected legislative assembly, and nine Union territories, administered by the central government (sometimes called the Union).

the party at the local and state levels had a powerful voice in how these allocations were made. There was a considerable amount of decentralization, so elected officials in state and local governments often had direct control over the way patronage was allocated. Factions, sometimes organized by a single caste, tribe, or religious group, but very often cutting across these social categories, fought for power within the Congress party in order to win seats in local bodies, legislative assemblies, and Parliament.

The party operated on the organizational principle that local elites seeking to mobilize their supporters would contest for power within the party at the village and *taluka* (an administrative unit smaller than a district) level. The winners (and losers) would battle once again for control over the district Congress committees, and still again for the *pradesh* (state) Congress committees. Those who lost one round of party elections might try in another. Losers might desert the party in elections to the legislative assembly and to Parliament but then return to the party to fight once more. Out of this process—inchoate, interminable, and opportunistic—emerged men who knew how to build coalitions within the party, influence the local bureaucracy, use the patronage of the state to maximize their support, and bargain with the central authorities for resources. The best of them also knew how to run state governments.

One result was the emergence of multiple power centers within the party. Prime Minister Jawaharlal Nehru dominated the center, but Congress party bosses flourished in the states. Among the most powerful figures in the party in the 1950s and 1960s were Atulya Ghosh and B. C. Roy in West Bengal, Sanjiva Reddy and Brahmananda Reddy in Andhra, S. Nijalingappa in Karnataka, Mohanlal Sukhadia in Rajasthan, K. Kamaraj in Madras, Kairon in the Punjab, and C. B. Gupta in Uttar Pradesh—men who were either presidents of their state Congress parties or chief ministers. These men built electoral coalitions within their states. They also provided electoral support for the national Congress party and thereby helped to create a stable national center. In return they were given financial resources from the center and the freedom to exercise power within their domain.

There was nothing inevitable about this institutional development. Indians might explain it as the result of the pluralism of Hinduism, with its traditions of diversity and tolerance, or of a nationalist movement that had existed since 1884 and grown deep roots under the leadership of Mahatma Gandhi and Jawaharlal Nehru. But these advantages would have been of little importance if, for example, the Hindu-Muslim bloodshed that accompanied the partition of India and Pakistan in 1947 had led the great powers to intervene; or if the conflict between Nehru as prime minister and Vallabhbhai Patel as party leader had split Congress in 1950; or if Congress had won, say, only 38 percent instead of 45 percent of the popular vote in the first parliamentary elections in 1952 and only been able to govern through a coalition; or if Nehru had responded to the demand for the reorganization of the states along linguistic lines in the mid–1950s by calling out the army instead of agreeing to restructure state boundaries. In other emerging nations, foreign intervention, intra-elite conflict, a military response to regional demands, or shifts in the electorate have too often brought an end to new and fragile democratic systems. India has managed, so far, to avoid all these pitfalls.

The price India paid for Congress party dominance, according to critics on the left, was that socially and economically dominant social strata were able, both locally and nationally, to prevent any effective redistribution of wealth and income. This elite, it was argued, permitted only enough land reform to take wealth from the large *zamindars,* or landlords; once they had benefited from this reform, the emerging rural classes (left critics called them kulaks while supporters called them peasant proprietors and farmers) prevented any further land redistribution. The Congress party also facilitated the development of a system of state capitalism that protected the large business classes from international competition. The Congress party, the left critics continue, was responsive to the demands of those who had or were acquiring local power and wealth, to the neglect of the populous low-income groups in both the cities and the countryside.

Conservative critics of Congress noted that virtually all factions within the government shared a dislike for the use of the market and were committed to state control over the private sector while using state controls to protect the public sector, and that the state put a disproportionate share of resources into industrial rather than agrarian development. The policy makers, moreover, placed excessive emphasis on an import substitution policy that encouraged inefficient noncompetitive industries while discouraging the growth of export-oriented industries. More generally, say the conservative critics, the expansion of the bureaucratic state, with its large public sector, substantial regulations, and distrust of the market, inhibited the creative impulse of private initiative. The result, so they conclude, is that India's economic growth has been below that of many developing countries in spite of its considerable resource potential, large business community, skilled manpower, and stable political system.

5

Charles E. Lindblom summarized the arguments of the critics on both sides when he wrote that "India's difficulties in economic development are in part the consequences of her leaders' inability to understand that growth requires growth mechanisms; if not the market, which Indian policy cripples, then the authority of government, which India has never chosen to mobilize."[3] The Congress party did in truth prove a weak instrument for bringing about social and economic transformation, though one should not underestimate the role of the Congress government in the 1950s and 1960s in creating an industrial infrastructure, an expanded educational system, a large modern sector, and a participatory political environment.

By the mid-1960s it was apparent that the Congress party was losing support from the classes that had prospered during the early years of its rule. The decline was a slow one. From a peak of electoral popularity in 1957, when Congress won nearly 48 percent of the vote (and three-fourths of the seats in Parliament), the party dropped below 45 percent in 1962, then to less than 41 percent in 1967. In the 1967 elections Congress emerged with a narrow majority of seats in Parliament. Growing unemployment among graduates of the universities combined with inflation to disillusion much of the urban middle class. Peasant proprietors were unnerved by Congress's proposals for land redistribution and were critical of the government's ineffectiveness in delivering services to rural areas and providing adequate price supports and sufficient credit. The government was losing support from lower-income groups. Pro-Hindu right-wing parties were growing in the North and regional nationalist parties in the South.

The state party bosses began to lose their electoral hold. Nehru was dead by 1966, replaced briefly by Prime Minister Lal Bahadur Shastri, then by Nehru's daughter Indira Gandhi. In the elections of 1967, Congress won only 54 percent of the seats in the national Parliament (compared with 73 percent in the three previous elections) and lost many of the state assembly elections to a variety of opposition parties. Fragile coalition governments took power in several states, and it looked as if the center itself would not remain for long under the exclusive control of the Congress party. Mrs. Gandhi had not yet shown her capacity to become a popular leader, or the skill to bring together diverse interests and factions within the party. The "old" Congress party, the party of patronage, party bosses, multiple power centers, consensual leaders and, in the Indian context, ideologically centrist politics, seemed to be coming to an end.

[3] Charles E. Lindblom, *Politics and Markets: The World's Political-Economic Systems* (New York: Basic Books, 1977), p. 6.

Congress entered a new phase after 1969, following an intense battle among many of the state party bosses (popularly known in India as the syndicate), and Mrs. Gandhi feared, probably correctly, that the party bosses might try to choose a new national leader. The party split, with most of the state leaders forming their own party, known as Congress (O), while Mrs. Gandhi led a Congress party that retained the support of most of the Congress members of Parliament. Mrs. Gandhi then launched a populist campaign against "big" business, the former ruling princes or ex-maharajas, and the syndicate, and for *garibi hatao*, the abolition of poverty. The result of these popular appeals was that Mrs. Gandhi's Congress won a very substantial victory in the 1971 parliamentary elections and, after winning a popular war against Pakistan over Bangladesh, further consolidated its position in the state assembly elections the following year. Mrs. Gandhi's Congress won back a large portion of the modern sector that it had begun to lose in the 1967 elections—the urban middle classes, the bureaucracy, the business community—while strengthening its electoral base with the scheduled castes and tribes, the religious minorities (especially the Muslims), and other low-income groups.

Since it had been the state leaders, the presidents of the *pradesh* Congress committees and the chief ministers, who had challenged Mrs. Gandhi between 1967 and 1969 (and whom she had defeated when they ran against her candidates in the 1971 and 1972 elections), she was eager to prevent new centers of power from rising within the party and the state governments to challenge her authority as prime minister and party leader. In the early 1970s, Mrs. Gandhi restructured and centralized the party. State leaders, including chief ministers, were no longer allowed to build an independent local base in the countryside or in the party, but were appointed (or dismissed) by the prime minister. As state party organizations and state governments became increasingly subservient to the center, democracy within the Congress party declined. Meetings of the All India Congress Committee and the Working Committee, the two important organs within the party, became infrequent and their political importance was reduced. Not only did state governments become less independent, but even municipal governments and village *panchayats* languished as local governments were superseded and local elections became infrequent. Most of the country's municipal governments were also suspended. In Bombay, Calcutta, Delhi, Hyderabad, Madras, and Bangalore, municipal power was shifted into the hands of officials appointed by the state or central governments. Under these circumstances, the local Congress party in the urban areas atrophied. Mrs. Gandhi may have reduced political threats to her power, but in doing so she also weakened the local and state party organizations. The result was that state governments became weaker and, between 1972 and 1975, less stable.

Many of the older functions of the Congress party—mobilizing local support, accommodating itself to local factions, providing opportunities for competing political elites, transmitting to state and central governments information about the local scene—were dissipated. In place of the party, Mrs. Gandhi turned to other institutions, to the intelligence apparatus of the government, the central reserve police, and various paramilitary institutions; and to advise her on political affairs she turned increasingly to a small band of trusted political advisers, a kitchen cabinet that came to be invidiously known as the caucus.

When Mrs. Gandhi declared a national emergency in 1975 it was, in a sense, the culmination of this move toward centralization within the party as well as within the government. The regime became increasingly unable to cope with the rising tide of public protest against the government, while the party itself was increasingly torn by dissidence over Mrs. Gandhi's centralizing tendencies. When on June 12, 1975, after four protracted years, the High Court of Allahabad declared Mrs. Gandhi's election to Parliament in 1971 null and void because she had violated the election law, Mrs. Gandhi evidently concluded that a declaration of emergency was necessary if she were to remain in office. Not only did the government arrest opposition leaders, impose censorship on the press, and suspend the electoral process, but all remaining independent centers of power within the Congress party were eliminated as critics were jailed and chief ministers made subservient to the prime minister, while the caucus used its position to extend its power into the intelligence services, the police, and the administration of central, state, and even local governments.

During the emergency, the party organization withered. In some localities it was displaced by the Youth Congress, a cadre-based organization led by Sanjay Gandhi, which could mobilize financial resources, exercise control over potential dissidents, and provide the clout necessary to influence the bureaucracy.[4]

[4] The story of the emergency and of the elections of 1977 that resulted in the defeat of the Congress party and the end of the emergency have been described in detail in Myron Weiner, *India at the Polls: The Parliamentary Elections of 1977* (Washington, D.C.: American Enterprise Institute, 1978).

The Rise of Janata: India's First Non-Congress Government

The key to understanding the 1977 elections is the emergence of the Janata party, a new political party formed on the eve of the elections, consolidating a variety of opposition parties in their determination to end Congress rule. Though various efforts had been made to form a united opposition party in 1974 and 1975 to bring down the Congress governments in the states of Gujarat and Bihar, it was not until January 1977, when Mrs. Gandhi made her surprise announcement that elections would be held and the emergency "suspended," that several opposition parties came together to form the Janata party. Some of these parties had been around for a long time or had split off from other opposition parties, and some were groups that had split away from Congress. In the past these groups had often fought one another as hard as they fought Mrs. Gandhi's Congress, but now they felt that their very existence had been threatened by the emergency. Many of the leaders of these parties were in jail together during the emergency and there they vowed to put aside their differences in order to bring down Mrs. Gandhi's government. Almost immediately after the election was announced and the opposition leaders were released from jail, they met to form a single party, Janata, with a single program and a single slate of candidates.

The Janata party consisted of six major identifiable groups.

1. Congress (O), the group that had split from Mrs. Gandhi's Congress in 1969. This group had the most well-known national leaders and, in the 1971 elections, the largest popular vote of any of the opposition parties. It won 10.4 percent of the vote, but only 16 seats (out of 518) in Parliament. Its leadership was generally regarded as conservative and aging. Among its prominent leaders were Morarji Desai, who subsequently became prime minister in the Janata government, and Sanjiva Reddy, who was subsequently elected president of India.

2. The Bharatiya Jana Sangh (or simply Jana Sangh). This was the oldest of the opposition parties, formed in 1951 and widely regarded as an anti-Muslim, anti-Pakistani, pro-Hindu party committed to *Bharatiya*, or Indian culture. It polled only 7.5 percent of the popular vote in 1971, but thereafter it appeared to be gaining popularity in the Hindi-speaking states of northern India, where it had support among shopkeepers, white-collar workers, professionals, and some of the peasantry in Uttar Pradesh. Closely associated with the Jana Sangh was the Rashtriya Swayamsevak Sangh (RSS), a militant

Hindu organization. The most prominent national leaders of Jana Sangh were Lal K. Advani and Atal Behari Vajpayee.

3. Bharatiya Lok Dal (BLD, or Lok Dal). The BLD was an amalgam of several small parties in northern India brought together by Charan Singh, a leader of the agricultural classes in Uttar Pradesh. The party had a considerable base in the rural areas of Uttar Pradesh, Bihar, Haryana, Rajasthan, and Orissa.

4. The Socialist party. Formed in 1971, this party was the descendant of the Congress Socialist party, founded in 1934 as a socialist group within the Indian National Congress. The Socialist party was the largest of the many splinter groups that came out of the original socialist movement. Ideologically, it brought together Marxist, Gandhian, and democratic socialist elements. In the 1971 parliamentary elections it won 3.5 percent of the vote and five seats in Parliament, with support primarily in Bihar, Uttar Pradesh, and Maharashtra. Among its leaders were George Fernandes, Madhu Limaye, and Raj Narain.

5. Two groups of Congressmen also joined the new party. One group, which included Chandra Shekhar, Kishan Kant, and Mohan Dharia, had been the Young Turks within the Congress party in the early 1970s. They were socialist in outlook and critical of Mrs. Gandhi's efforts to centralize the party. They were among the first to be arrested by Mrs. Gandhi's government when the emergency was declared.

6. The sixth group was Congressmen who had remained with the government during the emergency but deserted it when elections were called—denouncing Mrs. Gandhi not only for suspending democracy within the country but also for ending democracy within the party. This group included Jagjivan Ram, the most senior minister in Mrs. Gandhi's cabinet, and H. N. Bahuguna, a well-known left-of-center politician from Uttar Pradesh who, though a Hindu, commanded considerable support among Muslims. This group formed a party of its own, the Congress for Democracy (CFD), which supported Janata candidates and merged with Janata shortly after the elections.

The elder statesman of the new party was Jayaprakash Narayan, a widely revered socialist and disciple of Mahatma Gandhi, who was affiliated to no one political party but had played a leading role in bringing many of the opposition parties together against the Congress state and national governments in 1974 and 1975. Jayaprakash was arrested when the emergency was declared but subsequently released because of his ill health. Although he was physically unable to take any active role in the party or in its electoral campaign, he became the symbol around which divergent groups in the party rallied.

The Janata party and its CFD ally attracted support from all groups who opposed the emergency and feared that the reelection of Mrs. Gandhi and the Congress party would mean the end of competitive democratic politics for India. "The choice before the electorate is clear," said the Janata party election manifesto. "It is a choice between freedom and slavery; between democracy and dictatorship; between abdicating the power of the people or asserting it; between the Gandhian path and the way that has led many nations down the precipice of dictatorship, instability, military adventure and national ruin."[5] In spite of the enormous differences among the opposition groups, they were prepared to come together as a single party in an effort to restore the democratic framework.

Janata won the elections with a clear majority of the seats in Parliament, 298 out of 539, and a popular vote of 43.2 percent. Congress won 34.5 percent of the popular vote and 153 seats. The Janata victory was largely confined to northern India, especially the Hindi-speaking states (where it won 221 of its seats). Janata attracted support in both urban and rural areas, with some of its strongest support from Muslims and Harijan voters who had traditionally voted for the Congress party. Clearly the "excesses" committed during the emergency—particularly the compulsory sterilization and slum clearance programs—had antagonized Muslims, Harijans, tribals, and other low-income groups.

The Janata party chose Morarji Desai, former leader of the Congress (O), as its prime minister. Charan Singh, the elder leader of the former Bharatiya Lok Dal, was home minister; Atal Behari Vajpayee, one-time leader of the Jana Sangh parliamentary party, was minister of external affairs; Jagjivan Ram, the leader of the Congress for Democracy, was minister of defense; H. M. Patel, a former civil servant turned politician and a leader of the former Swatantra party (a unit of the BLD), was finance minister; George Fernandes, Socialist trade unionist, was minister of industries; Raj Narain, the Socialist politician who had defeated Mrs. Gandhi in her own constituency, was minister of health and family planning; Mohan Dharia, who had resigned from Congress on the eve of the emergency, was minister of commerce; and L. K. Advani, one-time president of the Jana Sangh, was minister of information and broadcasting.

[5] "Janata Party Manifesto," New Delhi, 1977. Selected portions are reprinted in Weiner, *India at the Polls*, pp. 134-40.

Chandra Shekhar, one of the Young Turk former Congressmen, was made president of the Janata party. In short, the new Janata government incorporated leaders from every important faction of the party.

There were no significant differences within the government on the need to dismantle the apparatus created by Mrs. Gandhi during the emergency. Freedom of the press was restored. A constitutional amendment was passed, which provided that an emergency could only be requested by the cabinet, not by the prime minister, that a presidential proclamation of an emergency required the approval of both houses of Parliament within a month, and that an emergency could be declared only in the event of an "armed rebellion," not merely an "internal disturbance," as the constitution had originally stated.[6] The government also appointed a commission, headed by a former chief justice of the Supreme Court, J. C. Shah, to investigate the conduct of government officials during the emergency.

The Janata party sought to consolidate its political position by calling state elections in the north Indian states where it had won so overwhelmingly in the parliamentary elections. In June 1977, elections were held in fourteen states and union territories—Uttar Pradesh, Bihar, Madhya Pradesh, West Bengal, Rajasthan, Orissa, Punjab, Haryana, Jammu and Kashmir, Goa, Himachal Pradesh, and Delhi, and in the south, Tamil Nadu and Pondicherry. Janata won all but four of the elections, and in these four it lost to regional parties or to the Communist party (in West Bengal) rather than to the Congress party. By mid-1977 the position of Janata seemed secure, and that of the Congress party hopeless.

Janata's Economic Policies and Performance

Considering how heterogeneous the new government was, its economic policies were unexpectedly coherent. By 1978 the government had adopted a new employment-oriented rural development program as part of the country's sixth five-year plan. To increase rural development, the government adopted its *antyodaya* scheme to provide self-employment for the poorest families, a food-for-work program to provide employment for the rural unemployed, government sup-

[6] For an analysis of the impact of the constitutional framework on Indian political development before, during, and after the emergency, see Henry Hart, "The Indian Constitution: Political Development and Decay," *Asian Survey*, vol. 20, no. 4 (April 1980), pp. 428-51. Hart persuasively argues that the force of constitutionalism is greater in India than in many other developing countries and that it may have been an important element in Mrs. Gandhi's decision to call elections in 1977. Mrs. Gandhi, he writes, had internalized the Western nineteenth-century belief in "the elective basis of legitimacy" (p. 445).

port for village and small-scale industries, a dairy development program, and a variety of block-level development projects. Raj Krishna, the chief economist of the planning commission, claims that from 1978 to 1979 these schemes increased rural employment by 5 million.[7]

Considerable new resources were invested in agriculture, particularly in expanding the country's irrigation capacity, increasing the amount of irrigated land by 2.5 million hectares. There was also a growth in institutional credit, which led to a considerable increase in fertilizer use.[8] Food grain output in 1978–1979 was 131 million tons, 3.9 percent higher than the 126.4 million tons in 1977–1978. The government had nearly 20 million tons of grain in storage in mid-1979, 3 million tons more than in the previous year. As a result of a drought, food grain production declined in 1979, but the losses were considerably less than had been expected. Though food grain production still fluctuated, the expansion of irrigation and improved agricultural techniques maintained production at a much higher level than before.

The good grain harvest in 1978 and the upsurge of remittances from Indian migrants abroad, especially in West Asia, gave India a favorable balance of payments in spite of a growing gap between imports (particularly of oil) and exports. India's foreign exchange position was further strengthened when Great Britain announced that it was writing off a $1.1 billion debt, and India received a record contribution for 1978–1979 of $2.3 billion from the Aid India Consortium (which includes the World Bank).

In 1978 the government initiated a new national adult education program to reach the largely illiterate rural countryside, and committed new resources to the expansion of primary and secondary schools in an effort to push closer to universal education.

There was some controversy over the decision by the minister of industries, George Fernandes, to order IBM and Coca Cola to leave India (IBM on the ground that it violated the requirement that a majority of shares of companies must be Indian-owned, and Coca Cola on the ground that its technology should be available to Indian

[7] Raj Krishna, "The Economic Malaise," *Seminar*, December 1979, pp. 42-45.

[8] For a sympathetic account of the rural development program of the Janata party government, see Marcus Franda, *India's Rural Development: An Assessment of Alternatives* (Bloomington: Indiana University Press, 1979). For an account of the efforts made by the Janata government to decentralize rural development by expanding the powers and financial resources of local institutions, see Shriram Maheshwari, "New Perspectives on Rural Local Government in India: The Asoka Mehta Committee Report," *Asian Survey*, vol. 19, no. 11 (November 1979), pp. 110-25.

companies), but even on these decisions there was considerable agreement within the government.

It was not policy but politics that divided and threatened to destroy the Janata party. Nor could one say that a deteriorating economy hurt the party, for the political divisions grew worse in 1978, at a time when the economy was doing comparatively well. The economy did worsen at the end of 1978 and in early 1979, in part because of poor performance in the coal industry, electric power, transport, and all public sector enterprises where management was poor and competition among the ministries precluded any effective reorganization. But the decline of the economy in 1979 (it grew worse after the fall of the government in the middle of the year) was rather a consequence of the breakdown in political authority than its cause: for most of 1979 politics was shaping economics.

The Failure to Consolidate the Party

From the very beginning it was unclear what kind of party Janata would become. One option was consolidation in the manner of the old Congress, with enrolled members and a hierarchy of elected bodies from the *taluka* to the district, state, and national levels. Alternatively, the party could permit each of its constituent units to retain its organizational identity and choose representatives for some kind of federal structure at the national level. Most of the national leaders preferred the former arrangement, but they were unsuccessful in their efforts to build a unified party. Nor did they create a federal party since, in theory at least, the constituent units lost their separate political identity. In practice, however, it was these units that battled for control over the party.

What made the struggle ultimately so destructive was the division at the national level among three senior rivals, Prime Minister Morarji Desai (eighty-one years old), Chaudhury Charan Singh (seventy-four), the leader of the BLD group, and Jagjivan Ram (sixty-eight), the leader of the CFD. The various political groups clustered around these men in an effort to protect or expand their positions. Moreover, each of these constituent units—once parties and now factions within a party—had an electoral base of its own, and it was these bases (often exaggerated by the leaders) that gave the factions their bargaining power.

Though Morarji Desai had been chosen by the leaders of the party as prime minister, he was not particularly well liked by the rank and file or indeed by most of the party leaders, who regarded him as a rigid person, guided by his own idiosyncrasies and impervious

14

to the viewpoint of others. Still, most of the former members of the Congress (O), the Young Turks led by Chandra Shekhar, and the leaders of the Jana Sangh preferred Morarji to the other candidates, for he had no major electoral base of his own and was far less threatening to their position in the party than Charan Singh, his greatest rival.

Charan Singh, in spite of his uncertain health and his age, was a formidable rival to Morarji Desai. He had had a long political career in Uttar Pradesh, where he had established himself as the leader of the "backward classes" (sometimes called the "backward castes"), a term loosely used to describe a variety of castes socially above the ex-untouchables, but behind the "forward classes," that is, the Brahmins, the Rajputs, and others. The strategic position of the backward classes had substantially improved in the late 1960s and early 1970s, through land reform legislation that ensured their land rights, the introduction of new agricultural technologies that improved their income, and access to education for their children, which increased their mobility. As the backward classes became economically and educationally better off, they became a politically mobilizable community, and Charan Singh, a leading figure in the Jat caste (not officially recognized as a backward caste, but one whose members regard themselves as spokesmen for the agricultural castes, including the backward castes), became their spokesman. He pressed for a more aggressive rural development program, for agricultural price supports, more credit, investment in irrigation, and an expansion of rural industries. And he appealed to the pride of the agricultural communities, especially the Jat castes of Uttar Pradesh and Haryana.[9]

In 1967 Charan Singh left the Congress party to form a regional party in Uttar Pradesh known as the Bharatiya Kranti Dal. Holding the balance in a divided legislature, Charan Singh skillfully played the game of parliamentary politics to bring down a minority Congress government in Uttar Pradesh. In 1969 a midterm election was held in which Charan Singh's party, now renamed the Lok Dal, won a little over 100 seats in the Uttar Pradesh legislature with 24 percent of the vote. Charan Singh then attracted support from both the Jana Sangh and the Communist party of India (CPI), that is, from both the right and left wings of the political spectrum, to help him become the chief minister of the state, leading a minority government.

[9] For an account of the increasingly important role played by the middle peasantry or backward castes of Uttar Pradesh, and the reasons why they turned away from the Congress party to support Charan Singh and his agrarian party, the BLD, see Paul R. Brass, "The Politicization of the Peasantry in a North Indian State," *Journal of Peasant Studies*, vol. 7, no. 4 (July 1980), pp. 395-426.

It was a lesson in coalition politics that Charan Singh was later to apply to national politics.

After the Janata party's election victories in 1977, Charan Singh argued that the victory of the party in three states, Bihar, Uttar Pradesh, and Haryana, was largely the result of the efforts of the Lok Dal. In these states, he said, the peasant classes—the Yadavs, Kurmis, Gujars, Koeris, and other backward castes—had supported the Janata party because of his leadership.

Charan Singh also had the backing of the Socialist party members within the Janata party. The founder of the Socialist party, Rammanohar Lohia (now deceased) had insisted that the Socialists should identify themselves with the cause of the backward classes against the upper castes. He opposed the spread of higher (as opposed to primary and secondary) education, denounced the use of English in higher education and in administration (for he saw English as the way the upper castes preserved their dominance in the administrative services), and advocated the use of Hindi. The Socialists described the backward classes as a "progressive" force standing for land to the tiller and the increase of agricultural productivity and income.

With the support of the Socialists, Charan Singh and his followers consolidated their position in Uttar Pradesh, Bihar, and Haryana while allying themselves with a group led by Biju Patnaik in Orissa. In each of these states a supporter of Charan Singh became chief minister; and in the Hindi-speaking states each sought to mobilize the backward classes behind the Janata party.

The Jana Sangh group within Janata was their major competitor. Its electoral base was largely in the states further to the West, in Rajasthan, Madhya Pradesh, Himachal Pradesh, and the Union territory of Delhi. In all four, Jana Sangh leaders became the chief ministers.

Jana Sangh was not without support in Uttar Pradesh or in Bihar, however, where it had a considerable following among the merchant communities, portions of the urban middle classes, and the landowning Rajputs. As a caste, the Rajputs were traditional rivals of both the upper-caste Brahmins (who tended to vote Congress) and the Jats, the largest of the middle-peasant castes, who supported Lok Dal.

Morarji Desai's electoral strength was confined primarily to Gujarat, while Chandra Shekhar had no significant electoral base of his own anywhere. It soon became clear to them that the balance of power between the BLD and the Jana Sangh was so precarious that any attempt to hold elections within the party might tear it apart and jeopardize their control of the state governments. To avoid a struggle for control over the party, the party leaders agreed not to hold elections for party officers, but rather to make ad hoc appointments, much as the Congress party had done under Mrs. Gandhi. Under this procedure the president of the party appointed state chairmen, who in turn appointed district party heads, who then appointed *taluka* party officials. The Janata party seemed no more able to operate democratically than the Congress party of Mrs. Gandhi, though for different reasons. From time to time party elections were scheduled, but when the rivalries became threatening they were postponed—indefinitely.

A balance among the various groups in the party was achieved in the distribution of central and state cabinet positions. This, however, ultimately proved unworkable. A political group that did not win power in a state was often reluctant to accept its subordinate position simply to further the interests of the group in another state. Moreover, every conflict within a state was seen in terms of its potential effects on the struggle for power at the national level.

Jana Sangh supported Morarji Desai, since its leaders believed that a victory for Charan Singh and the Lok Dal would undermine their position in the states they dominated, erode their electoral base in the states dominated by the Lok Dal, and reduce their chances of winning greater power at the national level when the elders, Morarji Desai, Charan Singh, and Jagjivan Ram, passed from the scene. Any attack by the Lok Dal on Morarji Desai, therefore, was seen as an attack on the Jana Sangh, and attacks on the Jana Sangh were seen as attacks on Morarji. Similarly, any attempt by the Jana Sangh to undermine the position of the Lok Dal in any state represented a threat to Charan Singh's desire to strengthen his national position.

"Aya Ram, Gaya Ram"—Ram Comes, Ram Goes

The movement of Indian politicians from one party to another—what Indians disdainfully call *aya Ram, gaya Ram*—was more prevalent in 1978 and 1979 than at any other time since independence.[10] One reason for the fluidity was that hardly anyone had any loyalty to the

[10] The growing disillusionment with the Janata government during its first year is described by the Indian political scientist Iqbal Narain, "India 1977: From Promise to Disenchantment," *Asian Survey*, vol. 18, no. 2 (February 1978), pp. 103-16. The decline of the party as a result of the growth of internal factional conflicts in 1978 is described by Iqbal Narain in "India in 1978: Politics of Nonissues," *Asian Survey*, vol. 19, no. 2 (February 1979), pp. 165-77.

Janata party. In the absence of party loyalty as a binding force, every imaginable conflict came to the surface. At one level there were the driving ambitions of Morarji Desai and Charan Singh, and the ambitions of many lesser figures as well. At another level, the struggle often seemed to be between two families, as Charan Singh and Morarji Desai each accused the other of using his position to permit family members to make private gains. At still another level, the struggle was between organized factions, as the BLD, the Jana Sangh, the Socialists, and the Congress (O) jockeyed for positions in the states and in the center. And the clashes involved the interests of different electoral groups, such as the ex-untouchables, the Jats and other backward castes, the Rajputs, and the Bania-merchant communities (or, as some people put it, the landless, the peasants, the landlords, and the capitalist classes).

There was no strong central authority around which groups could organize. Morarji Desai was too weak, for he lacked an electoral base of his own; he had been chosen not for his national popularity, but because his supporters wanted to prevent Charan Singh from becoming prime minister. Unlike his predecessors, Morarji was unable to influence the factional struggles, for as long as the center was weak, factional leaders who wanted to undermine state governments feared no political retribution.

Had Mrs. Gandhi and the Congress party been united against Janata, perhaps the various factions might have been drawn together for fear that she would once again take power. But by early 1978 the Congress party itself was split, and within the two new Congress parties (one organized around Mrs. Gandhi, and the other around her opponents) there were divided factions. As Mrs. Gandhi's star appeared to wane, there were rumors of more defections from Congress. Each of the factions within Janata envisaged a new realignment, and since none of the factions had a fixed ideological position that precluded collaboration with another group, there appeared to be no end of possible combinations around which some new party or government could be formed. Indeed, almost anything seemed possible, including a coalition between Mrs. Gandhi and Jagjivan Ram, or Mrs. Gandhi and Charan Singh, or a merger of the Congress party led by Y. B. Chavan (the Congress group that had split from Mrs. Gandhi) and Janata. Even the more ideological parties, like the Communist party of India and the more leftist Communist party of India (Marxist) appeared to be flexible in choosing whom to support. With so many actors, and with the boundaries of the parties so fluid, it was no wonder that those who were not playing the game found the struggle bewildering. It was an atmosphere that generated rumors (for some, rumor-mongering was a conscious strategy), uncertainty, and cynicism.

Throughout 1978 social tension was widespread in India. There were violent clashes between scheduled castes and caste Hindus over land rights, agricultural wages, and, in the state of Maharashtra, over the proposed renaming of one of the state universities after Ambedkar, a prominent deceased scheduled-caste leader. There were violent clashes between Hindus and Muslims, most notably in the industrial steel town of Jamshedpur in Bihar. And in the Punjab there were violent fights between the Sikhs and the Nirankaris, a small heterodox Sikh sect.

Divisions within the Janata party seemed to worsen and in some instances even created social cleavages and violence. In Bihar, for example, the conflict between the supporters of Karpoori Thakur, the chief minister, and his opponents moved from the legislative assembly and the party to the countryside and the campuses. Thakur, himself a member of one of the backward castes, sought to strengthen his political base in the state by adopting programs and policies that would mobilize the support of members of this community. He announced a program of reserving for members of the backward classes 25 percent of all admissions to colleges and universities and all jobs in the state administrative services in addition to the reservations already provided for the scheduled castes and tribes. His proposal was denounced by members of the upper castes, especially the Brahmins and Rajputs, who saw that this move would deprive them of educational and employment opportunities. The upper castes also attracted some support from members of the scheduled castes and tribes, who were persuaded that the government's policy of extending preferences to the backward classes would dilute their own preferential access to education and employment.

Demonstrations erupted at the colleges and universities where the upper castes were particularly numerous. As a result of clashes between upper- and lower-caste students, many of the colleges were closed, and it was not long before the violence spread to the towns and to the countryside. Karpoori Thakur may have succeeded in consolidating his support within the backward classes, but at the cost of eroding the precarious social coalition that had been put together behind the Janata party in the 1977 elections.

To what extent the conflicts between Hindus and Muslims and between scheduled castes and other Hindu castes were the result of intraparty or interparty disputes was less clear. The growing politicization of the scheduled castes and their increasing unwillingness to accept the old demeaning social and economic relationships, together

19

with the growing aggressiveness of some of the middle castes who supported the Janata party in the 1977 elections, were probably elements in the growth of caste conflicts. Whatever the cause, the political consequences were clear: the scheduled castes, who had supported the Janata party in 1977, were withdrawing their support and returning to Mrs. Gandhi's Congress party. The growth of Hindu-Muslim conflict became an issue in the Janata party because the Lok Dal group (which was blamed for growing caste conflict) held the Jana Sangh and the RSS responsible. Once again, though the causes may have been uncertain, the effect was to turn away from the party many Muslims who had supported Janata in 1977.

Each faction in the party appeared to be guided by one central goal—to build up its own electoral support while undermining that of other factions—even if the cumulative effect was to decrease support for the party as a whole. Underlying the strategy of each group was the assumption that the party center would not hold and that, as authority fragmented, the groups with the strongest electoral base would be in the best position to bargain for a share of power in the coalition governments that would soon emerge at both state and national level. As each faction adopted this assumption, the likelihood of its coming true increased.

Congress Splits

In the early months after her electoral defeat, Mrs. Gandhi's political standing declined precipitously as she and her close associates came under attack from within the Congress party. Many Congressmen held her and the "caucus" responsible for the excesses of the emergency and for the party's electoral defeat. Demands were made that Sanjay Gandhi, Om Mehta, Bansi Lal, and Narain Dutt Tiwari, all loyal supporters of Mrs. Gandhi, be expelled from the party. Bansi Lal was expelled, and in a countermove Mrs. Gandhi's supporters forced the resignation of their opponent, D. K. Borooah, as president of the party, then elected their own candidate, Brahmananda Reddy in his place.

It soon became clear that Mrs. Gandhi had no intention of retiring from politics and that she and her son Sanjay were eager to rehabilitate themselves as political leaders. Divisions within the party grew, as some concluded that Mrs. Gandhi could bring the party back to power, while others believed that both she and Sanjay were liabilities.

For a brief moment the party was united in October 1977, when the government of India arrested Mrs. Gandhi, only to release her a few days later when the court ruled that the charges filed against her were inadequate. But Mrs. Gandhi's arrest, followed so quickly by her release, enabled Sanjay Gandhi and his supporters to launch public demonstrations against the Janata government, accusing it of persecuting the former prime minister. As Mrs. Gandhi's standing as a persecuted martyr rose, the reputation of the government for political competence declined. Many Congressmen were convinced by this incident that Mrs. Gandhi had once again demonstrated her capacity to outmaneuver her political enemies and that eventually she would return to power.

Nonetheless, in January 1978 the party split as it became clear that Mrs. Gandhi wanted a party that was loyal to her. Mrs. Gandhi assumed leadership of the Congress (I)—for Indira—while her opponents formed their own party under the presidency of Brahmananda Reddy, who only a few months earlier had been her supporter. In February, a month after the split, elections were held for state governments in six states. Mrs. Gandhi's Congress (I) won an absolute majority in the two southern states of Andhra and Karnataka. The Andhra victory undermined the position of Brahmananda Reddy, who came from that state. The Karnataka Congress (I) victory appeared to strengthen the position of Devaraj Urs, the state party leader, who threw his support to Mrs. Gandhi. In Maharashtra, Congress (I) did well, and that was a blow to Y. B. Chavan, the Maharashtrian Congress leader who supported Mrs. Gandhi's opponents. (Chavan subsequently became the leader of the opposition Congress party nationally.) Elsewhere, neither Congress fared well. On balance, however, Mrs. Gandhi's Congress (I) had established itself as the stronger of the two parties.

Mrs. Gandhi further improved her position in November 1978, when she successfully stood for Parliament from Chikmagalur constituency in Karnataka. She won 55 percent of the vote in an election that received national (and international) attention, in part because so many Janata leaders chose to tour the constituency to campaign against her. The next month the Lok Sabha expelled Mrs. Gandhi from Parliament on the charge of breach of privilege and passed a resolution sentencing her to imprisonment till the end of its winter session. Following the passage of the resolution, Mrs. Gandhi was placed under arrest and jailed for a week, an act many believe strengthened her claim that she was being persecuted by the Janata government.

How to deal with Mrs. Gandhi was itself a divisive issue within the Janata government. Was it sufficient to discredit her through the public hearings held by the Shah Commission? Should the government take steps to prosecute her for actions committed during the emergency? Did she indeed break the law during the emergency (many of her critics doubted that she had), or would one have to find some minor infraction in order to take legal action against her? Should she have been opposed by national Janata leaders when she ran in a safe constituency and then been expelled from Parliament, or should she have been quietly allowed to return to elected office without the fanfare resulting from an election she was bound to win? And who had bungled by arresting her on inadequate legal charges—Prime Minister Morarji Desai, or Charan Singh, the home minister? Mrs. Gandhi's political rebirth was rapidly becoming a cause for recriminations within Janata.

The Fall of Janata

The struggle for control of the Janata party took place on two levels—nationally between Charan Singh and Morarji Desai, and at the state level, especially in Bihar, Uttar Pradesh, and Haryana, between the BLD and Jana Sangh factions.

Charan Singh, in an effort to prevent Morarji Desai's followers from charging him with mishandling Mrs. Gandhi's arrest, described the Janata leaders as a "pack of impotent people" for their failure to take more forceful measures against Mrs. Gandhi. Raj Narain, Charan Singh's closest associate, delivered a public speech attacking the Janata chief minister of Himachal Pradesh, a supporter of Morarji. Supporters of Charan Singh organized a mass "birthday party" of peasants in Delhi, busing in thousands from the nearby countryside, to demonstrate Charan Singh's enormous popularity. And both Raj Narain and Charan Singh became increasingly strident in their charge that Janata was falling under the control of the Jana Sangh and the RSS "communal elements," who, they said, were responsible for the growing clashes between Hindus and Muslims.

In an effort to undermine Morarji's reputation as a man of personal integrity, Charan Singh accused Morarji's son, Kanti Desai, of corruption. Charan Singh suggested that Morarji was protecting his son, who lived in the prime minister's residence, by blocking the appointment of a commission of inquiry. Morarji dismissed the charges as ill-founded rumors and saw no reason to appoint a commission simply in order to "cleanse our image."[11] In an effort to

11 The correspondence between Charan Singh and Morarji Desai over these charges is published as an appendix in L. K. Advani, *The People Betrayed* (Delhi: Vision Books, 1979), p. 136. Advani, minister of information and broadcasting in the Janata government and one-time president of the Jana Sangh, provides one of the more interesting "inside" accounts of the breakup of the Janata party.

demonstrate that Morarji was vulnerable to the charges, Charan Singh wrote him a public letter. Later he charged, "It is obvious that my letter has caused you some irritation—even anger. For, if it is not anger, how else is one expected to understand your reaction?" to which Morarji replied, "There was nothing in the letter to show that I was irritated or angry."[12]

In June 1978 Morarji Desai, confronted by continued public attacks from two leading members of his cabinet, dismissed Charan Singh and Raj Narain from the government.[13] The party now appeared to be on the verge of splitting.

But Jana Sangh leaders in the cabinet, L. K. Advani and Atal Behari Vajpayee, feared that the rift could split the party in several states, endanger the national government, and increase the chances of a return by Mrs. Gandhi. They therefore pressed Morarji to take a conciliatory line. In January 1979 Morarji brought Charan Singh back to the cabinet as finance minister and deputy prime minister in what proved to be the last major effort to hold the party together.

The struggle for power moved to the states. A factional struggle for control of the office of chief minister took place in Uttar Pradesh, in which the BLD emerged victorious over the Jana Sangh. The factional conflict spread to Bihar, then to Himachal Pradesh, Haryana, Madhya Pradesh, and Rajasthan. In April 1979 a coalition of Congress (O) and Jana Sangh members of the Janata legislative party in Bihar attempted to force the resignation of Karpoori Thakur, the chief minister and a supporter of Charan Singh. Karpoori Thakur lost the battle by thirty votes, and Ram Sunder Das, a Harijan and a former Socialist, was chosen chief minister with backing from both Morarji Desai and Jagjivan Ram. In mid-June a similar struggle took place in Haryana, and once again a coalition of Congress (O) and Jana Sangh members of the Janata legislative party brought down a chief minister, Devi Lal, who belonged to the Charan Singh wing of the party. A counterattack was launched by the Lok Dal group in Uttar Pradesh when Banarsi Das, the chief minister, with the support of Raj Narain and the Socialist leader, Madhu Limaye, sought to

[12] Ibid., pp. 133-34.

[13] The dismissal was precipitated by a statement by Charan Singh indicting the government for "its failure to put the former Prime Minister behind the bars" and claiming that people think "that we in the government are a pack of impotent people who cannot govern the country" (ibid., p. 12). Cabinet members, writes Advani, were particularly outraged because they believed that Charan Singh's arrest of Mrs. Gandhi on a minor charge pertaining to jeeps received from a private firm in the 1977 elections made the government look foolish. The dismissal of the charges by the courts, they believed, strengthened Mrs. Gandhi's position and was in fact a "turning point."

23

break the political back of the Jana Sangh by dismissing its members from the cabinet and launching a public campaign against the RSS. These developments in Uttar Pradesh, Bihar, and Haryana soon threatened the fragile stability of the national Janata party organization and the central government itself.[14]

If the Janata party seemed to be falling apart in June 1979, so did Mrs. Gandhi's Congress party. A conflict arose between Mrs. Gandhi and Devaraj Urs, chief minister of the state of Karnataka and president of the Congress (I). Urs became increasingly critical of Sanjay Gandhi's political role in the Congress party and as a personal adviser to Mrs. Gandhi. On June 25 Mrs. Gandhi expelled Devaraj Urs from the party. In a parting open letter, Urs denounced Mrs. Gandhi, saying, "we refused to be treated as bonded labour [an allusion, presumably, to Sanjay's role in the party]. . . . You have learnt nothing from your experience and the authoritarian bent of your mind persists, which is an anomaly in a democratic society. . . . You scare away all good, capable, and efficient men and women and then you hope to administer this vast nation with mediocres and sycophants."[15] To many, this split seemed like the political end of Mrs. Gandhi, since Urs appeared to control a large section of the Congress (I) in the two southern states of Andhra Pradesh and Karnataka, which provided Mrs. Gandhi with her largest bloc of supporters in Parliament. Devaraj Urs subsequently brought his supporters into the anti-Indira Congress party under Chavan which then constituted the largest single opposition bloc in Parliament.

The Congress split seemed to give an impetus to splitting within Janata. Raj Narain announced that he was leaving the party, Charan Singh resigned from the cabinet, and within a few days a number of M.P.s belonging to the Bharatiya Lok Dal group withdrew their membership from the Janata party. H. N. Bahuguna, a leader of the CFD group and a prominent politician from Uttar Pradesh, also resigned from the cabinet and the party.

The official ground for the defections was that Morarji Desai's government had failed to take steps to reduce the influence of the

[14] Advani, *The People Betrayed*, p. 39. For an alternate account of the fall of the Janata government, which attributes its breakup to the drive for ascendancy by the Jana Sangh, see Jyotirindra Das Gupta, "India 1979: The Prize Chair and the People's Share: Electoral Diversion and Economic Reversal," *Asian Survey*, vol. 20, no. 2 (February 1980). Das Gupta concludes that "supporters of Charan Singh openly resisted the Jana Sangh-Congress (O) combination . . . [Charan Singh] was extremely unhappy at the way his men were treated, particularly in his home state of Uttar Pradesh and in neighboring Haryana" (pp. 177-78).
[15] Ved Mehta, "Indian Politics: A Family Affair," *New Yorker*, March 17, 1980, pp. 119-20.

"right-wing," "Hindu nationalist" Jana Sangh and the RSS. The specific demand was that the Jana Sangh Janata members should be required to disavow any affiliation with the RSS or be told to leave the government and the party.

What role, if any, did Mrs. Gandhi and Sanjay play in the decision by Charan Singh and the BLD to break from Janata? Several weeks and months after the split, some of the participants spoke freely to reporters about the role they had played and the strategies they had pursued, and it is from these reports that we can reconstruct an account of what happened.

It is of some interest to note that those who left spoke with pride of the role they had played in bringing down the government. Indeed, Raj Narain's photo was published on the cover of the leading English-language newsweeklies as he boasted of the way he had maneuvered Morarji out of power. Privately and publicly, those who helped bring down the government were in a state of exaltation—especially those in Mrs. Gandhi's or Charan Singh's camp. The two groups had worked together to destroy the Janata party, and both anticipated that they would be the gainers.

In their efforts to break up the Janata party, Mrs. Gandhi and Sanjay were aware of two critical elements disrupting Janata: Charan Singh's unquenchable desire to become prime minister, and the concern of both the BLD and the Socialist factions that the Jana Sangh group was electorally and organizationally strong and threatening.

Sanjay Gandhi reportedly took the initiative in meeting with Raj Narain to assure him that if the BLD faction came out of the Janata party with a sizable bloc of M.P.s, then Congress (I) was prepared to help Charan Singh form a government. Sanjay endorsed Raj Narain's attack on Jana Sangh and RSS as the most effective way of winning the support of the Socialist and Congress (O) members of the party.[16] Sanjay, it is said, moved with some urgency because Parliament had passed the special courts bill under which the courts could try those accused of acting illegally during the emergency. As it was, Sanjay was already under indictment for his alleged role in destroying a film critical of Mrs. Gandhi.

Sanjay's efforts to woo Raj Narain and Charan Singh were welcomed by Madhu Limaye, a prominent member of the Socialist group in the Janata party, a supporter of Charan Singh, and regarded

[16] The role played by Sanjay Gandhi in widening the split between Morarji Desai and Charan Singh is described in detail by Barun Sengupta, a correspondent for the Calcutta newspaper *Anandabazar Patrika* in his book, *Last Days of the Morarji Raj* (Calcutta: Ananda Publishers, 1979), p. 42. Sengupta draws heavily on taped interviews he held with key participants.

by some as a pro-Soviet leftist. Barun Sengupta, a Bengali journalist, quoted Limaye as follows:

> Let me be very frank. From the very beginning I knew that this Janata party is dead. We had been given a mandate. I wanted the Party to implement the promises, do as much as it can. But I was also anxious to see that the Janata party did not fall into the hands of Jana Sangh. . . . They (Jana Sangh leaders) used to say that very soon these old leaders would die and they would not allow any young leader to come up and they would capture power. Their policy was to attack all the younger leaders of the Janata Party, Bahuguna, George [Fernandes], Biju [Patnaik of Orissa], myself and others. If you follow the issues of *Organiser* [a Jana Sangh journal] you will find enough evidence of this. Their policy was to capture power after the death of these three old men [Morarji Desai, Charan Singh, and Jagjivan Ram]. So, immediately after the state elections, my policy was to cultivate the anti-authoritarian Congressmen and the leftists. On the one hand, my attempts were to bring out the CPI men from the influence of authoritarian Indira Gandhi and to bring the CPI(M) closer to the secularist Janata men. And after, I could bring Bahuguna and Chaudhury [Charan Singh] together. I started working upon organizing the secular and anti-authoritarian forces of the country. . . . I was clear in my mind that by the 1982 election, ourselves and the Jana Sangh would not be on the same side.[17]

Madhu Limaye spoke of a realignment of political forces, bringing together the Lok Dal of Charan Singh, his own Socialists, the two Communist parties, and other "progressive forces." Splitting Janata was thus the first step toward bringing down Morarji Desai, forcing new parliamentary elections, and bringing about a national realignment.

Some figures within the Jana Sangh have speculated that Madhu Limaye and H. N. Bahuguna were primarily concerned with destroying Jana Sangh as a major political force in India, since they regarded it as a group whose substantial popular appeal and disciplined political organization represented the single greatest barrier to the growth of leftist forces in the country. As a member of a ruling coalition, Jana Sangh had acquired political respectability and many people regarded its leaders as likely successors to the aging Janata leadership. For the left, therefore, it was essential that the Janata party be divided in order to weaken Jana Sangh. For this reason, they suggested, leftist

---

[17] Ibid., pp. 57-58.

politicians within and outside Janata viewed Charan Singh and the BLD as their ally.

Whatever the varied motives, by mid-June Madhu Limaye, Charan Singh, Raj Narain, and H. N. Bahuguna were prepared to bolt from the Janata party, taking with them the Lok Dal, the Socialists, and some of the Congress for Democracy M.P.s, leaving behind in Janata the Congress (O), the Jana Sangh, and Jagjivan Ram's followers in the Congress for Democracy. The issue now was not whether they could bring the Janata government down—for they clearly had enough M.P.s to do that—but whether they could attract enough support from the left parties, the regional parties, Chavan's Congress, and Mrs. Gandhi's Congress to form an alternative government—the realignment of "leftist and progressive forces" of which Limaye and Bahuguna spoke.

Jana Sangh leaders recognized that these defections would bring down the government and destroy the Janata party—and thereby shatter their hope of becoming the country's dominant political force. They believed that if Charan Singh pulled out of the Janata party with forty or fifty members of Parliament, their best hope of keeping control of the national government was to attract the support of the Congress party of Chavan. They approached Chavan, offering to form a coalition government, but he refused.[18] Chavan had already decided to throw his support behind Charan Singh and the "progressive" camp. Chavan's decision proved decisive. Without Chavan's support for Charan Singh, the Janata government would not have fallen, elections would not have been held, and Mrs. Gandhi would not have been returned to power.

Chavan, as the leader of the opposition, moved a motion of no confidence against the Morarji Desai government. At this point it was not certain that Janata would lose, since only a handful of M.P.s had actually resigned from Janata. Mrs. Gandhi's Congress announced that it would support the no-confidence motion and Sanjay Gandhi reminded Raj Narain that if they could bring down the Desai government, the Congress (I) would support Chaudhury Charan Singh as the prime minister of a coalition government.

Raj Narain and Charan Singh then brought Karpoori Thakur of Bihar, Devi Lal from Haryana, and Ram Naresh Yadav from Uttar Pradesh to Delhi to persuade the BLD M.P.s from their states to resign from Janata. Raj Narain once again denounced the Jana Sangh and, in a further effort to split the government, announced

[18] Ibid., p. 76.

that his group would support Morarji as prime minister if he dismissed the Jana Sangh members of his government.

While Raj Narain was attempting to split the Janata party, Madhu Limaye and Bahuguna were trying to build a new alignment within Parliament that would make it possible to form an alternative government. They easily won the support of the CPI but were having more difficulty with the CPI(M), whose leaders were sympathetic to the proposal for a realignment of "secular and antiauthoritarian" forces but opposed to any alternative government that might include Mrs. Gandhi's Congress party.

More BLD members resigned from the party, and by the morning of July 11, the strength of the Janata party was reduced to 255.[19] The BLD members joined a new party formed by Raj Narain, which he called the Janata (Secular) party, to emphasize his differences with the "nonsecular" Janata party with its Jana Sangh support. Raj Narain's party had forty-five members.

Morarji understood that the issue was not the role of the Jana Sangh in the Janata party, for his opponents saw the removal of Jana Sangh as a device for removing him as prime minister. The defections continued. An important holdout, however, was Jagjivan Ram, who refused to leave the party in spite of the pressure from his one-time political associate, Bahuguna.

On the eve of the vote in Parliament on the no-confidence motion, the CPI(M) politburo issued an announcement that it would vote to bring down the Morarji Desai government. Still another blow was the announcement by George Fernandes, a member of the cabinet and a leading Socialist, that he too was deserting the government, though only a few days earlier he had spoken in the Lok Sabha to defend the performance of the Janata government.[20]

Last-minute efforts were made to save the government. Several Jana Sangh leaders met with Chandra Shekhar, president of the party, to see if Morarji Desai could be persuaded to step down, so that Jagjivan Ram could form a government in the expectation that he could win back defectors. But Desai refused to step down. Instead, Morarji proposed to Chavan that they form a coalition government. As Chavan said:

> He telephoned me and requested me to cooperate with him
> and take responsibility in the Government. But since I was

[19] Ibid., p. 87.
[20] Copies of Fernandes's speech in the Lok Sabha on July 12, 1979, in defense of the Janata government were widely distributed as election literature by the Janata party to counter the Fernandes criticism that the Janata government had become ineffectual.

clear in my mind that we cannot join or support a government which includes the Jana Sangh elements, I told him politely—no, we can't help you. I was not interested to discuss what he was offering and what role we were expected to play and things like that. Naturally he was offering some position in the Government, but we were not interested.[21]

On July 15, 1979, Morarji Desai submitted the cabinet's resignation letter to the president. The Janata party had been in power for only twenty-eight months.

The Twenty-one Day Government of Charan Singh

No single party or coalition of parties was in a position to form a government without the support of Mrs. Gandhi's Congress party. In the days following Morarji Desai's resignation there were frenzied negotiations among the various parties to build a majority coalition. The process was a new one for India, because this was the first time since independence that no party had had a majority of seats in Parliament (see table 1 at the back of this volume).

Chavan, as the leader of the opposition, attempted to win support from other groups to form a government, but Mrs. Gandhi made it clear that under no circumstances would she support a government led by her Congress opponents. On July 22, a few days after the government had fallen, Chavan informed the president that he was unable to form a government.

It was now Charan Singh's turn. He received support from the two left parties, the CPI and CPI(M), from the major regional parties in Tamil Nadu, Punjab, Jammu and Kashmir, and Kerala, and from Chavan's group. But without support from Mrs. Gandhi's Congress he lacked the 270 votes needed to form a government. After being persuaded by Charan Singh that he had the support of the Congress (I), President Sanjiva Reddy agreed to appoint him prime minister. On July 26 he was sworn in, with Chavan as deputy prime minister. Other members of the government included T. A. Pai, Brahmananda Reddy, C. Subramanian, and Karan Singh, all, significantly, former Congressmen who were now opponents of Mrs. Gandhi.

No sooner had the new government been formed than rumors spread that Mrs. Gandhi and Sanjay were displeased with the cabinet because it contained so many anti–Mrs. Gandhi Congressmen. Congress (I) leaders informed Charan Singh that they would not vote for

[21] Sengupta, *Last Days of the Morarji Raj*, p. 100.

his government unless he changed the composition of his cabinet and introduced legislation to end the special courts Parliament had established to try Mrs. Gandhi and other members of her government for acts committed during the emergency. But the socialists, the CPI, and many Chavan Congress supporters warned that they would withdraw from the coalition government if it took steps to abolish the special courts. Charan Singh quickly made it clear that he was unwilling (and politically unable) to end the special courts.

Morarji Desai resigned as head of the Janata parliamentary party and Jagjivan Ram was elected to replace him. Rumors spread that Mrs. Gandhi might be willing to support a Janata government if Jagjivan Ram were to become the prime minister. At the same time, Janata leaders starting wooing the CPI(M) and a number of Congressmen in the Chavan camp.

It was clear that Mrs. Gandhi had it in her power to bring down the Charan Singh government, to put Jagjivan Ram into office, or to force an election.

On the morning of August 20, a few hours before the Lok Sabha was to meet to vote on the Charan Singh government, the Congress (I) parliamentary board announced that it would not support the government. A few hours later, Charan Singh called an emergency meeting of the cabinet, which decided not to face Parliament but to resign immediately and ask the president to call a new election. Charan Singh's government had been in office for only twenty-one days.

In the days that followed there was a public controversy over whether the president should call new elections or first ask Jagjivan Ram to try to form an alternative government. Ram offered to form a government, but President Reddy, after consulting with members of Parliament, concluded that Jagjivan Ram lacked a majority, and he chose instead to dissolve Parliament and call elections. His decision was bitterly denounced by Janata leaders, who were convinced that the president had denied Jagjivan Ram an opportunity to form a government because he was a Harijan; others suggested that the president expected the elections to produce an unstable government that would place him in a powerful position as the head of state; and still others thought he was indulging a personal vendetta against Jagjivan Ram, who had opposed him when he had first contested the office of president in 1969.

President Reddy asked Charan Singh to stay on as the head of a caretaker government and instructed the Election Commission to set in motion machinery for national midterm parliamentary elections. Elections were scheduled for the first week in January.

At the end of three weeks of political gaming, only Mrs. Gandhi and Sanjay emerged as victors. In a country that admires politicians who manipulate others to their advantage, Mrs. Gandhi and Sanjay were given credit for the skillful way they had maneuvered the breakup of the Janata party and kept Charan Singh dangling, only to bring his government down. The Janata party was a shambles, deserted by the BLD, the Socialists, and some of the ex-Congress members. Only the Jana Sangh, of the major groups, remained fully intact. Many other Janata M.P.s had moved back and forth from one leader and one "party" to another. Party splitting and parliamentary defections, which had once only characterized state politics, now characterized national politics as well. Some observers said that for the first time politics in Delhi were like those in Lucknow and Patna, the provincial capitals of Uttar Pradesh and Bihar. Indeed, it was striking to see how much of the political game had been dominated by politicians from these two states—Charan Singh, Raj Narain, Madhu Limaye, H. N. Bahuguna, Chandra Shekhar, Jagjivan Ram, and, of course, Sanjay and Indira Gandhi. The exceptions were Morarji Desai (a Gujarati) and Y. B. Chavan (a Maharashtrian), but at every step they were clearly outmaneuvered by Hindi-speaking politicians. And in the end it was Mrs. Gandhi and Sanjay, commanding support from only eighty M.P.s and without power in either Uttar Pradesh or Bihar, who outmaneuvered everyone.

The Caretaker Government

President Sanjiva Reddy asked Charan Singh to form a caretaker government to run the country until the elections. Charan Singh's government, made up of members of the Lok Dal—renamed the Janata (Secular) party—Chavan's Congress party, and representatives from several of the smaller regional parties, was in office for five months. All observers agree that it was not a government that functioned well. Ministers were on the campaign trail much of the time, and a number of government decisions were made for the political benefit of Charan Singh's party. In the absence of ministerial authority, already mismanaged and uncoordinated government-run industries deteriorated. By the end of the year there were growing shortages of electric power, slowdowns in the railways and ports, declining coal deliveries, shortages of diesel fuel, a rise in the price of sugar, onions, and other commodities, and a slowdown in industrial

31

production. Inflation increased to an estimated 20 percent. Industrial strikes, already a problem, increased in number, particularly in the public sector. The rise in prices was made worse by a government decision to establish price supports of some commodities at higher rates than those recommended by the Agricultural Prices Commission, the official government body that determines the price the government should pay for commodities. Industrial production was seriously affected by shortages of coal and steel, inadequate power, inefficient transport, deteriorating industrial relations, and the lack of coordination among various ministries.

At times the government's price policies seemed almost calculated to create shortages. In sugar, for example, the government adopted what is known in India as a dual price policy, under which part of the sugar output is purchased by the government for distribution in fair-price shops while the remainder is sold on the open market. The government price is often set low to keep prices down for the poor; often it is even below the cost of production, so that producers actually sell to the government at a loss. The loss is then made up by selling sugar at a very high price on the open market, resulting in a considerable disparity between the controlled and the free price, which leads consumers to believe that producers are making exorbitant profits. Actually, the low prices on controlled sugar cause such heavy losses in the sugar industry that some of the smaller, less profitable units are forced to close down, leading to a decline in cane production and a rise in the price of sugar on the open market. One writer called it "a foolproof system for creating a shortage." [22]

Budgetary deficits grew, adding fuel to the inflationary fire. Since industrial growth rates were low and industries contribute the bulk of central and state revenues, there was little growth in tax revenues. Reluctant to increase its revenues by pushing up prices, the government artificially kept the price of kerosene and diesel fuel down, thereby worsening the budget deficit. Planned investment in the public sector, which accounts for some 60 percent of the country's capital formation, was virtually stagnant, with the result that there was almost no growth in employment in the organized sector.[23] For obvious reasons, the caretaker government was reluctant to resist pressures from employers in both public and private sectors to increase wages and benefits, and this contributed to the inflationary price rise. Moreover, the states and central governments were them-

[22] Pai Panandikar, "A Fair Question," *Hindustan Times*, January 8, 1980.
[23] Prem Shankar Jha, "Another Plan Holiday?" *Times of India*, February 1, 1980.

selves increasing emoluments to their employees, thus worsening the budget deficits.[24]

By the end of 1979 it was widely reported that many educated voters and members of the business community blamed the Janata party rather than the Charan Singh government for the deteriorating economic situation. After all, it was the Janata party that had been elected, and the politicians now running the country were renegade members of the Janata party. If the country now had an unstable government whose actions, or lack of actions, caused budget deficits, declining production, rising prices, and growing industrial disturbances, then wasn't it because the Janata party had failed to keep itself together? It was an argument that Mrs. Gandhi used effectively during the election campaign.

[24] For a detailed description of the deteriorating economic situation in the latter part of 1979, see N. S. Jagannathan, "Economic Notebook," *Statesman*, January 18, 1980; and Nabagopal Das, "After the Elections," *Statesman*, January 11, 1980.

2

The Campaign

Coalition-Making

From August 21, 1980, when President Sanjiva Reddy dissolved Parliament and ordered a general election, to January 3 and 6, when the elections took place, the central concern of party leaders was how to put together a winning coalition.

There were six nationally recognized parties, forming three "pairs." There were two Janata parties, one led by Jagjivan Ram and the other by Charan Singh, prime minister of the caretaker government. There were two Congress parties, one led by Mrs. Gandhi and the other by Devaraj Urs. There were two Communist parties, the Communist party of India and the Communist party of India (Marxist). At the regional level there were even two Tamil nationalist parties, the Dravida Munnetra Kazhagam (DMK) and the All India Anna DMK (AIADMK).

Each party within a pair, with the exception of the Communist parties, belonged to a different electoral coalition. One coalition centered around Charan Singh's Lok Dal. Charan Singh sought to keep together the coalition he had created to form his government. It consisted of the Lok Dal and the Congress (U) and two regional parties, the Akalis in the Punjab and the AIADMK in Tamil Nadu. This coalition had the support of both Communist parties. Madhu Limaye, the intellectual architect of the coalition, spoke of a "class realignment," focusing on the backward-caste middle peasants, agricultural laborers, and the working class. The coalition called itself "secular," to distinguish it from the alleged anti-Muslim "communalism" of the Janata party, and "democratic," to distinguish it from the "authoritarianism" of Mrs. Gandhi's Congress.

The electoral coalition proved unsteady. Efforts to bring Lok Dal and Congress (U) together with a single electoral manifesto failed, though the efforts continued through early December. Devaraj Urs, the Congress (U) leader, evidently concluded that his party had made a political mistake in bringing down the Janata government, supporting Charan Singh as prime minister, taking part in a coalition government, and allowing the country to slip into new elections. But Congress (U) leaders decided that, even if the two parties did not agree upon a single election manifesto, they had little choice but to continue the electoral arrangement. The weakness of the alliance and the near certainty that its electoral prospects were poor led a number of prominent leaders of the two parties to defect, most notably Brahmananda Reddy, the Congress (U) leader from Andhra, and H. N. Bahuguna, the Lok Dal leader from Uttar Pradesh.

Though the CPI supported the Lok Dal–Congress (U) coalition, it too was divided. S. A. Dange, long-time Communist leader and a powerful figure in the All India Trade Union Congress (AITUC), the CPI-controlled trade union federation, broke from his party to support Mrs. Gandhi.[1] During the campaign he sent a congratulatory telegram to Mrs. Gandhi when she reached an understanding with the shahi imam of Jama Masjid, the prominent Muslim leader.[2] Dange's endorsement of Mrs. Gandhi meant that the resources of the AITUC (which receives support from the World Federation of Trade Unions, one of whose vice-presidents is Dange) were not available to CPI-supported Lok Dal or Congress (U) candidates.

The CPI(M) supported the Lok Dal–Congress (U) coalition, but it was primarily concerned with the fate of its own governments in Kerala and West Bengal. The CPI(M) was reluctant to take part in any electoral arrangement that would involve giving up seats in either of these two states in return for seats elsewhere. From the CPI(M)'s point of view, however, the break between the CPI and

---

[1] According to R. L. Chaufla, in "Ramifications of Authoritarianism," *Mainstream*, January 5, 1980 (a Marxist magazine), S. A. Dange submitted a note to the Central Committee of the CPI in which he distinguished between monopoly capital and the national bourgeoisie. He identified Indira Gandhi as a "representative of patriotic national bourgeoisie" and alleged that the CPI had failed to understand the character of the national bourgeoisie and its leadership.

[2] H. N. Bahuguna, who had joined Mrs. Gandhi, mediated the agreement between the imam and Mrs. Gandhi. Since Bahuguna and Dange are regarded in India as pro-Soviet, observers concluded that the Soviets were eager to see Mrs. Gandhi reelected, particularly at a time when they were seeking Indian support for their role in Afghanistan. According to a report in the *Hindustan Times* (January 14, 1980), India's subsequent stand at the United Nations on Afghanistan and the Soviet reaction to the Congress (I) victory were seen in the CPI as a "vindication" of S. A. Dange's position.

Mrs. Gandhi enabled the two Communist parties to form a common electoral front. It was the CPI's support for Mrs. Gandhi in the 1977 elections that had prevented the two parties from working together. The CPI(M) had also moved closer to the CPI on international issues by its increasingly pro-Soviet views. In January, for example, the CPI(M) politburo defended the Soviet intervention in Afghanistan, which it compared to India's support for Bangladesh. The CPI(M) also called for recognition of the Soviet-backed government in Kampuchea.

The CPI(M) leaders backed the Lok Dal–Congress (U) alliance, but their particular anxiety was to prevent Mrs. Gandhi's return to power, for they feared that she would seek to undermine the two Communist governments. Many observers believed that, despite its denunciation of "communalism," the CPI(M) was likely to give support to any coalition in the national Parliament that would keep Mrs. Gandhi from becoming prime minister.

A similar concern for state politics dictated the behavior of the DMK and the AIADMK in Tamil Nadu. The AIADMK, which had supported Mrs. Gandhi in the 1977 elections, now allied itself with Janata—a clear marriage of convenience, particularly since the AIADMK was actually supporting the Lok Dal–Congress (U) coalition government and one of its members was in the national cabinet. But since neither the Lok Dal nor the Congress (U) had any political strength within Tamil Nadu, while Janata did, it seemed politically advisable to strike an alliance with Janata at the state level, regardless of the AIADMK's alliance at the national level. A local arrangement seemed all the more important since Congress (I) in Tamil Nadu had an electoral alliance with the DMK, though it should be noted that in 1977 the alliances had been completely reversed.

An equally bizarre electoral arrangement was made in Kerala, where Congress (U), Congress (I), and Janata, all opponents nationally, came together to form a single coalition in opposition to a Communist-led left front that controlled the state government. In Maharashtra, the state unit of the Congress (U) joined the Janata party and another independent splinter–Congress party to oppose Mrs. Gandhi's Congress (I).

These state alliances not only emphasized the priority given by local party leaders to considerations of state over national politics, they also indicated that there was a political logic to the process of coalition building that was independent of ideologies and economic interests, although political leaders often sought to find some public rationale other than self-interest to explain their party's electoral arrangements. Finding such a rationale was complicated by the fact that state units of parties did not always follow their national parties, and coalitions formed in November sometimes unraveled by December.

This confusing pattern of state and national alliances, and the movement of prominent politicians from one party to another, bred considerable cynicism even in a political system where the comings and goings of politicians have always been commonplace. The defections were now on a scale far beyond previous national elections and the alliances seemed more baldly based upon political self-interest than ever. What effect this had on the electorate it is hard to say, though it demoralized party workers and depressed much of the academic intelligentsia, the journalists, and other middle-class professionals.

On one thing everyone agreed. There was no possibility that either Janata or Lok Dal by itself could win an electoral majority; a government led by Charan Singh or Jagjivan Ram would be a coalition. Though Mrs. Gandhi's Congress might not win a majority of seats in Parliament either, her party was the only one with such prospects. Quite a few were convinced that Mrs. Gandhi would be able to form a stable central government, for she alone had the chance of winning a parliamentary majority and she alone had a record of holding a national government together.

Campaigning

The contest was not simply among three parties, or even three coalitions, but among three candidates for the office of prime minister. Each of the three parties announced in advance who would be prime minister if its party or coalition won, thereby focusing the attention of the media and voters on particular personalities as well as on the parties. The posters of the three major parties displayed photos of Indira Gandhi, Chaudhury Charan Singh, and Jagjivan Ram, and parliamentary candidates asked voters to cast their ballots for these leaders, not only for their parties.

For Mrs. Gandhi the emphasis upon choosing a national leader was, of course, advantageous since she alone of the three leaders could claim national stature. Moreover, she proved an indefatigable campaigner. She visited over 300 constituencies, traveled over 40,000 miles by plane, helicopter, and car, and addressed some 1,500 meetings. Her processions had a royal quality, with caparisoned elephants lumbering at the head of endless cars and jeeps. As she drove through the countryside at night, she sat in the front seat of a Peugeot switching on a battery-operated strip of fluorescent light when crowds appeared, revealing her familiar austere features and disheveled gray hair, modestly enveloped in her sari. It was, as one correspondent described it, an "exalted image" bathed in an eerie radiance.

The central slogan of Mrs. Gandhi's campaign was "Elect a government that works," a slogan that appeared on party posters everywhere. In her speeches she promised that Congress (I) would "restore stability" and "law and order." She spoke of the "harassment of Harijans and Adivasis" (tribals) since Janata took power, the increasing crime rate, especially in New Delhi, the downward trend in the GNP, the absence of industrial growth, the rise in the price of sugar, kerosene, matches, and salt, and what she asserted was the ineffective role of India in world affairs under the Janata government.[3]

Mrs. Gandhi made a special effort to reach out to Muslims, scheduled castes, and scheduled tribes. In Orissa, for example, she visited all five scheduled-tribe constituencies and the industrial steel town of Rourkela with its large tribal population. She attracted large and enthusiastic crowds, leading reporters to conclude (correctly) that there was a pro-Indira sentiment in the tribal belt extending from Orissa into portions of Madhya Pradesh and Bihar.[4]

In her speeches to minorities she emphasized not only her commitment to their economic improvement, but the need to bring to an end the violence against Harijans and Muslims, which she attributed to communalism—the anti-Muslim character of the Janata party and the anti-Harijan character of the Lok Dal. To emphasize her concern with law and order she campaigned in constituencies where there had been clashes between Hindus and Muslims and between ex-untouchables and caste Hindus. And to those ex-untouchables who may have been tempted to vote for the Janata party because of Jagjivan Ram, she said that "the Janata government would never make Jagjivan Ram prime minister."[5]

She did not repudiate the emergency but said instead that if returned to power she would "give the country a strong and stable Government, putting back the country once again on the rails of economic progress." The emergency, she said, had had to be promulgated because of "peculiar circumstances prevailing then"—but she added, "Those days will never come back again." She also reminded her audience that "the courts had cleared her of all blame despite the crores of rupees the Janata government had spent to convict her."[6]

[3] The statements are from an election broadcast on All India Radio, reported in the *Times of India*, December 22, 1979.

[4] Ibid., November 2, 1979.

[5] *This Fortnight*, January 7, 1980.

[6] *Statesman*, January 17, 1980.

Although the minorities had not forgotten the sterilization and slum clearance, concern for their own safety led many at least to forgive her. "The Emergency was good," said one Harijan to a journalist. "Only blackmailers were upset, not the *kisans* [peasants] and the poor. *Goondaism* [thievery] stopped and everything was available. Only *nasbandi* was bad for which Mrs. Gandhi has already apologized." An anti-Congress *kisan* exploded. "What are you saying? Don't you realize that the Emergency is dangerous. None of us were able to speak out and she will impose it again along with *nasbandi*. She cannot run the country without Emergency." "But," came the reply, "we have taught her a lesson. She has apologized for her mistakes. Besides, it was not her fault. She had 500 *netas* [leaders] to misguide her and who are now with the Janata party and the Lok Dal."[7]

In one speech after another, Mrs. Gandhi promised to restore "stable government," establish "law and order," and create more "discipline." These code words had multiple meanings. For the minorities, they promised security. For cultivators, businessmen, and the middle class, a "government that works" would turn the power on, move the trains, provide kerosene, and bring down prices. To many, the restoration of "discipline" meant bringing an end to the strikes that had paralyzed so much of the country's industry.[8] The emphases on electing a government "that works" and "law and order" were of course conservative appeals, quite different from the populist and radical slogans that Mrs. Gandhi had used in earlier elections.

[7] *This Fortnight*, January 7, 1980.

[8] In an article that interpreted her statements as antiunion, V. Balasubrahamian wrote: "Mrs. Gandhi seems to have got her priorities right. Even as the first round of election returns were being announced, she told a news agency that her first task would be to restore law and order and ensure security for the people. . . . The issue of law and order is much larger than a question of dealing sternly with communal flareups, caste feuding in the countryside or 'chain-snatchers' on city streets. The core of the problem is the restoration of a sense of responsibility to the community in the thinking and conduct of organised labour. We do not realize enough that farmers and other primary producers do not and cannot ventilate their grievances or enforce their claims on the community by withholding essential supplies. Workers in organised industry, however, have been permitted over a period to enjoy this privilege to an excessive degree. . . . Illegal strikes, go slow or work-to-rules have been merrily throttling the flow of essential utilities such as transport of vital supplies such as oil, and presently the country's banking system is being plagued by illegal and usually unaccounted stoppages of work. Unless this anti-social outbreak of aggression on the part of unions or employees in strategic industries is sternly dealt with, there can neither be restoration of law and order in the larger sense nor, in a more specific sense, the rehabilitation of crippled facilities such as coal, power, transport." "Forward with the People," *Hindustan Times*, January 9, 1980.

Janata's answer to Mrs. Gandhi was to remind the voters of the authoritarian regime imposed by Mrs. Gandhi during the emergency and to warn that the emergency might be reinstated. Because the election symbol of the Congress (I) on the ballot was a raised hand, Jagjivan Ram frequently warned his audiences that the raised hand would be converted, as he put it, into a "clenched fist" after the elections. One Janata poster depicted Sanjay Gandhi, scalpel in hand, standing over a fearful patient in a sterilization clinic. "Not now," said Mrs. Gandhi, with her hand raised, "after the elections." The poster was in Urdu, a language widely used by Muslims.

But try as he could, Jagjivan Ram, though a Harijan himself, failed to arouse fears that Mrs. Gandhi's election would mean a return to the emergency or to compulsory sterilization. Hadn't Mrs. Gandhi and Sanjay apologized for the "excesses," even while they blamed others?

Jagjivan Ram proved neither an effective speaker nor a good party leader. Though he had been in national politics since independence and had served as a cabinet member longer than any other public figure, he was not a man of mass appeal. Stories abounded of the personal wealth he had allegedly acquired in office, which did not contribute to the Janata party's effort to depict itself as a party of moral rectitude, committed to democracy, opposed to defections, authoritarianism, and corruption.

Rumors also spread that Jagjivan Ram, eager to become prime minister, would strike a deal with Mrs. Gandhi after the election if no single party won a clear majority, and might even desert Janata and join Congress (I) before the election. There were rumors that he would leave Janata if Congress (I) agreed to make him president of the party immediately, with an assurance that he would be made prime minister if they won the election.[9] There was also a rumor of a deal between Jagjivan Ram and Mrs. Gandhi in which she would become prime minister and he would become president of the Congress party, then president of India upon the completion of Sanjiva Reddy's term.[10] Jagjivan Ram repudiated these rumors, but they served to demoralize Janata party workers and strengthen the feeling that defections from Janata had not ended.

Janata made the issue of "defection" a major campaign theme. Candidates appealed to voters to "punish" those who left the party. Janata leaders emphasized that their government had fallen because of the defectors to the Lok Dal, and therefore the defectors, not

[9] *Times of India*, December 6, 1979, reported that such a proposal was considered but rejected by the Congress (I) parliamentary board.
[10] Ibid., November 2, 1979.

Janata, should be repudiated by the voters. The Janata party had run the government well, claimed Ramakrishna Hegde, secretary of the Janata party, but

> betrayers within the Janata party had succeeded in break-
> ing up the party and bringing down the government. None-
> theless, Janata had restored the Fundamental Rights sus-
> pended during the Emergency, abolished censorship, repealed
> MISA, released political prisoners, restored the independence
> of the judiciary, reestablished freedom of the press. The
> government had also increased investment in rural areas,
> removed many controls and pushed up production in such
> key industries as power, fertilizers and cement; foreign trade
> and exchange reserves had increased; most importantly, the
> government had launched the Antyodaya programme to
> provide employment for the poorest families; there was a
> major increase in irrigation, and in drinking water, and the
> growth rate had moved well ahead of the average growth of
> 3 percent during Indira Gandhi's "dynamic decade."[11]

It was an impressive list of accomplishments, but Janata spokesmen could not escape the central criticism that the party elected in 1977 to govern the country had fallen apart.

Charan Singh disavowed the charge that he and his supporters were "defectors," but emphasized that Janata had split because of the anti-Muslim communal character of a section of the party. Taking a more positive stance, he projected himself and his party as the spokesmen for India's agricultural classes. He promised that if the Lok Dal and Congress (U) were elected they would transfer power to rural India and pursue development policies that would benefit the countryside at the expense of the city. In a speech in Jaipur Charan Singh said that

> he would not allow machine-made consumer goods to be sold
> in the country as could be produced by artisans and manual
> laborers. He would only allow such factories to function if
> they exported all their produce. . . . There was no need to
> have factories for the manufacture of bread, biscuits, gar-
> ments, small tools, clothes and other such items as could be
> produced by manual labor. He said that he recently ordered
> the closure of a factory set up in Sultanpur near Delhi for
> producing pre-fabricated houses since such factories ren-
> dered thousands of workers and artisans unemployed.[12]

[11] Ramakrishna Hegde, "Why You Should Vote Janata," *Illustrated Weekly*, December 30, 1979, pp. 25-27.
[12] *Times of India*, November 19, 1979.

The Media and the Party Organizations

All the parties depended on public meetings, the visits and speeches of their best-known state and national leaders, the canvassing of their party workers, political processions, and posters. The mass media—radio, television, and the press—remained secondary as a means of reaching the electorate. Television and radio are government run, and they provided minimal opportunities for the parties to present their case.

Two of the four major English-language dailies leaned toward Mrs. Gandhi and two toward Janata. None of the English dailies, given their urban orientation, supported Charan Singh. The *Times of India*, whose coverage of the campaign, particularly its constituency-by-constituency reporting, was the most comprehensive and whose preelection assessments proved remarkably accurate, supported Mrs. Gandhi. The *Hindustan Times* was particularly strong in its support for the Congress (I). The *Indian Express*, which provided extensive coverage and has more regional editions than any other newspaper, was opposed to Mrs. Gandhi. Its anti-Congress (I) position colored much of its analysis, though many of its local reports from north India made accurate predictions. The *Statesman*, with editions in Delhi and Calcutta, was pro-Janata, though its uncertain mood was reflected in the report from one of its correspondents from Uttar Pradesh, who wrote in a reflective vein: "What guarantee is there that if either the Lok Dal or the Janata party is given a majority they will not quarrel again among themselves and fall like ninepins? And again, what is the guarantee that the dark days of the Emergency will not come back if the Congress (I) dons the mantle? An unenviable choice, indeed."[13]

None of the national parties could lay claim to effective local organizations with experienced party cadres. Janata had not held internal party elections, so at the local level it was a makeshift organization. Of the four senior national leaders who had toured the country in its support in 1977, Jayaprakash Narayan was dead, Morarji Desai was no longer the party's leader, Charan Singh had defected, and only Jagjivan Ram remained. The Jana Sangh segment alone had experienced cadres, and they were not enthusiastic about the party's choice of a national leader.

Charan Singh had considerable support among the middle peasants, and his followers were more enthusiastic, but the Lok Dal's

---

[13] *Statesman*, January 1, 1980.

organization was also makeshift, since it had been assembled only a few months before the elections. Yet in some areas it did command resources; its geographical base was more limited and it put up fewer candidates than the other two major national parties, but where it operated it had the capacity to reach out to the rural areas.

Mrs. Gandhi's Congress (I) had not held organizational elections either, and the split with the Congress (U) had left the party with few well-known state or national leaders. Before 1971 the district Congress committees and the pradesh Congress committees had had the dominant voice in the selection of parliamentary candidates, but after the Congress split of 1971 candidate selection had been centralized in the hands of the Congress Central Election Committee controlled by Mrs. Gandhi. In 1980, both Mrs. Gandhi and Sanjay personally played an active role in the selection of Congress (I) parliamentary candidates. The candidates themselves put together their own electoral organizations, drawing on what remained of the local Congress, their personal supporters, and, if they were associates of Sanjay Gandhi, the local Youth Congress.

How many of the Congress (I) nominees were associated with Sanjay was unclear. On the eve of the elections, the *Indian Express* surveyed its own correspondents, who reported that eighty candidates were "active aides or were personally favored by Mr. Gandhi" and another sixty-five were "known to be close associates of his aides."[14] The largest number, the reports said, were thirty candidates from Uttar Pradesh. They also noted that many of Sanjay's candidates were given relatively safe seats, which created some resentment among local Congress leaders. Though at the time Congress supporters criticized newspaper accounts that many Sanjay associates had been chosen as candidates by the Congress Central Election Committee (CEC), after the elections there was less reluctance to report the magnitude of Sanjay's personal support within Parliament.

Most of the Congress (I) candidates had never served in Parliament, and they were probably the youngest group to stand since the first elections in 1952. (Half the M.P.s elected in 1980 were new to Parliament, and only one-quarter had served in the sixth Lok Sabha, dissolved in August.) They were clearly not elected on the basis of their local standing, the strength of the local Congress (I) party organization, or any media campaign by the party. It was Mrs. Gandhi's popularity that proved important, and her capacity to draw back to the party groups that had been supporters in earlier elections.

[14] *Indian Express*, December 30, 1979.

How Honest Were the Elections?

Following the 1980 parliamentary elections journalists and losing candidates charged that there had been widespread fraud and violation of the election laws.[15] The election results, they said, did not accurately reflect voter preferences; attempts to "explain" the election results therefore assumed incorrectly that there was a relationship between voter preference and electoral outcome. Variations in the amount of money candidates spent, bribes of voters and election officials, and various types of rigging, they argued, had made the elections a farce. Charges were leveled at virtually all parties: the Lok Dal, it was said, did better in Uttar Pradesh than in Bihar because it controlled the state government and was able to manipulate the results in its favor. Elsewhere, it was said, local officials rigged results to benefit Mrs. Gandhi's candidates.

That elections were rigged in some constituencies is beyond doubt; that the police, the Election Commission, and the courts were unable to cope with all cases in which the vote was manipulated is also beyond doubt; but the magnitude of the fraud and whether it actually affected the outcome in more than a handful of constituencies are unknown. Charges were invariably exaggerated, for they were part of the campaign rhetoric; defeats were frequently explained by reference to the machinations of one's opponents, not to a loss of voter support.

Nonetheless, a review of the various devices employed by candidates and their supporters to influence the outcome of the elections illegally is important to our understanding of the election results and, more particularly, to our understanding of how candidates operated and what role the local police and administration played in the election. What follows, then, is a brief review of some of the ways in which candidates and parties attempted to fix election results, usually, though not always, by illegal methods.

Campaign Financing. Charges of "Arab," "Soviet," and "CIA" financing of elections are commonplace in India; they are a normal part of campaign rhetoric and, at least as far as the 1980 election campaign is concerned, remain unverified. Election law restricts the amount of money candidates can spend, but in India, as elsewhere, the sums

---

[15] For a list of such charges, see Nalini Singh, "Elections as They Really Are," *Economic and Political Weekly*, vol. 15, no. 21 (May 24, 1980), pp. 909-14. For this review I have drawn heavily from his article and on my own visits to polling stations, interviews with election and police officials and party candidates, and an extensive session at the Election Commission in New Delhi.

spent far exceed the legal limits, since there are no restrictions on what can be spent by friends of the candidates.[16] Earlier Congress governments had passed legislation aimed at restricting the flow of funds to opposition parties. In the late 1960s, for example, Mrs. Gandhi abolished the privy purses of the former princes, an act regarded by many as a device for preventing money from flowing to the Jana Sangh. Similarly, an act restricting election contributions by private companies was widely regarded as a way of preventing businessmen from contributing to the Swatantra party, a group that favored free enterprise.

A major source of campaign funds for most parties is "black money," from the large sector of the Indian economy that illegally escapes taxation. In an economy of government-regulated prices, much of what is sold enters the "free" or "black" market, where incomes are neither reported nor taxed. Much of it flows into the hands of bureaucrats as bribes, or to candidates for public office as "contributions." This illegal sector is so large and its influence on both bureaucrats and elected officials is considered so great that some observers have argued that this "intermediate class" of nonsalaried persons constitutes the real governing class in India, committed not to economic growth, but to the maintenance of a system of controls that enhances its own private gain.[17] This class, it is said, is interested not in the victory of any particular party or candidate but in the maintenance of close ties with whoever is likely to win. Thus, it is said, substantial sums were given to Mrs. Gandhi's candidates this time, anticipating the victory of her party. But the black market elements would have supported whoever had won, and they hedged their bets by providing money to candidates of several parties.

Fixing Electoral Rolls. In India voter registration is the responsibility of the Election Commission rather than of the voters themselves. Local officials, including school teachers, are recruited by returning officers to draw up voter lists by conducting a house-to-house canvass. The electoral lists are then made public and individual voters may check to see if they have been included. In practice, few voters check,

---

[16] Under law each candidate is permitted election expenses of up to Rs 100,000, approximately $12,000. Under the Companies Law, a bill passed in 1956, companies cannot make contributions to political parties or to candidates, but companies can indirectly (and legally) give funds by purchasing advertisements in "souvenir" volumes published by political parties.

[17] For a study of the political role of the "intermediate class," the self-employed in the trade, manufacturing, and service sectors, see Prem Shankar Jha, *India: A Political Economy of Stagnation* (Bombay: Oxford University Press, 1980).

even in urban areas. Only when the voters arrive at the polling stations do they sometimes discover that their names have been omitted, and by then it is too late. In some instances voters who have voted in previous elections find that their names are no longer on the electoral rolls.

Between 1971 and 1977 the number of Indians listed on the electoral rolls increased by 17.2 percent (an average increase of 2.9 percent per year), while from 1977 to 1980 the number increased by 10.2 percent (3.4 percent per year). The variations from one state to another and from one constituency to another were often considerable. These variations only partially reflect the number who have reached the voting age of twenty-one since the previous election and the effect of the local death rate and immigration or emigration. They are in fact often unrelated to demographic changes and seem to be determined more by "administrative" factors—including, some have argued, political pressures. In Bihar, for example, some constituencies actually experienced a decline in the size of the electoral rolls in 1980, while in other constituencies the increases were well above the statewide and nationwide averages. And in Assam the increase in the electoral rolls reflected the registration of illegal migrants from Bangladesh.

Influencing the Turnout. Parties have developed a variety of techniques for selectively affecting the local voting turnout. Nalini Singh provides one example of the way officers in charge of a polling booth can keep the turnout low in a locality where a party believes that its opponents are strong:

> In booths . . . located in villages inclining toward the leading "forward" candidate [member of the forward castes] the polling parties deliberately slowed down the polling by adopting dilatory procedures; delays in scanning the electoral roll to identify an elector, a long pause before the name was announced for cross-checking by polling agents, a manicurist's attention to detail in placing the indelible mark on the fingernail, fastidious folding of the ballot paper before handing it over with the franking stick. Against the normal one or two votes per minute the rate was slowed down to one vote in four minutes. Whenever there was a good turnout of voters, the presiding officer would hurl his baton at the end of waiting voters alleging that they were creating a disturbance in the booth area, and would detain some persons under "booth arrest." The timid villagers dispersed in panic, not sure of their crime, but sensitive enough to know

that "hakim" did not want voters near the booth. The message spread quickly through the village and nobody ventured to vote—and thus displease the presiding officer in a nearby block.[18]

Still another device for discouraging voters is for a candidate to bring his own voters to the polling station in large numbers early in the day. Thus, it was alleged, in some constituencies where Lok Dal was strong, backward-caste supporters would line up at the polling station, discouraging upper-caste supporters of other parties, who would arrive to find that they had to wait in a long line to vote. A similar strategy was often pursued in urban areas where a candidate with low-caste support believed that middle-class voters who were in opposition could be discouraged by finding a long line of low-caste people ahead of them. One more device for discouraging communities is for sympathetic officers to place a polling booth in an inconvenient location. The Election Commission has issued instructions that special attention be paid to the proper location of booths for Harijans and Muslims. But an officer who wants to discourage these communities from voting may locate their booths in the neighborhood of the dominant caste or place them several miles away from the minority's hamlet.

Are Voters Bribed? There is a variety of direct and indirect methods by which money is used to influence voters. Candidates recruit large numbers of young people to man voter booths, canvass voters, take part in bicycle processions, and drive the jeeps and other transport used to carry the candidates and their workers around the constituency or to bring voters to the polls. These "volunteers" are typically paid. Local *mukhiyas*, or village headmen, and *sarpanchs*, elected *taluka* officials, may be given sums to cover their "personal expenses" for participating in the election campaign. Similarly, sums may be given to officers of cooperative societies and other local associations, either for their own personal use or for distribution to voters. There are "vote banks" in India, that is, groups of voters under the influence of a local caste, faction, or community leader. These leaders are much in the tradition of ward heelers in American cities at the turn of the century. Payments to them, either in cash, in services performed, or in long-term influence assured, are presumed to result in the delivery of the voters.

[18] Singh, "Elections As They Really Are," p. 911.

Booth Capturing. Candidates are known to recruit "strongmen" who may forcibly prevent voters from voting or physically take possession of the polling stations. One such strongman explained:

> My men guard the booth. Yes, they are armed; some workers do the ballot stamping inside. What do the poor know about voting? Half of them can't even see the symbols on the ballot paper, their eyes are so bad. A few weeks before polling day hoodlums and bandits are booked by the leading candidates. The various agreements are common knowledge in the community. . . . The rates are in the range of Rs 1,500–2,000 per booth, plus a jeep on polling day. In other words, the candidate's outlay on bandit-labour is about one to two rupees per vote captured or about Rs 1.5 lakh for capturing 100 booths (about 80,000 votes). The rates for booth disturbance are somewhat lower— Rs 500–1,000 per booth disturbed. . . . In the standard procedure, the gang leader supervises the manufacturing of bombs . . . the normal requirement is one or two bombs per booth to be captured or disturbed.[19]

> The gangs swing into action 8–10 hours before the official commencement of polling, that is, around mid-night. The polling parties are already in position in the booth premises by that time. The gangs storm the flimsy structure, usually a school room or a portable shack. There is usually no resistance from members of the polling party who are not only out-numbered but are also unarmed. The intruders demand and obtain blank ballot papers, force the presiding officer to sign them by candle light, and arrange an efficient assembly line in which one person affixes the thumb impression, another stamps the ballot, the third man folds the paper correctly, and another inserts the folded ballots into the boxes. Despite the coordinated activity, the process is time-intensive and it takes about three hours to "poll" 500 votes. The job done, the team leaves for another booth, and later the members of the polling party enter the serial numbers and names of the "voters" on the ballot paper counter-foils and strike off corresponding names on the electoral rolls.[20]

To prevent booth capturing the returning officers work closely with the Inspector General of police. Because it is not always possible to have police officers at each polling station, there are a number of "flying squads" who are on call on election day to respond to

19 Ibid., p. 912.
20 Ibid., p. 914.

reports that booths have been captured. Moreover, if returning officers are informed after the fact that a booth has been captured, the ballot boxes for that polling station are impounded and reballoting will take place.

Prior to the 1980 elections, newspapers reported that a considerable amount of booth capturing was expected; Lok Dal and Congress (I) candidates accused each other of recruiting gangs for booth capturing, and in Uttar Pradesh and Bihar special precautions were taken by the Election Commission and the police. Immediately after the elections, several instances of booth capturing were reported, and repolling was ordered. The amount of booth capturing in fact proved considerably less than the newspapers had anticipated. It is said, however, that booth capturing by Lok Dal workers was particularly common in scheduled-caste localities in Haryana and western Uttar Pradesh and that this was a significant factor in Charan Singh's victory in a number of reserved constituencies.

Bogus Voting. An indelible ink mark is placed on the fingernail of each voter in order to prevent him from casting a second ballot. In spite of reports that parties had developed ways of erasing the ink mark, there does not appear to be any confirmed evidence of widespread double voting. Other methods of bogus voting have been developed, however, the most common being the use of young people below voting age to cast ballots in place of voters listed on the electoral roll. These voters—widely known in India as urchin voters—appear at the polling station early in the morning and give the names of voters on the list. Polling officials in collusion with a candidate permit the urchins to vote, then turn away the genuine voters who appear later in the day. Lok Dal candidates were widely reported as using this system of bogus voting in constituencies where a large number of scheduled-caste voters were expected to vote for Congress (I). The day after the elections several Delhi newspapers published photos of "urchins" standing in line at polling stations in western Uttar Pradesh. In one instance a truckload of Harijans from western Uttar Pradesh appeared at the office of the Election Commission in New Delhi to demand a repoll on the ground that they had been denied the right to vote by polling officials who reported that their votes had already been cast.

Dummy Candidates. A perfectly legal device intended to divide the votes of one's opponent is the use of dummy candidates.

> In one constituency in north Bihar the straight contest between a "backward" and "forward" candidate was given a

twist with the sponsorship of a Muslim candidate by the "backward" in order to erode the informal alliance of the "forward's" party with the ethnic minority. The "forward" candidate too shopped around for a "backward" dummy candidate, but was not successful because, one, the rate of compensation to the dummy was Rs 45,000 plus a jeep with free petrol; and two, the solidarity of the backward castes was difficult to splinter.[21]

The use of dummy candidates helps to explain why there were so many independent candidates standing for Parliament. In 1980 there were 4,611 candidates for 525 seats, of whom 2,868 were independents, or an average of 5 independents per seat.[22] Where there was a pattern of caste voting and the parties were highly fragmented and factionalized, the number of independents was considerably higher. In Haryana, for example, there were ten independents for each seat, and in Uttar Pradesh and Bihar there were eight. In contrast, there were comparatively few independent candidates in West Bengal, Tripura, Tamil Nadu, Kerala, and Gujarat.

Most of the independents, it should be noted, did so badly that they lost their deposits. Only eight independents were elected to Parliament in 1980. Altogether the independent candidates won only 6.6 percent of the vote, not much more than their 5.8 percent in the previous election. Evidently, party candidates, expecting the vote to be close, encouraged independent candidates to run in an effort to split the vote of their opponents. Though there were only a few constituencies where the vote for independent candidates made a difference, the sponsorship of an independent by party candidates appeared to be a low-cost investment that was particularly attractive in the 1980 parliamentary elections.

Counting the Ballots. Agents of each candidate are entitled to be present at the time of ballot counting. Ballots from the various polling stations are brought together at a central place, where they are counted in the presence of agents of the candidates and under police protection. Nonetheless, there are reports of collusion on the part of counting agents, who doctor the figures or place ballots of one candidate in the pile of another. There are, however, fewer charges of fraudulent ballot counting in India than in the elections of most other countries.

[21] Ibid., p. 911.

[22] There were nine contestants per constituency in 1980, as compared with five in the elections of 1977, 1971, and 1967. Elections were not held in 17 constituencies in 1980, most of them in the disturbed state of Assam.

50

Fear of Violence. Are variations in turnout related to the fear of violence on the part of voters or to the expectation that fraud, rather than honest ballot casting, will determine the election outcome? It is not uncommon for violent clashes to occur among party workers, for party workers and even candidates to be killed, and for violence to take place at some polling stations on election day.

On the other hand, violent clashes among religious, caste, and linguistic groups and among political parties are so pervasive in India that it is not easy to separate the violence that takes place during election campaigns from "normal" violence. In 1980, for example, according to official figures, 2,691 persons were injured and 372 were killed in 421 "incidents" of Hindu-Muslim violence throughout the country.[23] In early 1981 as many as 47 persons were killed and 68 injured in communal violence in the town of Biharsharif and the adjoining villages of the Nalanda district of Bihar.[24] The agitation in Assam in late 1979 and 1980 over illegal migration from Bangladesh resulted in hundreds of deaths and injuries. In Bihar, caste killings, the result of conflicts between high-caste Bhumihars and Brahmins and lower caste Yadavs, and between ex-untouchables and higher castes, are frequent, and it is not uncommon for dozens of people to be killed or injured in a single village clash.

Electoral violence should be seen, therefore, as another form of violent social conflict, not simply as a feature of electoral politics. In the 1980 election campaign twenty persons had been killed and scores injured by the end of December 1979. During election week itself, there was considerable violence in Andhra Pradesh, especially in Hyderabad, where six people died and fifty-two were injured, in Baghpat, Charan Singh's constituency in Uttar Pradesh, where twenty persons were injured, and in the Uttar Pradesh constituency of Amroha, where three persons were killed and nineteen injured.[25] There is no evidence that the level of violence was higher than in earlier elections, but apprehension that there would be violence at the polling stations was widespread.

Fear of violence may have been one reason for the low turnout in some constituencies in 1980, especially parts of Bihar and Uttar Pradesh, which have been troubled in recent elections. Except in 1977, the turnout in both states has rarely exceeded 50 percent and

---

[23] "Biharsharif," *Economic and Political Weekly*, vol. 16, no. 19 (May 9, 1981), p. 833, which quotes figures from the *Annual Report of the Ministry of Home Affairs, 1981*.

[24] Ibid.

[25] G. G. Mirchandani, *The People's Verdict* (New Delhi: Vikas Publishing, 1980), pp. 117-18.

has consistently been well below that of other states (although in the case of Uttar Pradesh the relative dearth of polling stations may be an additional factor). Clearly, then, substantial variations in turn-out from one constituency to another within a state, where consti-tuencies do not differ significantly in level of urbanization, literacy, some socioeconomic variables, or distance to polling stations, may in some instances be the result of bogus voting, booth capturing, coercion, or the threat of violence, although variations may also reflect differences in the efforts of parties and candidates to bring out the vote. In some constituencies fraud is very much a part of the electoral process, and even those who do not themselves engage in fraud must allocate resources to prevent fraud on the part of their opponents.

Analyzing Indian Elections

India is one of a handful of countries in the third world that have had numerous consecutive elections for both national Parliament and state assemblies, and where election data are available—and reliable. Conse-quently, a substantial cottage industry of research on Indian elections has developed, engaged in by American, British, and Indian scholars.

The analysis of the 1980 elections in this volume is based on data released by the Election Commission. Several newspapers and magazines and at least one polling organization conducted voter sur-veys, but these have not been incorporated into this study because they were limited to a few constituencies or were not published in any usable form.[26] A study confined to the election results themselves, based on returns from individual constituencies, has several limita-tions, the most important being that it is difficult to make inferences from the returns about the behavior of particular classes or ethnic groups. Ecological analyses are possible, using census data to relate constituency characteristics to voting patterns, but it is the con-stituency, not the individual (as in survey analysis), that is the unit of study. It is difficult, then, to describe how India's Muslims or its scheduled castes have voted, though it is possible to describe how constituencies with large numbers of Muslims or scheduled castes have voted. To infer the former from the latter is, of course, a well-

[26] There are several earlier studies of the Indian electorate based upon survey analyses, but these provide regrettably limited data relating ethnicity and socioeconomic characteristics to actual voting. See Sidney Verba, Bashiruddin Ahmed, and Anil Bhatt, *Castes, Race, and Politics: A Comparative Study of India and the United States* (Beverly Hills: Sage Publications, 1971); Anil Bhatt, *Caste, Class and Politics* (Delhi: Manohar Book Service, 1975); and John Osgood Field, *Consolidating Democracy: Politicization and Partisanship in India* (Delhi Manohar Book Service, 1980).

known statistical fallacy, and when we make such inferences it is largely to confirm what journalists and other observers in the field have said on the basis of their interviews with voters and local political leaders.

There are, however, at least two types of electoral units in India in which an ecological analysis can tell us something about categories of voters. We are able to look at the voting patterns for India's urban areas and compare them with the patterns of rural constituencies to compare and contrast urban with rural voters. And we are able to look at the voting patterns of India's tribals, who live in reserved constituencies overwhelmingly made up of tribal voters. In the case of Muslims, however, there are only a handful of constituencies where Muslims constitute more than 50 percent of the electorate; and in the case of scheduled castes, there are constituencies reserved exclusively for candidates from these communities, but typically only a fifth to a quarter of the voters in these constituencies belong to the scheduled castes.

Constituency-level analysis also precludes study of the relationship between class and voting. The industrial working class is concentrated in some localities, but the constituencies in which the workers live are so large that the proportion of the working class within them is too small to allow any inferences. Similarly, it would be difficult to make any judgments about how India's tenant farmers, agricultural laborers, plantation workers, or farmer-cultivators have voted on the basis of election data alone. Much of what we know, or think we know, about the voting patterns of various classes and castes in India (scheduled castes, Muslims, and Brahmins tend to vote for Congress; Rajput landowners in Bihar vote for Jana Sangh, farmer-cultivators in western Uttar Pradesh and Haryana support the Lok Dal; and so on) is drawn from local surveys, the observations of journalists, politicians, and scholars, or inferences from state assembly election results, rather than from a statistical analysis of parliamentary returns. One must be cautious in making inferences about the behavior of particular classes or ethnic groups on the basis of aggregate data.[27] How, for example, does one interpret a high correlation between scheduled-caste constituencies and voting for the Lok Dal? One possible explanation is that members of scheduled castes voted for the Lok Dal, but an alternative explanation is that the backward castes were better organized in scheduled-caste con-

[27] The classic attack on such inferences is the article by W. S. Robinson, "Ecological Correlations and the Behavior of Individuals," *American Sociological Review*, vol. 15 (June 1950), pp. 351-57.

stituencies than other castes and turned out in larger numbers to vote for the Lok Dal.

Paul Brass gives us another useful example of the problems involved in drawing inferences about the determinants of electoral behavior from high correlations.[28] There is in India a high correlation between voter turnout and population density: the highest turnouts are in the states of West Bengal, Kerala, Punjab, Haryana, Delhi, and Tamil Nadu, all with population densities well above the national average. Does this signify greater discontent? More interpersonal contact leading to more voting? That it is easier for party workers to organize and bring out the vote? Perhaps the high correlation is simply the result of the fact that the Election Commission has established more polling booths in high-density areas, reducing the distance voters have to go to the polls.

Precisely because the analysis of voting patterns in India must rely heavily upon ecological analysis, in which socioeconomic and demographic data are correlated with election results to identify patterns in turnout, interparty competition, and party support, there has been a considerable refinement of this mode of analysis.[29] Use has been made of data from individual polling stations, from state assembly constituencies (on the average one-sixth of the population of a parliamentary constituency) and from assembly "segments" of parliamentary constituencies. For this volume, however, we have only had access to the results from entire parliamentary constituencies.

For each of India's 525 parliamentary constituencies in which elections were held in 1980, data were available on the size of the electorate, the number of voters who cast their ballots, the number of valid and invalid votes, and the number of votes cast for each candidate. Exactly the same data were available for these constituencies for the 1977 elections. All of this information was put into the computer by DCM Data Products and the Systems Group, computer-management consultants in New Delhi. The results were used in the reporting of United News of India, a national news agency, and were

[28] Paul R. Brass, "Indian Election Studies," *South Asia*, vol. 1, no. 2, p. 93. For a plausible demonstration of the relationship between number of polling stations and voter turnout, see R. Chandidas, "Poll Participation Slump," *Economic and Political Weekly*, vol. 7, no. 29 (July 15, 1972), pp. 1359-68.

[29] For a comprehensive review of much of this literature, see Brass, "Indian Election Studies," pp. 91-108. The most comprehensive ecological analysis, using parliamentary data, is Biblap Dasgupta and W. H. Morris-Jones, *Patterns and Trends in Indian Politics: An Ecological Analysis of Aggregate Data on Society and Elections* (New Delhi: Allied Publishers, 1976). For an analysis of state assembly elections, see Myron Weiner and John O. Fields, eds., *Studies in Electoral Politics in the Indian States*, 4 vols. (Delhi: Manohar Book Service, 1974-1977).

available to India's newspaper readers within a few days of the elections. The computer printouts and the discs containing the data were then made available to me for further analysis.[30]

In the statistical analysis of Indian election results conducted here, one contextual variable has proved of central importance—the region or state in which a constituency is located. Though, as we have seen, there are national trends from one election to another, there are substantial variations between regions and states. Attempts to isolate how urban India votes or how predominantly Muslim, scheduled-caste, or scheduled-tribe constituencies vote nationally have rarely proved useful. When constituencies with a particular set of characteristics are aggregated nationally, they rarely look different from the country as a whole. The reason is that constituencies are influenced by whatever factors influence the voting pattern of the state (or region) in which they are located.

To illustrate this point with data from West Bengal, we find that constituencies in West Bengal with a large Muslim population tend to vote Communist—as do other constituencies in the state. Since there are proportionately more Muslim constituencies in West Bengal than in most states, a correlation based upon national data erroneously reveals that a higher proportion of Muslim constituencies vote Communist than do non-Muslim constituencies. A headline writer might report "India's Muslim Constituencies Lean toward the Communists," but the conclusion would be false. In fact, within West Bengal the Congress party actually has a slightly higher vote in constituencies with Muslims than in non-Muslim constituencies.

National correlations for India rarely produce any interesting findings. Strong correlations are procured only for smaller units— either the state or a region of the state. Thus, one finds a strong correlation between constituencies with backward-caste farmer-cultivators in Haryana and western Uttar Pradesh and support for Lok Dal candidates, but no such correlation on a national scale. We are able to show a negative relationship between turnout and Con-

---

[30] For another analysis of the 1980 elections using the DCM data, see G. G. Mirchandani, *The People's Verdict* (New Delhi: Vikas Publishing House, 1980). Mirchandani is the director of the United News of India. For a study of the 1977 elections, see G. G. Mirchandani, *320 Million Judges* (New Delhi: Abhinav Publications, 1977). The official results for the 1977 parliamentary elections are available in *Report on the Sixth General Election to the House of the People in India, 1977*, vols. 1 and 2 (statistical) (New Delhi: Election Commission of India, 1978). Other relevant reports are: *Report on the General Election to the Legislative Assemblies, 1977* (statistical) (New Delhi: Election Commission of India, 1979); and *Report on the Sixth General Election to the Lok Sabha and General Election to the Kerala Legislative Assembly, 1977*, vol. 1 (New Delhi: Election Commission of India), 1978.

gress support in many north Indian states, but not in the South; a relationship between scheduled-caste constituencies and Congress voting in Andhra in 1977, but not in 1980 and not in northern India; a correlation between predominantly Muslim constituencies and Congress voting in Bihar, but not elsewhere; a relationship between tribal constituencies and the Congress vote in Madhya Pradesh, Rajasthan, Maharashtra, and Gujarat, but not in Bihar, Orissa, West Bengal, and Tripura. One could go on, but by now the point should be clear. For this reason, many of the tables in this book are arrranged by state, and judgments about the voting patterns of particular religious, ethnic, and class groups are made from an analysis of state rather than national data.

Local factors often play such an important role in voting that neither aggregate election data nor national surveys convey a satisfactory picture of why and how Indians vote as they do. While, as we shall emphasize later, some national trends override local factors, significant local variations in voting result from different community power structures, variations in social structures and socioeconomic conditions from one locality to another, different linkages between local leaders and their factional, caste, class, and religious supporters, and alliances among national, state, and local community leaders. Precisely how these local factors are affected by national factors, how and why some linguistic, class, religious, and caste groups swing with the national trends but others do not, and what these variations tell us about the political attitudes and behavior of various social groups can best be understood through detailed studies of particular communities. For this reason, anthropological studies of selected communities are an important complementary tool of voting analysis in India, a distinctive addition to survey research and aggregate data analysis. Regrettably, there are few such studies for each of the general elections and no communities that have been regularly studied from one election to another.[31]

[31] Indian social scientists could make a substantial contribution to the study of voting and other forms of political behavior if they could develop an institutionalized system of monitoring a panel of villages and urban communities. While individual communities have been studied in particular elections, none as far as I know have been systematically studied over time. For examples of micro-level community studies see Myron Weiner and Rajni Kothari, eds., *Indian Voting Behavior: Studies of the 1962 General Election* (Calcutta: Firma K. L. Mukhopadhyay, 1965). Among the scholars who have contributed to the study of voting behavior at the community level are V. M. Sirsikar, D. L. Seth, Ramashray Roy, Yogesh Atal, D. N. Pathak, K. D. Desai, Imtiaz Ahmed, Rajni Kothari, Rushikesh Maru, S. H. Somjee, Harold Gould, and F. G. Bailey. For a review of their writings, see Norman D. Palmer, *Elections and Political Development: The South Asian Experience* (Durham: Duke University Press, 1975), chap. 10, pp. 269-301.

3
National Results

Voter Turnout

In the parliamentary elections of 1980, 201.7 million Indians cast votes, or 57 percent of an electorate of 354 million. Turnout was lower than in 1977 (60.5 percent) or 1967 (61.6 percent) but higher than in India's four other parliamentary elections (see table 2).[1] Attendance at political rallies during the campaign was low; there was little enthusiasm among party workers; and none of the middle-class groups so active in the 1977 elections—students and lawyers— were in evidence: nevertheless, the elections did not demonstrate that voters were apathetic. What they proved was how special the elections of 1977 and 1967 had been. Indeed, state by state, a comparison of voter turnout for 1980 with that of the more typical election of 1971 shows how similar these two elections were, with the turnout a few percentage points higher in some states and a few points lower in others. A further matching of 1977 and 1967 suggests one significant conclusion: major increases in voter turnout are often accompanied by a decline in the vote for candidates of Mrs. Gandhi's Congress, while lower voter turnout (as in 1980) is correspondingly accompanied by an increase in the vote for Congress.

[1] There are differences between the figures for the 1977 election in this volume and those in the author's *India at the Polls, 1977*. The earlier figures were based on data made available by the Press Information Bureau of the Government of India, while those in this volume are based on the official report of the Election Commission. Fortunately, the differences are usually small and they change none of the findings in the earlier volume. The data used for the 1980 elections were provided by the Press Information Bureau and computerized by DCM Data Products of New Delhi. For further details on the sources and methods employed in this book, see the section on "Analyzing Indian Election Results" in chapter 2.

These conclusions do not hold for all of India's states, but mainly for the Hindi-speaking states of the Gangetic heartland. The turnout in these states in 1980 was similar to the turnout in 1971, and so was the vote for the Congress party, while the massive increase in turnout in 1977 was accompanied by an increase in the vote for the opponents of Congress. (This was also the case in 1967, when Congress did badly in the Hindi-speaking states.)

This appears to suggest that the Congress defeat in 1977 reflected the opposition of new voters, who did not vote in 1980. But such a conclusion can be overdrawn. In Orissa and Himachal Pradesh, there was little or no decline in turnout, yet the Congress vote in 1980 increased substantially; while in Madhya Pradesh, Rajasthan, and Tamil Nadu, the growth in the Congress vote exceeded the modest decline in turnout. The argument holds best for Bihar, Haryana, Punjab, and Uttar Pradesh, where turnouts declined from six to nine percentage points, while the Congress vote increased by eleven to seventeen percentage points—though even in these states the increase in the vote for Congress far exceeded the decline in turnout, reflecting an absolute increase in the number of Congress voters, not simply a change in their percentage (see tables 4 and 5).

In any event it is important to separate the long-term trend toward increasing voter turnout in India from the particular spurts shown in any one election or in any single state. Voter turnout in India's first election in 1952 was 46.6 percent, and the trend has been upward. This suggests that India's population has become increasingly political or that political parties have increased their capacity to bring voters to the polling stations. One should also note, however, two "mechanical" factors that affect the number of voters. The first is the question of voter registration. Since 1951 the Election Commission has enrolled a larger proportion of the population of voting age for each election. The Election Commission prepares the electoral rolls through a house-to-house canvass, registering all citizens twenty-one years of age or older. There are no literacy, educational, or property requirements. Table 3 indicates how effective the Election Commission has been in expanding the electoral rolls.

The increase in the number and percentage of adults registered by the Election Commission has enabled an increasing number of Indians to vote. What is striking, moreover, is that the proportion of adults actually voting has increased more rapidly than the registered electorate.[2] From 1952 to 1980, the electorate increased by 181 mil-

2 The decline in voter turnout from 1977 to 1980 (60.5 percent to 57.0 percent) may be inflated by the particularly high increase in the number of voters reg-

lion (104 percent), but the number of actual voters grew by 121 million (an increase of 150 percent). To put it another way, in 1952 21.9 percent of India's population voted (approximately half the population, of course, was below voting age), whereas in 1980 30.4 percent of the population went to the polls.

The second "mechanical" factor is the increase in the number of polling stations, which also helped to increase voter turnout. In 1952 there were 132,560 polling stations in the country, while in 1980 the number had been increased to 437,166, giving voters a shorter distance to go to vote (see table 2). The Election Commission provides one polling station for approximately every 800 voters, but where the population is dispersed it often provides more. In Orissa, for example, there is one polling station for every 780 voters, while in densely populated Kerala each polling station services an average of 940 voters. Yet in Orissa, Madhya Pradesh, and Rajasthan, voters must travel longer distances and for longer periods than in the more densely populated states of Kerala, Haryana, and West Bengal.

In most of India turnout declined in 1980, but there was a marked increase in voting in the Northeast. To some extent this reflected the growing political agitation in the region, but it may also be explained by the change in the number of polling stations. In Manipur, for example, the turnout leaped from 60.2 percent of the electorate in 1977 to 81.9 percent in 1980 (the highest in India) after the Election Commission increased the number of polling stations from 910 to 1,316: this was a 45 percent increase while the national increase in polling stations was 17 percent. The Election Commission, one assumes, sought to reduce the distance for voters to travel in a state with a low population density. Similarly, the increase in voter turnout in Tripura, from 70.1 percent to 80.0 percent may be related to an increase in the number of polling stations from 1,055 to 1,443 (a 37 percent increase). And in Arunachal Pradesh, voter turnout rose from 56.3 percent to 68.6 percent as the number of polling stations tripled, from 304 to 911.[3]

---

istered by the Election Commission in 1980. The percentage of the total Indian population voting in 1971 was 27.6 percent; in 1977, 31.0 percent; and in 1980, 30.2 percent. If one measures turnout by the ratio of actual voters to actual population (rather than registered voters), then the 1977 election produced the highest turnout of any election in India, 31.0 percent of the population; in 1967, 30.4 percent of the population voted or 61.1 percent of the electorate.

[3] Not every increase in the number of polling stations brings an increase in voter turnout. The number of polling stations in Bihar, for example, was increased by 33 percent in 1980 over 1977, but voter turnout declined by 9.1 percentage points, well above the nationwide decline of 3.5 points.

Only in West Bengal was there a significant increase in voter turnout in 1980 unrelated to an increase in the number of polling stations, the result it would appear of the successful effort of the Communist party of India (Marxist) to mobilize large numbers of new voters.

But northeastern India was the exception in 1980. Virtually everywhere else the turnout remained the same or reverted to the earlier voting patterns. The largest declines were in Kerala, Jammu and Kashmir, Bihar, Haryana, Punjab, Uttar Pradesh, and Delhi. How closely linked are these declines to the change in the Congress vote? The story of the Congress party's defeat in 1977 and its victory in 1980 centers largely on developments in the north Indian states, where turnouts and votes for Congress appear to be inversely related. In 1971 these states (including Bihar, Haryana, Himachal Pradesh, Madhya Pradesh, Orissa, Punjab, Rajasthan, Uttar Pradesh, and Delhi) cast 66.8 million votes. In 1977 turnout in these states rose to 89.9 million, then to 92.1 million in 1980. From 1971 to 1977 turnout increased by 23 million, the Congress vote declined by 5.9 million, and the Janata vote increased by 31 million. The 1977 results suggest that Janata picked up the voters who deserted Congress and some who earlier had supported independents and candidates of smaller parties, *plus* a very large proportion of the new voters. The Congress vote in these states was 29.9 million in 1971, 24 million in 1977, and 36.3 million in 1980. Between 1977 and 1980 Congress gained 12.3 million votes, and Janata and Lok Dal (which won 22.4 million in these states in 1971, 53.4 million in 1977, and 38.4 million in 1980) dropped 15 million votes.

These figures suggest that millions of Janata voters of 1977 switched to Congress (I) in 1980 but that another several million switched to independents and to other parties. In most of these states the combined percentage of votes for Janata, Lok Dal, and Congress (I) in 1980 was below the combined Janata-Congress percentage of 1977. Many Janata supporters, evidently disillusioned with their party, were equally disillusioned with Congress (I). It should also be noted that the number of voters in 1980 was well above the 1971 total and that the share of this increase won by Janata and Lok Dal was greater than that won by Congress (I).

In other words, increases in voter turnout in northern India have generally benefited the opponents of Congress, especially in 1977, but even in 1980 when a comparison is made with 1971. In fact, in every election since 1957, a rise or decline in turnout in northern India has been accompanied by an inverse decline or rise in the Congress vote. Uttar Pradesh, India's largest state, with eighty-five members of Parliament, provides us with a clear example: A decline in the percentage of voters in both 1971 and 1980 was accompanied by a rise in the Congress vote, just as in earlier elections; while in 1977 increases in turnout were accompanied by a decline in the Congress vote (see table 18).

Once again, it is important to understand that the relationship between turnout and the Congress vote is not the whole story. The change in the vote for Congress in each election can only partially be explained by changes in turnout; quite clearly some voters switched from one party to another. In 1980, for example, the Congress vote increased by 12.3 million in northern India, the number of voters increased by 2.2 million (though the percentage of voters actually declined), and the combined vote for Janata and Lok Dal dropped by 15.0 million. Though some former Janata voters stayed home and many voted for Congress (U) or independents, a large proportion (two-thirds to three-quarters, one might surmise) switched to the Congress party of Mrs. Gandhi.

The Election Outcome

In the 1980 parliamentary elections, Indira Gandhi's Congress party won 351 out of 525 seats. Lok Dal came in second with 41 seats, the Communist party of India (Marxist) third with 35, and the Janata party trailed with only 31 seats, an enormous decline from its parliamentary majority of 298 seats in 1977. Congress (U) won 13 seats (see table 8).

In popular votes, the Congress (I) victory was less impressive. Congress won 42.7 percent of the vote, compared with 34.5 percent in 1977 and 43.7 percent in 1971. By increasing its popular vote by 8.2 points, Congress (I) increased its share of parliamentary seats from 153 to 351 (see table 7). The massive seat increase was the result not only of an increase in its share of votes, but also of the fragmentation of the Janata party. Nationally Janata won 18.9 percent of the vote and the Lok Dal 9.4 percent, a combined total of 28.3 percent, while in 1977 the combined figure had been 43.2 percent. As in the previous election, the Janata and Lok Dal vote was largely confined to northern India. The only national party other than Congress whose position improved was the Communist party of India (Marxist), which won 6 percent of the vote in 1980 as against 4.3 percent in 1977, but this increase was confined almost entirely to the states of West Bengal and Tripura. The CPI's position declined

FIGURE 2

1980 Election Results: The Popular Vote, by State

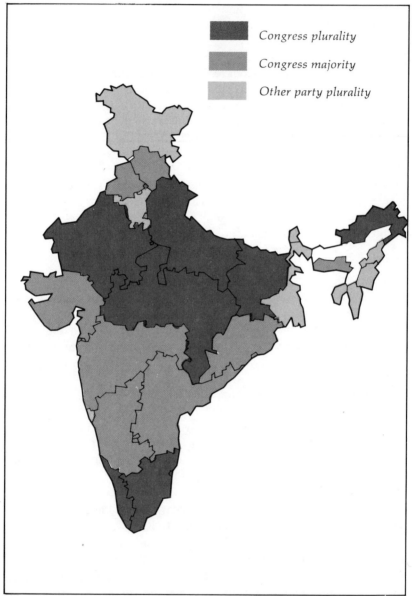

Congress plurality

Congress majority

Other party plurality

NOTE: Assam is left blank on this map because elections were held in only two of the fourteen constituencies in 1980.

SOURCE: Based on Survey of India maps, government of India, 1970.

slightly from 2.8 percent to 2.6 percent (see tables 14 and 15). The vote for the regional parties also went down, from 9.9 percent in 1977 to 8.5 percent in 1980. And the Congress (U), which had set out to demonstrate that it, not Mrs. Gandhi's Congress, was the "real" Congress, won only 5.3 percent of the vote.

The performance of each of the parties, including Mrs. Gandhi's Congress, varied, of course, from state to state (see tables 9 and 11 and figure 2). Yet perhaps the most striking feature of the 1980 election is that it confirmed a pattern established in earlier elections: once again there were *national* voting shifts. These national patterns are expressed in the swings to and from the Congress party in each of the states.

Consider the following: of the fourteen major states (each with ten or more parliamentary seats), Congress increased its share of the popular vote in eleven in 1980. (These states had 436 seats.) In 1977, when the national vote turned against Congress, the Congress vote declined in ten out of these fourteen. A comparison by state of the voting shifts for Congress from 1967 to 1971, from 1971 to 1977, and again from 1977 to 1980 shows how geographically widespread the national swings have been (see table 12). In fact, in 1980 only three major states did not increase their vote for Congress—Andhra Pradesh, Karnataka, and Kerala—but in each of these the combined vote of Mrs. Gandhi's Congress and the Congress (U), which had split from it, was well above the 1977 Congress vote. In the 1977 swing against Congress only five states had resisted the national trend—Andhra Pradesh, Gujarat, Kerala, Tamil Nadu, and West Bengal—and in two of these there had been special local circumstances. A purely local Congress split in Andhra in 1971 made it look as if the party had improved its position in 1977; and in Tamil Nadu there had been an "artificially" low Congress vote in 1971 because Congress had formed an electoral alliance that year and contested a smaller number of seats than in previous elections. If we go back one more election, to 1971, when there was a national swing to Congress, there were only four states where the Congress vote did not go up—Gujarat, Kerala, Tamil Nadu, and West Bengal.

A look at the vote for the Janata party in its various guises also confirms the view that there are national tendencies. Janata won 43.2 percent of the national vote in 1977, well above what its constituent parties won in 1971 (27.7 percent). The swing toward Janata in 1977 took place in every major state except Tamil Nadu (see table 13). Even in the two large southern states where Janata lost, Andhra and Karnataka, there had been a considerable swing toward it.

The same tendency held in 1980, when the combined vote for Janata and Lok Dal declined to 28.3 percent; the decline took place in every Indian state without exception.

To put it another way, when Bihar swings, so does Uttar Pradesh in the North, Madhya Pradesh in the center, Maharashtra in the West, Orissa in the East, and very likely either Andhra or Karnataka in the South.

Two features of the 1980 elections further demonstrate the importance of national factors in the election outcome. The first is that in 1980, as in 1977, many well-known state and local leaders were defeated simply because they stood on the ticket of a losing party, while their seats were won by relatively unknown candidates. In 1980, for example, many Congress candidates chosen because of their relationship to Sanjay Gandhi won easily, though they were often not well known or, in some instances, even well regarded. (Jagdish Tytler, for example, a local Delhi businessman and a friend of Sanjay Gandhi, defeated a popular M.P. in the New Delhi constituency in which the university is located; and in one constituency in Rajasthan, a Calcutta business friend of Sanjay's, Kamal Nath, was elected.) Moreover, Janata lost parliamentary seats even in several states where the Janata state government was generally well regarded. Madhya Pradesh and Rajasthan had what were generally viewed as competent and even popular Janata governments, but the electorate chose to vote for Congress.

What accounts for the existence of national trends in a country of such extraordinary diversity? The first factor is a national communications network that exposes a large part of the electorate to a common pool of information. Clashes, for example, between the police and Muslims in Uttar Pradesh, between backward castes and scheduled castes in Bihar, and a split within the Janata party in New Delhi were quickly known throughout the country. To the extent that religious, linguistic, caste, economic, and occupational communities have similar political perspectives, events affecting them in one part of the country become known and politically affect them in other parts.

A second factor is shared national economic experiences that spring from the growth of a national market. Rising prices and food shortages are less local than they were. In the 1980 elections, for example, the high price and shortage of onions and sugar was a national, not a local issue. Similarly, shortages of electric power, diesel fuel, and fertilizers have an impact on agriculturalists every-where. Government policies on dearness (cost-of-living) allowances, bonuses for industrial labor, and procurement prices for the purchase of agricultural commodities affect classes that are geographically widely dispersed.

One structural factor may also be important. The tendency of each state to follow the national swing was less pronounced before the 1967 elections. While the national vote for Congress declined from 1962 to 1967, the vote for Congress actually increased in Maharash-tra, Madhya Pradesh, Rajasthan, Haryana, Kerala, and Assam and in the smaller states of Tripura and Manipur. Earlier elections show similar deviations by state from the national trend. The 1971 elections appear to have been a turning point; since then the number of states deviating from the national trend has been smaller than in 1967. Until 1971 national parliamentary elections were held at the same time as assembly elections, and the same factors often influenced voting in both. The delinking of state and national elections in 1971 made it possible for candidates to run for Parliament as repre-sentatives of national parties, with national leaders, national pro-grams, and national campaigns. One indication of the importance of delinking is that even in the election of 1967, described by many observers as a national election in which inflation, the balance-of-payments deficit, devaluation, and a widespread disillusionment with the Congress party seemed to affect the entire country, the state voting paterns, as we have seen, were erratic by the standards of 1971, 1977, and 1980. With the delinking of parliamentary and state elections, most of the states that had deviated from the national voting trend in 1967 and earlier followed the national trend in voting for Parliament in 1971 and in all subsequent elections.

India's Electoral Geography

It is customary in Indian electoral analysis to divide India into four major geographic regions—southern India, with four states; western India, with two; northeastern India, with Assam, West Bengal, and several small hill states; and the Hindi-belt, or "northern" India, which would include the Punjab and Jammu and Kashmir as well as the Hindi-speaking states. Orissa is sometimes included in the north-east, but more often in north India.[4] A review of the voting for the

[4] For a particularly useful and detailed analysis of regional voting see C. P. Singh, "The Seventh Parliamentary Election in India (A Geographical Analysis)," report submitted to the Indian Council of Social Science Research, December 1980 (manuscript).

Congress party from 1967 to 1980 suggests that these regions do not form electorally cohesive units.

In south India, Andhra and Karnataka have usually been only one or two percentage points apart in their voting for the Congress party (except in the election of 1971), while Tamil Nadu and Kerala both have quite distinctive voting patterns. In western India, the votes for the Congress party in Gujarat and Maharashtra are usually one or two percentage points apart, although in the elections of 1971 the divergence was considerable. In the Hindi-belt, the spread is very large, a range of 33.7 to 48.3 percent for Congress in the 1967 elections moving up to a range of 29.3 to 50.7 percent in 1980. The swings from one election to another, however, are quite similar in all these states. From 1967 to 1971, for example, the vote for Congress increased in all of them, from a 5.3 point increase in Bihar to 25.7 points in the case of Delhi. From 1971 to 1977, the total vote for Congress decreased in all of these states, from 13 points to 34.6 points, and in 1980 the vote went up by 11 points to 20 points (see table 12). In no other regions have the swings been so large and so uniformly unidirectional.

In contrast, there is no clearcut pattern in the Northeast. West Bengal, Tripura, and Manipur show considerable similarities in their swings, which, by and large, have been counter to the national trends. In all three states the vote for Congress dropped from 1967 to 1971, when everywhere else it went up; and in 1977 the Congress vote increased in all three states while declining elsewhere. In 1980 the Congress vote increased in West Bengal but declined in Tripura and in Manipur. Assam, on the other hand, has moved with the national tide, at least until 1980, when for special local reasons it did not take part in the election.

If, instead of looking at India from the point of view of its four geographic regions, we consider instead the question of which states conform to the national voting pattern and which do not, we arrive at quite different geographic groupings (see figure 3). From this point of view, India can be divided into two distinct groups. In all the states in Group 1, the Congress party vote increased from 1967 to 1971, dropped in 1977, then rose again in 1980, following the national pattern. These states largely determined the election outcomes, and their electorates consistently shifted along parallel lines and appeared to be influenced by similar forces. Group 1 includes Karnataka, Maharashtra, Punjab, Himachal Pradesh, Orissa, Delhi, Madhya Pradesh, Rajasthan, Bihar, Uttar Pradesh, Haryana, and Jammu and Kashmir. Though it did not participate in the 1980 elections, Assam can be included in this group, for it followed the national

FIGURE 3

Electoral Swings: The Vote for Mrs. Gandhi's Congress, 1962–1980

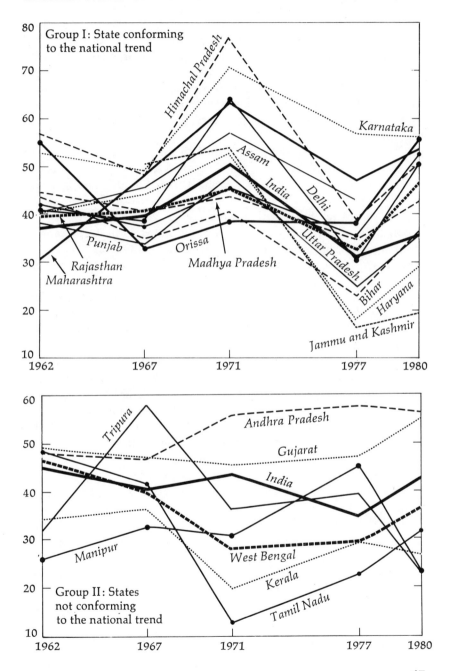

trend in earlier elections. It should be noted that all thirteen states have been swinging together since 1967, but five of them failed to follow the national swing against Congress from 1962 to 1967.

Group 2 has not conformed to the national pattern even since 1967. In all but one state (Andhra), the vote for the Congress party declined from 1967 to 1971, while it increased nationally; and perversely, the vote for Congress increased in all of these states in the 1977 elections. The picture was more variegated in the 1980 elections, with the vote for Congress declining in Tripura, Manipur, Kerala, and Andhra but following the national trend in Gujarat, West Bengal, and Tamil Nadu.

In Group 1 every state conformed to the national trend—or, to put it another way, helped create the national trend. Group 2 consists of states that ran counter to the national trend in 1977 and in 1971, 1980, or both. According to this division (illustrated in figure 3) thirteen states in India, with 67 percent of the population, set the national electoral trend, while seven other states, with 32 percent of the population, have electoral shifts that more often run counter to the national trend. The Group 2 states are all geographically far from India's center. The five larger states—West Bengal, Andhra, Tamil Nadu, Kerala, and Gujarat—are all littoral states. This suggests that as far as India's electoral geography is concerned, the more interesting analytical distinctions are not North, South, Northeast and West, but rather the heartland versus the periphery.

The resistance of the periphery to national voting trends does not suggest that these areas are either more or less politicized than the rest of the country. West Bengal, Tamil Nadu, and Kerala have above-average voter turnouts, Andhra and Gujarat are average, while there are other high-participant states, like Haryana and the Punjab, that follow the national trend in voting for the Congress party.

It should be noted that we are not suggesting that the states on the periphery are more anti-Congress than the heartland states, for some states like Andhra and Gujarat have been more pro-Congress than many of the Hindi-speaking ones. Our central distinction is different: The heartland states tend to swing together from one election to another whereas some of the states on the periphery experience electoral shifts that are counter to the national results.

How does one explain why some of the states in the periphery have not followed the national swings in most elections since 1967? Perhaps their distance from some central "core" (Delhi perhaps?) is a factor, though some states such as Karnataka and Assam that have followed the national trend are as far away. It may be that West

Bengal, Kerala, Tamil Nadu, Andhra, and Gujarat deviate from the national voting patterns for many different reasons. Particular historical circumstances or local factors may be at work, either acting on their own or reinforcing a center-periphery distinction that has been successfully overcome elsewhere.

Partisanship

Nationally, the Congress party has never won less than 34.5 percent of the electorate (in 1977) or more than 47.8 percent (in 1957).[5] The swings from one election to another, while not insignificant, can hardly be described as massive: Congress declined by 9.2 percentage points from 1971 to 1977 and increased by 8.2 percentage points in 1980 (see table 16). The Congress vote has fluctuated substantially in some states (in Delhi, between 1967 and 1980, 38.8 percent, 64.5 percent, 30.2 percent, and 50.4 percent) and narrowly in others (in Gujarat, in the same years, 46.9 percent, 45.3 percent, 46.9 percent, and 54.8 percent). Congress appears to have a solid base of partisan voters who have stayed with the party in every election. In Andhra, for example, the Congress vote has never fallen below 46.9 percent, and even in Bihar and Uttar Pradesh, it has not fallen much below a quarter of the vote. Similarly, there has been a core partisan vote for Jana Sangh in the Hindi-speaking region and for Communist parties in West Bengal and Kerala, the DMK and AIADMK in Tamil Nadu, and the Akali Dal in the Punjab.

Partisan attachments predate independence. The Congress party, of course, predates independence and has successfully maintained support in every region of the country. The Socialists, though they have moved from one party to another in recent years, still retain their political base among the middle peasantry in Uttar Pradesh and Bihar, where they established their base well before independence. The Jana Sangh was created after independence, but its various predecessors before independence, particularly the RSS, won support from Hindus in central and western India in opposition to separatist Muslims. The Communists continue to have their political base in Kerala and West Bengal, the states in which they operated before independence. The two Dravida parties in Tamil Nadu are of recent vintage, but they grew out of the Justice party, which emerged in the 1920s as a Tamil nationalist movement opposed to the dominant

[5] For some data on the characteristics of partisans in India, see John Osgood Field, *Consolidating Democracy: Politicization and Partisanship in India* (Delhi: Manohar Book Service, 1980), especially chapter 4, "Partisanship in India: A Cross-national Comparison and Social Overview," pp. 75-118.

Brahmin classes. And finally, the Akali Dal established itself as the party of Sikh nationalism in the Punjab well before independence.

These preindependence attachments persist and evidently have been transmitted to a new generation of voters, lending a remarkable degree of stability to India's elections by providing each party with an irreducible core. Table 10 indicates the actual number of voters belonging to each of the major national parties or groups of parties since 1967 and demonstrates the persistence of electoral support.

From 1967 to 1980, the number of valid votes increased by 34.9 percent, the Congress vote by 41.3 percent, the "Janata" vote by 46.9 percent, the Communists by 24 percent, and the Dravida parties by 61.3 percent. We can best understand changes from one election to another, therefore, by studying the relatively small proportion of voters who appear to have changed their preference. "Appear" is an important qualification, since the persistence of an unchanging core vote may in fact hide the movement of some voters to and an equal number from a particular party. At a minimum, however, it is clear that in the 1980 elections Congress gained 19.2 million votes over 1977, Janata lost 25.4 million, and the CPI and CPI(M) together gained 3.7 million votes. The Congress (U), which did not stand in 1977, won 10.5 million votes. In all, then, the gainers added 33.4 million voters while the losers lost 25.4 million. The difference is accounted for primarily by an increase in the number of voters.

One can assume that some of the new voters in 1980 cast their ballots for the Janata and Lok Dal; if the new voters voted in the same proportion for these parties as did other voters, then Lok Dal and Janata received 2.3 million of the new votes. In that case, as many as 27.7 million of the 1977 Janata voters (25.4 plus 2.3 million) switched to other parties in 1980. In other words, a minimum of 14.7 percent of the 1977 electorate changed their voting preference in the 1980 elections. Mostly they switched to the Congress party of Mrs. Gandhi, though in Andhra, Karnataka, and Kerala many voted for the Congress (U), while in West Bengal and Tripura many voted for the CPI(M). To these 27.7 million "old" voters, we would add 5.9 million "new" voters who voted for parties other than Janata—for a total of 33.6 million voters whose vote made the election results of 1980 different from the results of 1977. Who these voters were, what states and regions they lived in, to what castes, religious communities, and economic classes they belonged, and to which parties they gave their votes, needs to be known if we are to explain the elections of 1980.

The Effect of the Janata–Lok Dal Split

Before examining the changes in voting patterns, we must consider how the split in the Janata party affected the elections. In the Indian electoral system the candidate with the largest number of votes in a constituency wins, so that the more candidates there are for a particular seat, the fewer votes are generally needed to win. How many seats Congress won, therefore, is partly a matter of how many votes its candidates won, but also how divided or unified the remainder of the voters were. Because of the extreme fragmentation of parties in India in 1980 there were many anomalies, with the same number of votes yielding very different numbers of seats from one state to another. Consider the following: In Haryana in 1980, Congress, with less than 33 percent of the vote, won 50 percent of the seats; but in 1977 the Congress party of Madhya Pradesh, also with a third of the vote, netted less than 3 percent of the seats. In West Bengal, Congress won 36 percent of the vote in 1977 (higher, it should be noted, than in Haryana) but netted less than 10 percent of the seats. Finally, in 1977 Congress failed to win a single seat in Bihar with 23 percent of the vote, while three years later, with 36 percent of the vote, the party won 57 percent of the seats.

One essential difference between the parliamentary elections of 1980 and earlier elections was in the number of candidates per seat—8.8 in 1980—but only 4.5 in 1977, 5.4 in 1971, and 4.6 in 1967. The number of candidates was especially great in many north Indian constituencies. In Uttar Pradesh, for example, there were 1,005 candidates for 85 seats (nearly 12 candidates per seat), and some 443 candidates in 1977. In Bihar there were 594 candidates for 54 seats in 1980, 340 in 1977.

Congress won a number of seats as a direct result of the split between the Janata party and the Lok Dal. Nationally, Janata won 18.9 percent of the vote and Lok Dal 9.4 percent, a combined total of 28.3 percent, but in four states their combined vote equaled or exceeded that of Congress, as the following percentages show:

	Congress	Janata	Lok Dal	Lok Dal plus Janata
Bihar	36.4	23.6	16.6	40.2
Haryana	29.3	28.1	33.5	61.6
Rajasthan	42.7	30.4	12.1	42.5
Uttar Pradesh	36.5	22.6	29.0	51.6

The combined vote for Janata and Lok Dal was higher than that for the Congress candidates in 54 of the 221 constituencies in the

Hindi-speaking states in which they put up competing candidates (see table 20).[6] More than a third of the 145 seats Congress won in the Hindi-speaking states were won because of the split.[7] Without these seats, Congress would have won only 91 seats, a united Janata and Lok Dal would have taken 115, and the Congress majority in Parliament would have been 297 instead of 351 seats.

There were a number of other seats in which the combined Janata–Lok Dal vote was only a few points less than that of Congress and where a unified ticket might have brought out more voters, or attracted some of the Congress (U) or independent vote, but one can only speculate as to whether the number of Congress victories would then have fallen below the 263 needed for a parliamentary majority.

Congress won 203 of its 351 seats with a majority of votes and 148 with a plurality. In the 1971 parliamentary elections, by contrast, Congress had won 262 of its 352 victories with a majority and 90 with a plurality. Congress won approximately the same number of seats in 1980 as in 1971, but with a slightly smaller overall vote (42.8 percent in 1980, 43.6 percent in 1971) and fewer of them with a simple majority (see table 17).

What headline writers described as "smashing" victories for the Congress party in 1971, the Janata party in 1977, and the Congress (I) in 1980 were a consequence as much of the degree of party fragmentation as of a shift in the preferences of the electorate. Thus, a 9.1 percentage point decline in the vote for Congress in 1977, combined with a unified opposition, led to a "smashing" defeat for Congress in 1977; while an increase of 8.2 percentage points in 1980, combined with a splintered opposition, resulted once again in a "smashing" victory for Congress.

Dividing the opposition is thus an important element in any Congress strategy. As the party with the largest single "core" vote of committed partisan voters, it reaps enormous benefits when a large number of candidates run and its major opponents compete for the same seats. A considerable amount of political skill, therefore, must be expended by Congress leaders at the national, state, and constituency levels on encouraging dissension in the opposition parties.

[6] Congress (U) put up candidates against Congress (I) in eighty-three constituencies in these states, but it is not possible to say how many of these votes would have gone to Congress (I) or to Janata if a Congress (U) candidate had not been standing. Congress (U) won only 3.6 percent of the vote in the Hindi-speaking states and 5.3 percent of the national vote.

[7] Janata and Lok Dal also split the vote in many constituencies outside the Hindi-speaking states, namely in Orissa, Gujarat, Andhra, Karnataka, Maharashtra, and West Bengal, but their combined vote never exceeded that of Congress.

The Congress party's involvement in the affairs of other parties *and its need for such involvement* have led many commentators to describe the Indian party system not simply as a one, two, or multiparty system, but as a "Congress system," in which the *Congress party sustains its position as the dominant party through its involvement in the internal affairs of the opposition parties.* Its failure to do this in 1977—when the conduct of the party and the government served to unify the opposition—proved a costly error. It was an error that Congress did not make again in the 1980 elections.

4

Regional Results

The popular vote for the Congress party increased in all four regions of India—the Hindi belt in the North, western India, the Northeast and East, and the South. The major increases for the party were in the North and West. In the Hindi belt, the Congress vote increased from 25.9 percent in 1977 to 39.5 percent in 1980 and the seats won from 2 to 145. Indeed, in terms of seats won, it was the party's performance in this region that accounted for both its defeat in 1977 and its victory in 1980. With a less dramatic increase in the popular vote in western India (46.5 percent to 53.8 percent) the Congress party doubled its number of seats, from 30 to 64, and this accounted for all the remaining seats gained by Congress.

In terms of seats won, the position of the Congress party remained the same in both south India and the Northeast, although in both regions there was some improvement in the popular vote for Congress (see table 19).

The Hindi-Speaking Region

Virtually all the major political actors in the 1980 parliamentary elections are from Uttar Pradesh and Bihar. Two of the three contenders for the prime ministership, Mrs. Gandhi and Charan Singh, are from Uttar Pradesh (although Mrs. Gandhi has spent most of her adult political life in Delhi), while Jagjivan Ram is a Bihari. Chandra Shekhar, the president of the Janata party, is from Uttar Pradesh, as is the Lok Dal leader, Raj Narain. Madhu Limaye and George Fernandes, though both are from Bombay, stood in constituencies in Bihar. The Lok Dal has support primarily in three Hindi states, Uttar Pradesh, Bihar, and Haryana; and the Janata party is also a party of the Hindi region, with some additional strength in western India.

Two-fifths of the voters reside in the Hindi-speaking states and, of course, two-fifths of the M.P.s are elected from this region. In the 1980 election two-thirds of the M.P.s elected in the Hindi-speaking states were Congressmen. Janata's share of seats dropped from 215 to 21, while Lok Dal won 40 seats. The Hindi belt gave the Congress party its national victory in 1980, just as it had given the Janata party its national victory in 1977. The impact of the Hindi region on the national outcome is shown in the regional breakdown of Congress seats:

	1971	1977	1980
Hindi region	161	2	145
Non-Hindi region	191	151	206
Total Congress seats	352	153	351

Congress lost 40 of its parliamentary seats in the non-Hindi region in 1977 and gained 55 seats in 1980; but neither the losses in the one election nor the gains in the other decided whether Congress won a parliamentary victory. The results in the Hindi states are shown in tables 34 and 35.

The change in the number of seats won by Congress was the result of two factors. The first and obvious one was the decline in the party's vote in 1977 and its increase in 1980, a roller-coaster pattern reflected in each one of the six states in the region. It is worth noting that, in Madhya Pradesh, the 1980 Congress vote remained below that of 1971. The second factor is the relationship between votes received and seats won. With 46.4 percent of the votes in 1971, Congress won nearly three-quarters of the seats, while in 1977, with 25.9 percent of the vote, Congress won only two seats. In 1980 the party won only 39.1 percent of the vote but two-thirds of the seats. As we saw in the last chapter, had the Janata party not been fragmented in 1980, it would have won a majority of the seats in the Hindi region in spite of the overall decline in votes from 65.4 percent to 46 percent for the Lok Dal and Janata combined. In a majority of constituencies, the combined Lok Dal/Janata vote exceeded that of Congress.

In the Hindi-speaking states, the Congress vote increased by fifteen percentage points over 1977. The swing occurred in every one of the states, ranging from eleven percentage points in Uttar Pradesh, the largest state, to twenty points in Delhi, the capital city. Which groups shifted and which social groups remained firmly with Janata and Lok Dal will become clearer as we briefly review the electoral results in each of the states in the region.

Uttar Pradesh. Uttar Pradesh, with eighty-five seats in Parliament, is the most populous state in the region and in the country. Organized agrarian interests have increasingly played a role in the state's political parties, but much of the political strategy of the parties and much of the local political rhetoric and activity still center on particular castes and religious communities. The largest communities are the scheduled castes, who constitute 21 percent of the population, the Muslims, another 16 percent, and a variety of backward castes—Ahirs, Kurmis, Gujars, Koeris, Lodhis, and others who constitute about a third of the population. Associated with this group are the Jats, a particularly large and important peasant community in western Uttar Pradesh. The Jats are not officially listed in Uttar Pradesh as backward, but many of the Jats, including Charan Singh, identify themselves with the cause of the backward-caste middle peasantry. The forward castes make up most of the rest of the population, and these include the Brahmins, the Thakurs or Rajputs, and the Vaishya or trading castes.

The electorate is divided into what observers of Indian electoral politics have called "vote banks," each of which tends to be linked with one of the political parties. Political parties make "withdrawals" from their "accounts," depending on whom they nominate, how well the local party organization mobilizes its supporters, and a variety of exogenous factors. In Uttar Pradesh, the Congress party vote banks include Brahmins, scheduled castes, and Muslims. Lok Dal has its support among the backward castes and the Jats. Janata, particularly its Jana Sangh group, has support from the Rajputs and the Vaishyas, and it has proportionately more followers in urban than in rural areas.[1]

When a party chooses members of its vote bank as candidates, it reduces the chances of winning votes from another party's vote bank. By nominating many Rajput candidates, Janata created a Harijan backlash even though the party was led by a Harijan, Jagjivan Ram. In contrast, Lok Dal won an unexpected number of Muslim votes

[1] In an analysis of the role of castes in Indian elections, it must be emphasized that the main caste groups are themselves divided. The scheduled castes, for example, consist of many castes, including the Chamars (Jagjivan Ram's caste) and the Mahars, their traditional rivals. Similarly, the backward castes, the Yadavs, Kurmis, Koeris, etc., are often antagonistic to one another, as are the Shi'ite-Sunni branches of Islam. Moreover, there are often factional rivalries within each of the castes and religious sects that may preclude bloc voting. When we speak of "voter banks," it does not mean that a particular group necessarily votes as a cohesive unit, for it rarely does; it does mean that the castes or religious communities, or their subsections, are the units around which political leaders plan their campaign strategies. They influence the choice of candidates, the coalitions, and the electoral appeals.

by nominating Muslim candidates and yet retained the loyalty of its Jat and backward-caste voters.

We can get a sense of what factors were at work in Uttar Pradesh from a brief review of some of the reports by journalists. Many reporters emphasized the role of caste in the campaign. "Wherever one goes," wrote the correspondent for the *Statesman,* who noted that he had traveled over 2,000 kilometers in Uttar Pradesh, "every calculation, every prediction, is based on the caste factors. It is unabashed casteism in its most naked form."[2] S. K. Tripathi, the *Indian Express* correspondent who has been covering Uttar Pradesh politics for many years, wrote that casteism had been promoted by Charan Singh and the Lok Dal state government, which had sought to build its power base among the backward castes through its proposal to introduce reservations in government employment.[3] Still another correspondent wrote that each of the party leaders had become a symbol for a particular caste: Charan Singh attracted the Jats; Chandrajit Yadav, the Lok Dal chief minister, attracted the Ahirs; Raj Narain, the Bhumihars; Chandra Shekhar, the Thakurs; while Kamalapati Tripathi, the Uttar Pradesh Congress leader, and Mrs. Gandhi herself attracted the Brahmins.[4]

Other correspondents emphasized the role of economics and the performance of the government as factors affecting the electorate. Sunanda K. Datta Ray, the correspondent for the *Statesman,* sent this report from Rae Bareli, Mrs. Gandhi's constituency:

> Rows of stalled tractors speak of the virtual impossibility of getting diesel oil. Queues at kerosene shops are long and weary. Sugar has disappeared from fair price shops and can be bought only at exorbitant rates. The land lies withered under a cruel drought which has gripped Uttar Pradesh for several months, with authority not bothered by village distress. The tubewells, which might have helped to pump water out of rocky soil and bring life to barren fields of cane, cannot be operated because of the power crisis. It is as if man had conspired with divinity to discredit Government which found absorbing fruition only in vendetta and intrigue.
>
> It made little sense in this wilderness for Rajmata Vimay Raje Scindia of Gwalior [Mrs. Gandhi's opponent], stately

[2] *Statesman,* January 1, 1980. For a useful detailed analysis of the Congress (I) victory in northern India that explores the role of caste and class, see Harold A. Gould, "The Second Coming: The 1980 Elections in India's Hindi Belt," *Asian Survey,* vol. 20, no. 6 (June 1980), pp. 595-616.

[3] *Indian Express,* January 1, 1980.

[4] *Patriot,* December 18, 1979.

and genial, to wind down the glass of her white estate car and inform a group of women and children that the choice lay between democracy and dictatorship.[5]

Raj Narain, the sitting M.P. who defeated Mrs. Gandhi on a Janata ticket in 1977, declined to stand for reelection in Rae Bareli, apparently aware of how little chance he had of defeating Mrs. Gandhi. Reporters noted that there was considerable resentment against Raj Narain for failing to serve his constituency, and that many of the development programs initiated by the central government in the constituency had come to an end with Mrs. Gandhi's defeat.

Western Uttar Pradesh, reported the *Times of India* correspondent,

> suffered from severe power and diesel shortages, resulting in production losses in both factories and farms. In Aligarh, an election meeting to be addressed by Jagjivan Ram was held in the light of petromax, and it was much later that power supply was resumed. . . . Besides causing great inconvenience to the consumers, breakdowns in power supply have rendered idle many cottage units like steel smelters. Because of a lack of demand by these units the prices of scrap have registered a steep fall, depriving many a small trader of his means of livelihood.[6]

Tractors were also short of diesel. "Since large farmers are highly mechanised and tractors are used even by middle ranking cultivators, agriculture suffers and the land is starved of water for lack of diesel to run pumping sets."[7]

Another report from western Uttar Pradesh concluded that many Muslims were now supporting Congress. "The Emergency, the main cause of Muslims' disenchantment with the Congress, has become a non-issue, largely because of the infighting in the Janata party leading to the great split and the malfunctioning of the government. Communal violence in the country has caused among the Muslims as much disillusionment with the Janata and the Lok Dal as have the rising prices and scarcities."[8]

The *Hindustan Times* reporter in eastern Uttar Pradesh wrote that many voters were disenchanted with the government because of

[5] Sunanda K. Datta Ray, "Return of the Gandhis: View from Rae Bareli and Amethi," *Statesman*, January 9, 1980. Mrs. Gandhi won her seat with 56 percent of the vote.

[6] *Times of India*, December 18, 1979.

[7] Ibid., December 25, 1979.

[8] J. D. Singh, "Grim Contest in West U.P.," *Times of India*, December 26, 1979.

severe shortages. "The average voter blames the Government for non-availability of diesel and kerosene and a long queue at dealer points. They are easily available at exorbitant prices in the black market. While complaining against the Government, the voter does not distinguish between the Janata and the Lok Dal."[9]

In a similar vein, the *Indian Express* correspondent in Lucknow wrote, "The Emergency and its excesses, particularly the forced sterilisation which swept Mrs. Ghandi and her party from power are dead issues. On the other hand the increasing lawlessness, growing insecurity, rising prices and halting supplies of diesel, kerosene and power capped by the incompetence of the Government are issues which are leading an angry common voter to endorse the Emergency minus forced sterilisation."[10]

In fact, the economic conditions notwithstanding, there was no evidence from the electoral returns that many voters were prepared to "endorse" the emergency, for the swing to Congress was hardly overwhelming. Congress won only 35.9 percent of the vote, well above its 25 percent in 1977, but also substantially below the 48.6 percent it had won in 1971. Mrs. Gandhi and Sanjay were easily elected and Congress won most of the seats in central and eastern Uttar Pradesh, but almost always with a plurality. Together, Janata and Lok Dal won a majority of the votes in the state, but the split enabled Congress to win fifty-one of the eighty-five seats.

Observers of the Uttar Pradesh elections concluded that Congress had rebuilt its traditional Brahmin-Harijan-Muslim base. The Harijans, it was said, "had largely forgotten or forgiven Congress for the family planning excesses,"[11] although Congress had to share some of the Harijan vote with the Lok Dal. According to most observers, Janata failed to win any significant portion of the Harijan vote.[12] Muslims, it was also reported, voted for Congress in larger numbers than in 1977 or 1967, when they had deserted the party; yet the Muslim vote for Congress was still considerably less than in 1971.

[9] *Hindustan Times,* December 30, 1979.

[10] *Indian Express,* January 1, 1980.

[11] Kapil Verma, "Congress-I Regains Vote Banks," *Hindustan Times,* January 12, 1980.

[12] Several journalists writing in the *Patriot* from Uttar Pradesh in January 1980 reported that party workers within Janata were unhappy that Jagjivan Ram was their leader, for they felt that they thereby lost their upper-caste votes and did not get the Harijan votes either. According to the correspondent of the *Hindustan Times,* many Jana Sangh-RSS members of the Janata party did not work for non-Jana Sangh candidates in Uttar Pradesh (*Hindustan Times,* January 24, 1980). These charges against Jana Sangh members of the Janata party were an important element in the postelection split in the party.

Lok Dal, not Janata, emerged as the second most important party in the state. It won twenty-nine seats, while Janata took only three, and it came in second in thirty-two other constituencies. It swept the constituencies in western Uttar Pradesh. Charan Singh easily won Baghpat constituency with 65.2 percent of the vote, compared with 63.5 percent in 1977. Surprisingly, Lok Dal did well in the scheduled-caste reserved constituencies and in constituencies with substantial numbers of Muslims, but its major support was from the backward castes and the Jats. Why it did so well among the middle peasantry in the face of reported widespread disillusionment with the economic performance of the government (which was, after all, a Lok Dal government led by Charan Singh) tells us a great deal about the role of both class and caste in the politics of north India.

The Middle Peasantry and the Lok Dal. In the past fifteen years, the middle peasantry or landowning cultivators (as distinct from larger landowners on the one hand and tenant farmers and agricultural laborers on the other) have become an increasingly articulate and organized political force in north Indian politics. They are particularly influential in the politics of three states—Uttar Pradesh, Haryana, and Bihar.

The middle peasantry grew in importance in Uttar Pradesh after legislation transferred title to the land from rent-collecting *zamindars*, or noncultivating landowners, to tenants. In place of rent, the new owner-cultivators paid land-revenue taxes directly to the state. By the end of the 1960s the economic situation of the middle peasants had improved as a result of the new technology associated with the green revolution—new varieties of seeds, pesticides, commercial fertilizers, and irrigation. The cultivators wanted low-interest credit and agricultural inputs at low cost, and they sought agricultural procurement prices that would ensure a profitable return on their investment. What had emerged was a class of small capitalist farmers producing grains and other commodities for a commercial market.

The middle peasants were also sufficiently numerous to have electoral clout. In many areas they formed 30 to 40 percent of the electorate. Almost everything they needed in agriculture—credit, diesel fuel, storage facilities, tubewells, agricultural machinery—involved dealing with the government or quasi-governmental institutions (such as banks and cooperatives). An elaborate system of state patronage had developed that required peasants individually or collectively to deal with the state.

The bulk of the middle peasantry belonged to the backward castes, that is, those Hindu castes who lie between the scheduled castes and the upper-caste Kshatriyas and Brahmins. In Uttar Pradesh, under an executive order of the government, there were thirty-seven Hindu backward castes. An overlapping of caste and class enabled political leaders to appeal alternately to the one or the other, depending on the kind of claim the class wanted to make upon government and administration.

In north India, the middle peasants were effectively organized by Charan Singh, a member of the Jat caste, one of the largest and certainly the most articulate, if not economically the most powerful, of the middle-peasant castes. In the early 1960s, Charan Singh criticized Nehru's emphasis on rapid industrialization. He opposed policies that gave benefits to urban areas at the cost of rural India (such as low prices on agricultural commodities), and he was an advocate of dispersing industries to rural areas to provide employment for the children of the middle peasantry. In 1967 Charan Singh broke from Congress to organize his own party, the Bharatiya Kranti Dal (BKD) as the spokesman for the middle farmers. The BKD won 99 seats out of 425 constituencies in the Uttar Pradesh state legislature in the 1969 elections, with 21 percent of the vote, coming in second to Congress. The party was particularly strong in western Uttar Pradesh, the heartland of the Jat community.[13] Skillfully taking advantage of the fragmentation and factional conflicts within the state Congress party, Charan Singh built a coalition around his BKD to form a government. In a state in which parties are not well institutionalized, where social fragmentation along caste and factional lines is acute, where individual loyalties to parties are not enduring,

---

[13] For an account of the BKD, its performance in the 1967, 1969, and 1971 elections, and an analysis of its social base, see Craig Baxter, "The Rise and Fall of the Bharatiya Kranti Dal in Uttar Pradesh," in Myron Weiner and John Osgood Field, *Electoral Politics in the Indian States: Party Systems and Cleavages* (New Delhi: Manohar Book Service, 1975). In a particularly prescient statement, Baxter concluded his essay by writing that "the B.K.D. represents an important rural force of peasant proprietors—especially in the western parts of the state—which is not likely in the near future to reconcile itself to upper caste dominated parties like the Congress and the Jana Sangh. This force will continue to have importance in U.P. politics, perhaps increasing as the Green Revolution continues, and it will be heard whether as a separate party or as a faction within the Congress" (p. 142). For an attempt to relate caste to the class structure of Uttar Pradesh, and assess its impact on the rise of the BKD, see Francine Frankel, "Problems of Correlating Electoral and Economic Variables: An Analysis of Voting Behavior and Agrarian Modernization in Uttar Pradesh," in Myron Weiner and John Osgood Field, *Electoral Politics in the Indian States: The Impact of Modernization* (New Delhi: Manohar Book Service, 1977). According to Professor Frankel, the BKD's support came from the backward communities, the Muslims, and the Jat caste, all belonging to the class of small peasant farmers in Uttar Pradesh.

Charan Singh demonstrated that a party with only a fifth of the electorate could dominate state politics.

Though Charan Singh's government was short-lived and the BKD failed to increase its vote in the state assembly elections of 1974, his party continued to retain the support of the middle peasants. When the emergency was declared, Charan Singh and the BKD were among its fiercest opponents, and when the Janata party was formed on the eve of the 1977 elections, Charan Singh's party (renamed the Lok Dal) became one of its largest constituents. After the 1977 elections for Parliament and the state assemblies, the Lok Dal share of seats in the assemblies of Bihar, Uttar Pradesh, and Haryana was sufficiently large for Charan Singh's group to claim the chief ministership in each of these states. Charan Singh himself, as we have said earlier, aspired to be prime minister, but he lacked sufficient support in Parliament.

The Lok Dal made a great effort to strengthen its position among the backward castes and the Jats. On the eve of the elections, Charan Singh moved to reserve 25 percent of the jobs in the central services for backward classes, though the proposal was dropped when the president of India made it clear that he would be unwilling to sign such a controversial order. The Lok Dal platform promised reservations, which appealed to many middle peasants who wanted government jobs for their educated sons and daughters, particularly when there were so few new employment opportunities in industry.

Lok Dal won only 9.4 percent of the popular vote nationally in the 1980 elections, but it demonstrated that it commanded the allegiance of a large part of the electorate in four north Indian states. These four were Bihar (16.5 percent for the Lok Dal), Haryana (33.5 percent), Orissa (19.5 percent), and Uttar Pradesh (29 percent). In Haryana, the Lok Dal actually emerged as the largest party in the popular vote, and in Uttar Pradesh it was second only to Congress.

How mobilized the supporters of the Lok Dal were is suggested by the turnout in the constituencies it won. The *average* turnout in the twenty-nine constituencies won by the Lok Dal in Uttar Pradesh was 54.9 percent, while the statewide turnout was 50 percent. In Bihar the average turnout in the five seats won by Lok Dal was 58.1 percent; it was 51.7 percent for the state as a whole. And in Haryana, where Lok Dal won a larger vote than any other party, the entire state turnout was 64.8 percent (65.5 percent in the four constituencies won by Lok Dal), the highest of any state in northern India and well above the national turnout of 57 percent.

These same constituencies, it should be noted, had had a similarly high voter turnout in 1977. In Uttar Pradesh their turnout was 60.9

percent, while the state turnout was 56.5 percent; in Bihar the difference was even greater, 71.3 percent and 61.1 percent, and in Haryana it was 73.9 percent, and 73.3 percent in a state that had the highest turnout in northern India.

The electoral strength of the Lok Dal is more concentrated than that of other parties. The middle peasants are particularly numerous in western Uttar Pradesh and in Haryana. In a study of the middle peasants in Uttar Pradesh, Paul Brass reported that they are most numerous in the region known as Upper Doab and Rohilkhand.[14] According to Brass, the Upper Doab is the domain of the prosperous peasantry, with 17.4 percent of the cultivators owning 54 percent of the acreage in holdings that are at least 7.5 acres. Brass also notes that while in some of the western districts the larger landowners are Rajputs and Brahmins, the middle or backward castes, such as the Ahirs and Kurmis, have smaller holdings and were themselves tenants of the elite castes before the abolition of the *zamindari*. The Lok Dal attracted the support of peasant proprietors holding between 2.5 and 27.5 acres of land, a class that is particularly large in the wheat and grain growing areas in the West. The geographic concentration of this class enabled the Lok Dal to win seats proportionate to its share of votes. In the Hindi-speaking states, Lok Dal won 18.1 percent of the seats with 20.1 percent of the vote; in contrast, Janata, whose supporters were more widely dispersed, won only 9.5 percent of the seats with 25.9 percent of the vote.

It should also be noted that, while the Lok Dal is widely regarded as the party of the middle peasants, it successfully attracted Muslims and even scheduled-caste voters. Its attack on the Janata

[14] Paul R. Brass, "The Politicization of the Peasantry in a North Indian State: Part I," *Journal of Peasant Studies*, vol. 7, no. 4 (July 1980), pp. 395-426. This article provides a fine analysis of the way class, caste, and parties are linked in rural Uttar Pradesh. In the late 1960s the Swatantra party, according to Brass, appealed to the former *zamindars* and large farmers; the Jana Sangh, while appealing to the former landlords, also tried to win the support of the smaller farmers holding five to thirty acres of land; the BKD made the most direct appeal to the small peasant proprietors (with 2.5 to 27.5 acres); the Socialists appealed to the landless and the poor peasants and advocated reduced ceilings on land holdings. "The Janata party in U.P.," concludes Brass, "was an attempt to pull most of these groups together to appeal to the interests of the market-oriented, input-oriented farmers. Much of the increased vote for the B.K.D., and subsequently the Janata party, came from the vote that previously had been given to independent candidates, one indication of the failure of the Congress party in U.P. to successfully attract the middle peasants." (p. 426). For other interpretations of the economic and political role of the middle peasantry, see Pradhan H. Prasad, "Caste and Class in Bihar," *Economic and Political Weekly*, vol. 14, nos. 7 and 8 (February 1979), pp. 481-84; and Susanne H. Rudolph and Lloyd I. Rudolph, "The Centrist Future of Indian Politics," *Asian Survey*, vol. 20, no. 6 (June 1980), pp. 575-94.

party for its Jana Sangh and RSS association may have been a factor in its remarkably good performance among Muslim voters. However, since most of the heavily populated Muslim constituencies are located in Upper Doab and Rohilkhand, which also have a large middle-peasant, backward-caste population, it is difficult to infer from the election data that it is the Muslims in these constituencies who have voted in substantial numbers for the Lok Dal. But there are at least three indications that Lok Dal did receive a substantial share of the Muslim vote: (1) Lok Dal did as well in the two constituencies with the highest proportion of Muslims (Moradabad and Rampur) as in other districts in Rohilkhand; (2) Lok Dal received an above-average vote in two of the three constituencies in the central and eastern part of the state (Bara Banki and Basti) that have large numbers of Muslims; and (3) seven of the twenty-nine successful Lok Dal candidates for parliamentary seats were Muslims.

Lok Dal also apparently did well among the scheduled castes, winning nine of the eighteen reserved constituencies. Whether many Harijans were "buying" peace with the Jats by voting for Lok Dal candidates or were coerced, or there was a great deal of "bogus" voting, we cannot say. Once again, it is difficult to infer that Lok Dal received a substantial share of the scheduled-caste vote in the re-served constituencies, since several of these constituencies are located in the western part of the state, where the Lok Dal victory may have reflected the voting strength of the middle peasantry. Lok Dal did carry several reserved constituencies in the eastern part of the state, but it may have done well because of substantial support from the Yadavs, one of the backward castes.

Bihar. The interplay of caste, class, and party is equally a central theme of Bihar politics. Inder Malhotra of the *Times of India,* a keen observer of the Bihar social and political scene, wrote shortly after the elections:

> Caste has played a part in . . . the struggle for political power all over the country. But nowhere has this happened so consistently and virulently as in Bihar. . . . The configuration of caste forces arrayed against one another in Bihar has undergone such a change over the years as to exacerbate the caste conflicts. Gone are the days when the Brahmins, the Bhumihars and the Rajputs were overwhelmingly dominant, both economically and politically, and could torment others, especially the Harijans, at will. Their power has not ended but it has been eroded. They are being seriously challenged by the so-called backward castes—the Yadavs,

the Kurmis, the Koeris and so on—which are economically well off and politically assertive to the point of being aggressive. Though there is still no dearth of Bhumihar and Rajput landlords, the balance of power in the countryside has shifted to the landowning backward castes. The so-called upper castes have to some extent moved away from land to professions, industry, trade and government and commercial jobs and unlike the Bhumihar or Rajput landowners, the backward caste landlords work in the fields themselves and are apt to treat the landless labourers and sharecroppers more harshly. Indeed, the backward castes are as militant in confronting the "upper castes" as they are in terrorising the poor Harijans. It is no mere coincidence, for instance, that, according to the findings of responsible inquiry committees, all the major atrocities on the Harijans in Bihar during the last three years—at Belchi, Bishrampur, Pathda and Baljitpur—have been committed by Yadavs and Kurmis.[15]

Malhotra went on to explain that the Janata ministry that took power in Bihar in June 1977, under the chief ministership of Karpoori Thakur, set out to "pander to the aggressiveness of the backward castes" by its move to reserve jobs for them. Thakur, who later joined the Lok Dal, proposed that the backward castes be given 25 percent reservations, a percentage equal to the reservations for Harijans and tribals. The proposal was greeted with a violent protest movement by the forward castes in a state with so much unemployment. The policy further polarized the forward and backward castes.

Reporters noted that the upper castes in Bihar voted for Congress.[16] In addition to the Brahmins and other forward castes, Congress reportedly won support from a large proportion of the Harijans (particularly those not of the Chamar caste) and the tribal population in southern Bihar as well as a larger proportion than elsewhere of the Muslim vote. Malhotra also reported that some of the higher-caste supporters of Janata switched to Congress to prevent Lok Dal candidates from winning.[17] Congress won 36.4 percent of

[15] Inder Malhotra, "Caste Carnage in Bihar: Wages of Whipped Up Tensions," *Times of India*, February 14, 1980.

[16] *Indian Express*, January 16, 1980.

[17] Malhotra, "Caste Carnage." Coercion, according to many local journalists, has often been used in Bihar elections. "In the past elections," writes the *Times of India* correspondent (December 14, 1979, "Election Eve Survey: Bihar Voter is Disillusioned"), "goondas carrying guns, knives and other lethal weapons—often hired by upper caste or affluent contestants—are known to have prevented Harijans from going to polling booths in many areas. The Yadavs too are known to have displayed their muscle power in electoral battles."

the vote and a majority (thirty out of fifty-four) of seats. As in Uttar Pradesh, Congress did not do as well as the combined Janata–Lok Dal vote (40.2 percent), and in both votes and seats it fell short of its performance in the elections of 1971.

In Bihar, Muslims constitute 13 percent of the population, scheduled castes 14.1 percent, and scheduled tribes 8.8 percent. The remaining 64 percent of the population is caste Hindu, a third (say local observers) belonging to the forward castes (Bhumihars, Rajputs, Brahmins, and Kyasthas), and the remainder to the backward castes.

Both Congress and Lok Dal did disproportionately better in the scheduled-caste reserved constituencies than elsewhere in the state, while Janata, though led by a Bihari Chamar, actually did worse. Congress and Janata did as well in the scheduled-tribe constituencies as elsewhere, while Lok Dal did less well; but there was also considerable support in some of the tribal constituencies for independent candidates advocating the creation of a separate tribal (or "Jharkhand") state. And in the constituencies with a substantial Muslim population, both Lok Dal and Congress did unusually well, while Janata was below its state average.

Lok Dal won only 16.6 percent of the vote in the state, but it did substantially better in the northern half of the state, where the backward castes reside. (The southern portion, with its large tribal population, gave little support to Lok Dal.) Lok Dal reportedly did particularly well among the Yadavs, one of the largest of the middle-peasant backward-caste communities.

The absence of agrarian radicalism in Bihar (and in Uttar Pradesh) puzzled many observers. Some analysts expected the middle peasantry to be radicalized, while others looked to the poor tenants and agricultural laborers to provide the mass base for a revolutionary movement. Both classes have been mobilized by political parties in Bihar, the one by the Lok Dal and the other by Congress, but neither party can be described as revolutionary. The tradition of patron-client relations based on a system of attached laborers persists in much of Bihar, with attendant political consequences for the way the lowest castes vote. The middle peasants in Bihar are mobilized by the Lok Dal to make demands upon government and administration for better terms of trade between the countryside and the city and for a greater share of government benefits—but not for revolutionary change.

Haryana. "Jatland," as some portions of Haryana are called, has a high proportion of Jat-caste voters and is the center of Lok Dal strength in northern India. Jats in Haryana are described by reporters and politicians as an aggressive community, who force lower-caste voters either to stay at home or to vote for Jat candidates. There are a variety of rival Jat subcastes—Miliks, Dehyas, Rathis, Ahlawats, and Dalals—and violence may be used by one Jat group against another as well as against "outsiders." The Jats in Haryana, most of whom are owner-cultivators, want higher prices for their produce and an adequate supply of water, power, kerosene, and other agricultural inputs at low cost.

Because the Jats are themselves divided, they forge political alignments with locally influential non-Jat groups such as the Rajputs, Brahmins, and the various trading castes. The Jats constitute as much as 40 percent of the electorate in some constituencies but may nonetheless nominate a non-Jat candidate. In spite of their divisions, the Jats provided the Lok Dal with an impressive victory in the state.

Lok Dal won 33.5 percent of the vote in Haryana, a larger vote than either Congress or Janata and the largest vote won by Lok Dal in any state. But once again, because of the fragmentation of the non-Congress parties, Congress won more seats than any other party; it won five seats (Lok Dal won four and Janata one) with only 29.3 percent of the vote. Moreover, the vote for Congress was an enormous improvement over 1977, when it was a mere 18 percent, the lowest vote in any of the Hindi-speaking states.

During the campaign, Bansi Lal, once the most powerful politician in Haryana and a close associate of Mrs. Gandhi, toured the state, blaming the former chief minister and now Janata supporter Banarsi Dasgupta for the excesses of the emergency but at the same time speaking of his own "repentance." "Repentance," he is reported to have told his audiences, "is the ultimate punishment."[18] Reporters said that he visited the homes of many prominent Jats "with folded hands," seeking forgiveness for what he had done during the emergency; he also approached many Harijans seeking their forgiveness for the "excesses" in family planning.[19]

Some Jat voters credited Bansi Lal with having played an important role in the development of the economy of Haryana and improving the position of the Jats. "Bansi Lal," said one correspondent, is a "bigger god for them than Charan Singh. . . . To see Jats hotly arguing over the question of support to Mr. Bansi Lal or the Lok Dal is not an uncommon sight. At village Sirsee . . . there was an open division in the community after Mr. Bansi Lal's visit, and the two sides virtually came to blows."[20] Bansi Lal won his seat in Bhiwani

[18] *Pioneer,* December 31, 1979.
[19] *Hindustan Times,* December 20, 1979.
[20] *Indian Express,* December 18, 1979.

constituency with 194,000 votes; his Janata opponent took 144,000; and the Lok Dal candidate 100,000.

"Bansi Lal," said another correspondent, "succeeded in denting the Lok Dal offensive" [21] in Haryana. Congress increased its vote by 11.3 percentage points, and the combined vote of Lok Dal and Janata declined correspondingly, by some 9 percentage points over 1977.

Madhya Pradesh. The Congress victory in Madhya Pradesh was spectacular, for the party not only increased its vote from 32.5 percent to 46.5 percent (the highest vote it received in any of the large Hindi-speaking states) but even succeeded in surpassing its 1971 vote. There was probably no state in which the results were as surprising, particularly since most observers gave the Janata ministry in the state credit for its effectiveness in increasing irrigation and electric power. The Janata government had launched an aggressive "food for work" program and, with Jagjivan Ram as its leader, was expected to do well among the Harijans. Janata also had a firm hold on the cooperative banks and in local government (*panchayat*) institutions. Moreover, Lok Dal was not a significant force in the state, so the contest was primarily between Congress and the Janata party, with its strong Jana Sangh–RSS base.[22]

As it turned out, these factors were not as significant as had been expected. Janata did do well in the scheduled-caste reserved constituencies (where it won 42 percent of the vote), but Congress did even better. Congress also swept the reserved tribal constituencies. An important element here was the division within the former ruling families, the ex-maharajas, in Madhya Pradesh. The Scindia family, historically strong supporters of Jana Sangh, had split, with the mother contesting the seat against Mrs. Gandhi in Uttar Pradesh while her son ran on the Congress ticket in Madhya Pradesh.

A striking feature of the Congress campaign in Madhya Pradesh was its success in winning support from both the lowest economic groups and the wealthiest, while leaving the middle groups to Janata. One correspondent, assessing the prospects for the Congress party a few weeks before the elections, wrote, "It sounds strange but the fact is that everywhere the really rich and the really poor are with

[21] *Statesman*, January 12, 1980. See also Paul Wallace, "Plebiscitary Politics in India's 1980 Parliamentary Elections: Punjab and Haryana," *Asian Survey*, vol. 20, no. 6 (June 1980), pp. 617-44.

[22] Madhya Pradesh is the historic stronghold of Jana Sangh. The party won a third of the vote in the state in 1971, and eleven seats in Parliament. In 1977 Janata won 57.9 percent of the vote and all thirty-seven seats, a majority of which were reportedly won by former Jana Sangh members.

Indira Gandhi. In almost every city you go you soon come to discover that the rich local 'biri king' [producers of local cigarettes] or the 'rice king' is with Indira Gandhi. In Jabalpur the 'biri king' Hagovind Patel is on her side and so is the 'rice king' of Chhattisgarh, Naimchand Jain. . . . And so are the poor whether they be in the cities and towns or in villages."[23]

Other States in the Hindi Belt. The Congress victory in Rajasthan illustrates both the effects of the Janata–Lok Dal split and the role played by Muslims, scheduled castes, and scheduled tribes in the Congress victory. The vote for Congress was about the same as the combined Lok Dal–Janata vote, but the split made it possible for Congress to win a disproportionately large number of seats, eighteen out of twenty-five, with 42.7 percent of the vote. All seven reserved constituencies—three tribal and four scheduled-caste—went to Congress, and with substantially higher votes than the party received elsewhere in the state. In fact, Congress won a majority of votes in the reserved constituencies, whereas in 1977 it had lost all seven constituencies with about one-fourth of the vote. Congress apparently also won back a substantial portion of the Muslim electorate. Since 35 percent of the population in Rajasthan is scheduled caste, scheduled tribe, or Muslim, the shift in these communities accounts for a substantial portion of the increase in the Congress vote.

Janata, which continued to run the state through the elections, hoped that its *antyodaya* program to assist the most impoverished in each village and its food for work program would attract the support of the lower-income groups, but the results were disappointing. Janata had the support of some of the ex-maharajas, but the electoral influence of this class upon lower-income groups, which once loomed so large in the state, has declined.

Congress swept Delhi, the capital city, with an absolute majority of the votes and won six of the seven parliamentary seats. Three years earlier Janata had won all seven seats.[24] However, Congress did not do nearly as well as in 1971, and in several constituencies the margin of victory was not very great. As elsewhere, the scheduled castes appear to have voted for Congress, as evidenced by the overwhelming Congress victory in Karol Bagh, the city's only reserved constituency. The sole Janata candidate to win in Delhi was Atal

[23] *Patriot*, December 23, 1979.

[24] In the election before that, in 1971, Congress had won all seven. In 1967 Congress had won only one seat. In no other major city of India have the swings been so great over the four elections.

Behari Vajpayee, the foreign minister in the Janata government and a leading figure in the Jana Sangh.

In the Punjab, a non-Hindi-speaking state located within the Hindi belt, Congress won 52.5 percent of the vote, more than the party received in any of the Hindi-speaking states, and a greater percentage than the party had received in either 1977 or 1971. A special feature of the Punjab is the importance of the Akali Dal, a regional party with a secure political base in the Sikh population. In 1977 the Akali Dal and the Janata party had formed an alliance that easily defeated Congress. In 1980 there were acute factional divisions within the Akali Dal and conflicts between the Akalis and Janata; a last-minute electoral pact between the two parties did not materially change the picture. The Akalis won less than a quarter of the vote and Janata about a tenth. Congress won twelve of the thirteen seats.

Since 1967 only Congress and the Akali Dal have had a significant electoral base in the state. The Akalis won 27 percent of the vote in 1967, 30.8 percent in 1971, 34.8 percent in 1977. The 1980 election marked the first time the Akalis had declined in over a decade; it was also the first time Congress had won an absolute majority.[25]

Conclusion. The 1980 parliamentary elections revealed how dependent the Congress (I) in northern India is upon the personal popularity of Mrs. Gandhi and how relatively unimportant local party organization has become. What proved critical—as we shall see in some detail later—was Mrs. Gandhi's success in winning back many of the party's former supporters, particularly among the scheduled castes, scheduled tribes, and Muslims. But the position of the party in the North remains fragile. Indeed, even with Mrs. Gandhi as its leader, the Congress party in 1980 won only 39 percent of the vote in the entire region. The party's popular following is less than it was in 1971 and only slightly better than it was in 1967, when it barely won.

Both Lok Dal and the Janata party have more solid positions in north India than their share of parliamentary seats indicates. The Lok Dal has a base among the middle peasants, and it may be less dependent on its leader, Charan Singh, than the Congress party is on Mrs. Gandhi. The middle peasants do have a set of interests, and it seems likely that the Lok Dal—or some other political party—will

[25] The Akalis ran the state government at the time of the 1980 elections. It is noteworthy that in 1980, as in 1977, control over a state government did not apparently give the governing party any edge in the parliamentary elections in the state.

continue to mobilize them. Similarly, the Janata party, or at least its Jana Sangh segment, has a base in the trading community, among the former landowning castes, and in a substantial section of the middle class in the towns and cities. In spite of the party's recent efforts to emphasize its secularism, it retains an important link to Hindu nationalism, which gives it a particular vitality that other parties, apart from the Communists, lack. It too, in one guise or another, seems likely to remain a significant force in the politics of northern India.

The poor, or at least those sections of the poor that belong to the scheduled castes and scheduled tribes, provided Mrs. Gandhi's Congress with a significantly large vote in 1980, as they did in all previous elections except 1977. But the Muslims remain a more volatile group; their return to the Congress party in north India was less enthusiastic and complete. They seem peculiarly available to whichever party or leader can find the right appeal. How they move politically, and how cohesive or divided they become, may have a significant impact on future elections in northern India.

The educated unemployed in the countryside may prove to be the Achilles' heel of any government and the source of support for one or more opposition parties. But it will make a difference whether the educated young are from the backward castes, the scheduled tribes, the scheduled castes, the Muslims, or the forward castes, for attachment to community is still a more potent force for political organization than class interest for aspiring middle-class youth. Indeed, it is as likely that the middle classes of each ethnic community will demand a share of public goods for their own community as that they will band together around some common class interest, ideology, or party.

The Hindi-speaking region, by virtue of its population, size, geographic position, and historical role in national politics, is the place where the fate of a national government is decided. The 1980 election once again demonstrated that political control over the Hindi heartland is the key to national power.

Western India

The Congress victory in the Hindi belt was given a strong boost in both Gujarat and Maharashtra, where the party won twenty-five out of twenty-six seats in one state and twenty-nine out of forty-eight in the other. In both states Congress won an absolute majority of the votes, faring better than in most of the Hindi-speaking region. Throughout western India the Congress party has traditionally had a strong electoral base. In fact, even in the 1977 elections the two states gave 47 percent of their combined vote to Congress and a respectable thirty out of seventy-four seats. And when the Congress party has been challenged, as it was in 1977, the opposition has come from people who split from Congress in order to create a competing Congress organization.

In Maharashtra, the split after the 1977 elections between the pro-Indira and anti-Indira groups in the Congress party threatened to weaken, if not destroy, Mrs. Gandhi's electoral position in the state. Y. B. Chavan, the most prominent Maharashtrian Congress leader in the state, led his group against the former prime minister, and his withdrawal came on top of that of Sharad Pawar, the Congress chief minister, who subsequently formed a coalition government with the Janata party.

Pawar and Chavan were regarded as the leaders of the "sugar lobby," the sugar mill owners who operate a network of rural cooperatives. These cooperatives process sugarcane and they control vast economic resources; since their earnings are largely determined by the government's sugar pricing policy, their members form an active political lobby. The cooperative sugar movement grew under the patronage of Chavan and the Congress party, and the cooperatives in turn contributed to the election funds of Congress politicians. Most of the members of the sugar cooperatives belong to the Maratha caste, a highly influential rural caste that played an important role in the governance of the region in pre-British times and continues to be the dominant political elite in the state.

Although the state government run by Sharad Pawar and other Congress groups had a good record of maintaining law and order, supporting the sugar cooperatives, and providing work schemes for the rural poor and loans to the scheduled castes, the Maratha community and others who traditionally vote Congress nevertheless deserted these groups to support the Congress party of Mrs. Gandhi. "As far as the Maharashtra Congress is concerned," wrote the *Statesman* correspondent from Bombay after the elections, "the verdict is unmistakable. The traditional Congress voters have recognized the Congress (I) as their own party and have totally rejected the curious combination of the Congress (U), the parallel Congress, and the Prajatantra Congress [the three Congress splinter groups in Maharashtra]." [26] The Maratha leaders were apparently split between those who felt personally loyal to Pawar and Chavan and those who concluded that they had best go with the likely national

[26] *Statesman*, January 13, 1980.

winner. The sugar lobby in particular was split. One reporter noted that some of the sugar factories had employed more workers than usual, assigning some to campaign work, and that money from the mills was going in substantial amounts to various candidates of different parties.[27]

Mrs. Gandhi's Congress (I) swept the state with thirty-nine victories and 53.3 percent of the popular vote. Congress (I) apparently retained support among the scheduled castes,[28] the scheduled tribes, and the Muslims. Congress (I) was, however, unable to regain its position in urban Bombay. It won only two of the six seats, losing four to Janata. (In 1971 a united Congress had swept all six of the parliamentary seats.) The Congress (I) share of votes in the city was 39.2 percent, less than the 40.2 percent won by Janata. Janata fared badly elsewhere in the state, with a statewide vote of 20.6 percent. But Janata also did well in Poona, suggesting that the Janata party, its split and the soaring food prices notwithstanding, still retained the support of a large proportion of the urban voters in Maharashtra. Congress (U) won 11.6 percent of the vote in the state, much of it from the Maratha community.[29]

In Gujarat, the parliamentary elections were seen as a preparation for the more important state assembly elections due to be held within a few months. In spite of defections from the Janata party to the Congress (I), Janata controlled the state government. There were really two Congress parties in Gujarat, dating back to the 1969 split in the party, and they have been electorally well matched. In the 1971 elections, the Congress led by Mrs. Gandhi won ten of the twenty-four seats, and the Congress led by Morarji Desai won eleven. In 1975, Morarji Desai's Congress (O), joined by Jana Sangh and several other groups, won control of the state assembly, but with the advent of the emergency their government proved short lived. In the 1977 election, Janata won, but with only a few percentage points more than Mrs. Gandhi's Congress and thirteen seats, while the Congress took eleven. In terms of votes, Congress actually did better in 1977 than in 1971.

The defeat of Morarji Desai in Delhi and the breakup of the

[27] *Times of India*, December 21, 1979.

[28] The Maharashtra Dalit Panthers, an organization of ex-untouchables, campaigned for Mrs. Gandhi's Congress, though a smaller faction of the organization decided to support Janata in view of its promise to make Jagjivan Ram prime minister.

[29] Congress (U) won 20.8 percent of the vote in the state assembly elections in June 1980, but Mrs. Gandhi's Congress won easily with 186 assembly seats out of 288 and 44.5 percent of the vote.

Janata party nationally had its repercussions in Gujarat as a number of local leaders defected to join Mrs. Gandhi. The morale of party workers plummeted. Morarji Desai, though not himself a candidate for reelection, toured the state on behalf of Janata candidates, and many Janata leaders made a special plea for the Harijan vote. But the scheduled-caste and scheduled-tribe constituencies, which had not deserted Mrs. Gandhi in 1977 as they had in north India, remained loyal to her in 1980. So apparently did many Muslim voters, her traditional supporters in Gujarat. The increase in the Congress vote, from 46.9 percent in 1977 to 54.8 percent in 1980, was sufficient to enable Mrs. Gandhi's party to sweep the parliamentary constituencies. Janata dropped to 36.9 percent and won only one seat. The state assembly elections a few months later confirmed the parliamentary results. Congress won three-quarters of the assembly seats and an absolute majority of the votes, bringing down the Janata state government.

The Northeast

The electoral patterns of northeastern India in 1980 differed from the rest of the country in three respects. First this region contained a state, Assam, politically so disturbed that elections could not be held in twelve of its fourteen constituencies. Assam thus became the first state in postindependence India unable to participate in a national parliamentary election. Second, the Northeast was the only region that failed to give Congress a majority of its parliamentary seats. Indeed, Congress won a mere ten of the fifty-two seats, while the CPI(M) took twenty-nine, the CPI four, independents two, and local parties seven. Neither Janata nor Lok Dal won a single seat. Third, while turnout declined in every other region of India, in the Northeast it improved, ten percentage points each in West Bengal and Tripura, and as many as twenty percentage points in Manipur (see table 23).

This is not to suggest that the Northeast was entirely uninfluenced by developments in the country; in West Bengal the Congress vote did increase between 1977 and 1980. But elsewhere in the region the Congress vote actually declined, a further indication that the region marches to a different political tune from that of the rest of India. How the region differs, and why, are the issues to be looked at in each of the states.

Assam. The decision not to hold parliamentary elections in Assam was made by the government of India after it became clear that political agitation, which had already prevented nominations from being filed with the Election Commission, had become so disruptive that free and fair elections were not possible. The political crisis had been precipitated by a statement by Chief Election Commissioner S. L. Shakdher that the electoral rolls for Assam had been inflated by the registration of illegal Bengali migrants from neighboring Bangladesh.[30] The number of voters on the electoral rolls in 1979 was 8.5 million; this was an 18 percent increase over the 1977 figure of 7.2 million; the national increase was 10 percent.[31] In 1971 there had been 6.3 million voters on the electoral rolls, giving Assam an increase over the eight years of 36 percent while the national increase was 29 percent.

On the eve of the parliamentary elections, a political movement was launched by the All Assam Student Union (AASU, which claims to represent the 1.3 million school and college students in the state), several regional parties, and the state's major literary association demanding that the electoral rolls prepared by the Election Commission be screened to eliminate the names of those who had entered India illegally. The Election Commission agreed in principle, but a conflict arose over how to decide who was a citizen, whether it was sufficient to scrutinize the new names on the electoral rolls or whether it would be necessary to reassess the status of all those entered in 1971 or 1967 or even, as many Assamese demanded, since 1951. It soon became clear that what was at issue was not only the status of illegal migrants who had crossed the borders from Bangladesh after the Indo-Pakistan war of 1972, but also that of Bengalis who had fled East Pakistan after partition in 1947, many of whom were entitled to citizenship, and even of Bengalis who had moved to Assam from West Bengal.[32] In a country in which few people have birth certificates, school certificates, or other documents to prove their citizenship, any procedure for scrutinizing the electoral rolls would have created anxieties among all the Bengalis in the state. The natural anxieties were intensified as the movement took an increasingly anti-Bengali turn, and anti-Indian slogans began to be heard ("Get out Indian Dogs

[30] L. K. Sarin, *India's North-East in Flames* (New Delhi: Vikas Publishing House, 1980), p. 36.
[31] *This Fortnight*, December 22, 1979, p. 13.
[32] East Bengalis who came to India before July 26, 1949, automatically became Indian citizens and, under an agreement between India and Bangladesh, those who entered India between that date and March 25, 1971, could secure citizenship certificates, though few did. However, the AASU and the All Assam Gana Sangram Parishad, the council of Assamese organizations, viewed this latter agreement between Indira Gandhi and Mujib Rahman, the prime minister of Bangladesh, as illegal and unconstitutional.

from Assam" and "Assam for the Assamese").[33] Assamese political leaders expressed the fear that the influx of Bengali voters was so changing the demographic and political structure of the state that the indigenous Assamese were in danger of losing control over its political system.

The migration of Bengalis into Assam has been going on for more than a century, but several elements made the influx from Bangladesh particularly disruptive.[34] For one thing, precisely because there had been a long history of migration, the number of Bengalis in Assam was already so large that this new influx threatened to tip the balance of the population away from the Assamese. The situation had been obscured for many years by the tendency of Bengali Muslims who migrated to Assam from what is now Bangladesh to report to the census authorities that they were Assamese speakers. Most of the 3.6 million Muslims in the state told census enumerators in 1971 that they were Assamese-speaking Muslims—although most were of Bengali origin.[35] Their apparent motive was the desire to avoid land confiscation and possible deportation. In return, Assamese Hindus received Bengali Muslim support for state government policies to make Assamese the state language, enforce the teaching of Assamese in schools and colleges, and ensure Assamese job preference in the administrative services. Moreover, the governing Congress party received political support from the Bengali Muslims. Even in 1977, when Congress was defeated throughout northern India, the Congress party in Assam won 50.6 percent of the vote, much of it from Bengali Muslims.

[33] For a vivid account of the agitation and photos of the anti-Indian graffiti, see "The Danger of Secession: Assam and the North-East," *India Today*, North American edition, vol. 2, no. 1 (1980), pp. 20-26.

[34] For a detailed history of the various migrations into Assam and an account of its impact on Assamese politics, see Myron Weiner, *Sons of the Soil: Migration and Ethnic Conflict in India* (Princeton: Princeton University Press, 1978), chapter 3, "When Migrants Succeed and Natives Fail: Assam and its Migrants," pp. 75-143.

[35] The Assamese-speaking population (which includes Bengali migrants and tribal tea plantation workers from Bihar who report Assamese as their mother tongue) is reported in the census as 56.7 percent of the population in 1951, 62.4 percent in 1961, and 61 percent in 1971. The corresponding figures for Bengali speakers are 16.5 percent, 18.5 percent, and 19.7 percent, and for the Hindi-speaking population 3.8 percent, 4.8 percent, and 5.4 percent. See Susanta Krishna Dass, "Immigration and Demographic Transformation of Assam, 1891-1981," *Economic and Political Weekly*, vol. 15, no. 19 (May 10, 1980), p. 855. Dass suggests that the substantial increase in the number of Bengali speakers between 1961 and 1971 (a 43.5 percent increase) was due to the migration of Hindu refugees from East Pakistan as a result of communal disturbances there in 1965.

It was an uneasy alliance' since many Assamese Hindus feared that Bengali Muslims might someday reassert their Bengali identity and join politically with Bengali Hindus. The census reported that nearly 20 percent of the population of the state claimed Bengali as its mother tongue, and if the Bengali Muslims who did not report Bengali as their mother tongue were added, the position of the Assamese would be precarious. Moreover, many Assamese Hindus were becoming concerned at what they viewed as an alarming increase in the proportion of Muslims in the state. By 1971 the Muslims were 24 percent of the population, at least twice what they had been in the first census of 1871. And if the growth in the electoral rolls accurately reflected the population increase in the state since 1971, then Assam's population had increased approximately 7 percent more than that of the rest of India—a growth rate that might reflect a higher rate of natural population increase but almost certainly reflected migration into the state from other parts of India or illegal migration from Bangladesh.

The political response to these demographic changes should be seen in the context of the breakup of the Congress party in Assam after the 1977 elections. In Assam, as elsewhere in India, Congress split into pro— and anti—Indira Gandhi factions, with the result that for the first time since independence, Congress failed to win a majority of seats in the state assembly elections of March 1978. In an assembly of 126 seats, Congress (I) won only 8 seats and the anti-Indira Congress won 26. This split within Congress ended the post-independence coalition of Assamese Hindus and Bengali Muslims, for what had attracted Bengali Muslims to Congress was the certainty that Congress would govern the state. Many Bengali Muslims subsequently shifted their support to other parties, and so did many Bengali Hindus who had earlier supported Congress. In the 1978 state assembly elections, the CPI(M) won 5.6 percent of the vote (and eleven seats), and the CPI 4.1 percent of the vote (and five seats), more than twice the combined vote of 4.3 percent won by the two parties in the parliamentary elections only a year earlier. Many Assamese regarded the Communist parties as Bengali because of the pro-Communist vote in both West Bengal and Tripura.

The Congress (I) was excluded from the various coalition governments that governed Assam in 1978 and 1979. The Janata party (which won 53 out of 126 assembly seats) initially formed a government that included the CPI(M). During its eighteen months in office, Janata supported a policy of screening voters to ensure that noncitizens were not on the voter lists. Leading the movement for taking aliens off the rolls were several Assamese organizations, particularly the AASU, the Asom Jatiyotabadi Dal (AJD, Assam Nationalist party), the Purbanchaliya Lok Parishad (PLP, Eastern Regional People's Council), and the Assam Sahitya Parishad (Assam Literary Association). When the Janata coalition government fell in mid-1979 a new coalition government, led by J. N. Hazarika, was formed with the support of Congress (U) (which held twenty-two seats). The Hazarika government was torn, as the various Assamese nationalist organizations pressed for removing aliens from the electoral rolls before the 1980 parliamentary elections, while the Congress (U), the Congress (I) and the Communist parties, all competing for the votes of the migrants, refused to join the agitation. Congress and Communist leaders argued that it was not simply illegal Bangladeshis who were threatened by the agitation, but Indian citizens who had come to Assam from West Bengal, and Bengali Hindus who had come to Assam after independence and were entitled to citizenship; these would be excluded from the electoral rolls by government screening. Moreover, the movement to exclude foreigners from the electoral rolls soon took on ominous anti-Indian overtones. Many members of the Asom Jatiyotabadi Dal adopted a secessionist stance, arguing that Assam with its oil and tea had been exploited by the central government. The Purbanchaliya Lok Parishad called for the secession of the entire northeastern region, including Manipur, Meghalaya, Nagaland, Tripura, Arunachal Pradesh, and Mizoram, as well as Assam.

The agitation also took an anticommunist turn when the All Assam Gana Sangram Parishad (AAGSP), an organization consisting of eleven constituent organizations supporting the agitation, denounced the left parties in Assam as "agents of the Bengalis." [36] There were reports too that many members of the Assamese urban middle class, who owned agricultural land leased to tenant farmers, were hostile to the CPI(M) for its support of the demand by the tenants, many of whom are Bengali Muslims, for title to land they had cultivated for several years. [37]

Some Assamese nationalists were concerned simply with reducing the number of Bengali voters, and therefore they advocated measures that did not distinguish carefully between Bengalis from West Bengal and Bengalis from Bangladesh. The impact on Bengalis of Indian citizenship of scrutinizing the electoral rolls did not trouble some of the Assamese nationalists. "My party," said Giri Barua,

[36] *Statesman* (Calcutta), January 15, 1980.
[37] Yogi Agarwal, "Left in Waiting," *Economic and Political Weekly*, vol. 15, nos. 24-25 (June 14-21, 1980), p. 1046.

president of the Asom Jatiyotabadi Dal, "demands that each person staying in Assam must have two certifications of citizenship, one for India and the other for Assam." When told that dual citizenship was against the constitution, he replied, "Get the Constitution changed then." [38]

AAGSP and AASU took the position that the government should review the legal status of all those who had entered the state after 1951. Bengalis and other non-Assamese would have to produce some evidence of their citizenship. Foreign nationals who had come between 1951 and 1961 should be screened and probably given citizenship. Those who came between 1961 and 1971 should be declared stateless and distributed throughout the country. And those who had come after 1971 should be returned to Bangladesh. Some of the Jana Sangh members of the Janata party advocated a cutoff date of 1971 for revising the electoral rolls, for that would force many Muslims to leave but permit Bengali Hindus to remain. Though all the organizations participating in the agitation disavowed the attacks on Muslims and insisted that their opposition was not to Muslims but to any foreigners illegally residing in the state, in some areas clashes took a communal turn. Many opponents of Mrs. Gandhi also saw a reduction in the size of the Bengali Muslim electorate as a means of undermining what had been a major source of her electoral support.

The end of the alliance between Assamese Hindus and Bengali Muslims thus appeared to result from a concatenation of events: the continued influx of Bengali Muslims from Bangladesh, the split in the Congress party, the shift of some Bengali Muslims to the left parties, the opposition of Assamese Hindu middle-class landowners to the demands of their Muslim tenants, and the efforts by political parties and groups opposed to the leftist parties and the Congress to reduce the size of the Bengali electorate.[39]

The agitation paralyzed much of the economic life of Assam and soon had a major impact on the country as a whole when the Gana Sangram Parishad and the All Assam Student Union took steps

[38] "The Danger of Secession—Assam and the Northeast," *India Today*, North American edition, vol. 2, no. 1 (1980), p. 24.

[39] For a Marxist interpretation of the agitation, see the articles by Hiren Gohain in *Economic and Political Weekly*, vol. 15, no. 8 (February 23, 1980), and vol. 15, no. 21 (May 24, 1980); and Ghanshyam Pardesi, "Internal Colony in a National Exploitative System," *Economic and Political Weekly*, vol. 15, no. 22 (June 7, 1980). For an analysis by an Assamese who believes that the left underestimates the importance of the demographic changes resulting from the influx of Bengalis, see Sanjib Kumar Barua, "Cudgel of Chauvinism or Tangled Nationality Question?" *Economic and Political Weekly*, vol. 15, no. 11 (March 15, 1980).

to prevent the movement of both crude and refined oil out of Assam. Because Assam is a major oil-producing center, the Indian government was forced to import more of its oil from the Middle East which worsened the balance of payments. The movement against outsiders also spread to Meghalaya, Mizoram, Arunachal Pradesh, and even across the Indian border to the Chittagong Hill Tracts district of Bangladesh, where the tribal population took arms against "Bengali expansionism."

The agitation also had a noticeable impact on Tripura, a Bengali majority state bordering on Assam, where the local Chakmas, a tribal group, had become a minority as a result of the influx of Bengalis from both India and Bangladesh. The CPI(M) strengthened its hold in the state, winning both parliamentary seats with 47 percent of the vote; it had taken only 34 percent in 1977. But the Tripura Upajati Yuba Samity, an organization of militant tribal youth resentful of the domination of the state by Bengalis, doubled its vote from 6 percent in 1977 to 12 percent in 1980. Even more ominous to the central government were reports that members of the Upajati Yuba Samity were working closely with Mizo rebels and receiving armed training somewhere in Bangladesh.[40]

Elsewhere in the small northeastern states, the regional parties played an even bigger role in electoral politics—the Hill State People's Democratic party and the All Party Hill Leaders' Conference in Meghalaya, the People's party of Arunachal in Arunachal Pradesh, the National Convention of Nagaland and the United Democratic Front in Nagaland, and the People's Conference in Mizoram. Congress won four of the nine parliamentary seats in this region, two went to the CPI(M), and the remaining three to the regional parties.

In terms of popular vote the regional parties or independents won all of the votes in Nagaland and Mizoram, 45 percent of the vote in Arunachal Pradesh, 26.4 percent in Manipur, 28.4 percent in Tripura, and 18.9 percent in Meghalaya (see table 24).

The inability of the Election Commission to hold elections in most of Assam; the minority position of the Congress (I) in the hill states; the strength of regional parties, some with separatist and even secessionist tendencies; the agitations throughout the region against "outsiders"; the sense of economic backwardness and isolation that characterizes much of the Northeast; and the vulnerability of the region to influences and support from the three countries on its borders, China, Bangladesh, and Burma—all these factors make this area a point of particular concern for Mrs. Gandhi's government.

[40] *Times of India*, January 15, 1980.

West Bengal. The electoral fight in West Bengal was between Mrs. Gandhi's Congress and the Left Front, a coalition of left parties led by the Communist party of India (Marxist). In the parliamentary elections of 1977 the left parties had joined with Janata to fight against Congress and the CPI, but in the assembly elections a few months later they had demonstrated that they could win without the support of Janata. In 1980 the left again demonstrated its electoral superiority over all the nonleft parties by winning, for the first time since independence, more than 50 percent of the popular vote.

The Left Front won 53.7 percent of the vote, Congress won 36.5 percent, and Janata a mere 4.6 percent. The left won thirty-seven of the forty-one parliamentary seats, as compared with twenty-three in the previous elections. The CPI(M) alone won 39.4 percent of the vote and twenty-seven seats (see table 26).

How did the left do it? It is important to note that the left was united while the nonleft was divided among four competing parties—Congress (I), which contested forty seats; Janata, which contested thirty-five; Congress (U), which contested eighteen; and the Lok Dal, which contested seventeen. Further, the Left Front took no position on whom to support for prime minister if no one party received a majority in the national elections; they chose instead to emphasize their achievements in governing the state, and they sought a mandate for a Left Front delegation to the national Parliament. The Left Front thus appealed to regional sentiment, even as it also used the rhetoric of class interests and ideologies.

The national CPI(M) had supported Janata in 1977, but in mid-1979 the party's politburo announced its withdrawal of support from Morarji Desai. The politburo declared that "authoritarianism" (i.e., Mrs. Gandhi's Congress) and "communalism" (i.e., the Janata party and its Jana Sangh component) constituted equally dangerous threats to Indian democracy. This declaration by the party's politburo was not well received by the West Bengal unit of the party, which feared that the fall of the Janata government and new elections might bring Mrs. Gandhi back to power. Promode Dasgupta, the secretary of the West Bengal CPI(M) and its strategist, feared that a Congress government under Mrs. Gandhi would threaten the position of a left government in West Bengal. Many members of the politburo, whose interest was in national strategy, believed that an electoral arrangement with the Lok Dal would net the party more seats in the Hindi-speaking states. West Bengal party leaders, on the other hand, argued that the interests of the local left government should not be sacrificed for unlikely and meaningless gains for the party elsewhere.

In the West Bengal elections, the Left Front set out to win the support of the agricultural laborers, whom they regarded as the main beneficiaries of the government's agrarian policies. The government's land reform program (called Operation Barga) provided that share-croppers (*bargadars*) be given assured tenure (through a system of registration of rights) and an assured percentage of the crop, 75 percent if the sharecropper provided the fertilizers and seeds as well as the labor, and 50 percent if the farmer-owner provided the inputs. As a result of these reforms, the CPI(M) and its allies swept the *panchayat* elections in the state; they won 80 percent of the seats in the *gram* (village) *panchayats* and *panchayat samities* and took control of all the district councils (*zilla parishads*) in the state. The government dispensed more development funds to the *panchayats*, thereby increasing the power of its elected members and decreasing the political influence of the local bureaucracy and the landed classes.

The leftists further strengthened their hold among the rural poor by effectively distributing relief during the floods and by establishing a food for work program that provided employment for the unemployed and underemployed in the villages. The Left Front attracted party cadres in the rural areas and soon built the most effective political organization in the state.

In its campaign, the CPI(M) not only appealed to the rural poor for their votes but sought to deepen the cleavage between the rural poor and the "rich" peasantry. The left stressed class rather than caste or communal identification and accused the Congress of seeking to divide the electorate on communal lines, especially in constituencies with a large proportion of Muslims. The party also appealed to the middle peasantry, whose interests, it argued, were closer to those of the sharecroppers and the landless than to those of the "rich" peasantry.

The strategy worked. The CPI(M)'s electoral support in the rural areas of West Bengal increased sharply. The increase was particularly noticeable in places that had not earlier been centers of the party's electoral strength—Midnapore, Bankura, and Purulia—while it made significant gains in the districts of Murshidabad, Nadia, West Dinajpur. Local observers in these districts reported that the party succeeded in winning support not only from the sharecroppers and landless laborers but from much of the middle peasantry as well.[41]

[41] One measure of the CPI(M)'s success in mobilizing the rural poor was the substantial increase in voter turnout in the state, from 60.2 percent to 70 percent, an increase that ran counter to the national decline and was unrelated to any increase in the number of polling stations. It is also noteworthy that the Calcutta turnout of 62.2 percent was well below that of the rural areas.

The CPI(M) did not, however, do as well in the urban constituencies—Barrackpore, Diamond Harbour, Howrah, Durgapur, Asansol—or in Calcutta. Congress (I) won 41.3 percent of the Calcutta vote, 36.5 percent in the state of a whole. Congress (I) did best in constituencies with large migrant populations from neighboring states and in constituencies with a large proportion of Muslims (the few seats won by Congress (I) in the state had a higher than average proportion of Muslim voters). The business and trading communities of the city also threw their support behind Congress (I). The Burra Bazar section of Calcutta's northwest constituency, the major trade and commercial center of the city, voted overwhelmingly for the Congress (I) candidate. In the countryside, Congress (I) apparently won the support of many of the traditional village leaders and landowners resentful of the government's land reform program. Congress (I) party workers were also particularly active in Muslim areas, to such an extent that critics described the Congress (I) as the "Muslim Congress." [42]

Class appeals and a touch of regional pride were the ingredients of the CPI(M) and Left Front victory in West Bengal. These appeals by the left apparently turned the Muslims, the non-Bengalis, the rural wealthy, and the urban business and trading communities to the Congress (I). The result was a greater polarization of the vote in West Bengal in 1980 than in 1977. While in 1977 the Congress, Janata, and CPI(M) together won 77.1 percent of the vote, in 1980 the combined vote for Congress (I) and the CPI(M) alone was 75.9 percent (see table 25).

South India

The electoral position of the Congress party in the four states of south India hardly changed between 1977 and 1980. Congress won 92 out of 129 seats in the earlier election, and 93 seats in 1980. In two of the states, Andhra Pradesh and Karnataka, the popular vote for Congress hardly changed at all, in Kerala the Congress vote declined, while in Tamil Nadu there was a substantial increase. The breakup of the Janata party had less impact on south than on north

[42] *Times of India*, December 26, 1979. The report from rural West Bengal is by Sivadas Banerjee, their regular correspondent. While there is evidence that a larger proportion of Muslims than of other voters voted Congress, it is not conclusive. The seats won by Congress did have a higher proportion of Muslims, and in the three Muslim majority constituencies in the state the Congress vote was several percentage points higher than elsewhere. But the vote for Congress in other constituencies with substantial numbers of Muslims proved no greater than the statewide vote for Congress.

India, if only because Janata had never succeeded in establishing itself in much of the South.

In analyzing the party system and electoral behavior of south India, it is useful to distinguish between the "upper" South and the "lower" South. The former consists of two states, Andhra Pradesh and Karnataka, and the latter of the two states of Kerala and Tamil Nadu. In the upper South, the Congress party is so dominant that in the last three elections it has won an absolute majority of the votes—in spite of the emergency and in spite of splits within the party. In these two states, Congress has won all but one or two constituencies in every recent election. In contrast, Congress is weak in the lower South, and it faces more formidable competition from other parties. Congress has won less than half the parliamentary seats in Kerala and Tamil Nadu in all recent elections including 1980, and since 1967 it has not won the support of even a third of the electorate in either state.

The Upper South. Mrs. Gandhi felt so secure in the upper South after her national defeat in 1977 that it was to this region that she turned in her search for a "safe" constituency to return her to Parliament. The Congress chief minister in Karnataka offered Chikmagalur constituency, and with the support of the resources of the Karnataka Congress party Mrs. Gandhi easily won the seat. The victory was a significant first step in her campaign to return to national power, even though she was subsequently expelled from her seat by Parliament.[43]

Devaraj Urs, the chief minister, had been a strong, persistent supporter of Mrs. Gandhi. Indeed, in his campaign for Mrs. Gandhi in Chikmagalur, he frequently described the accomplishments of his state government as the result of the leadership and support of Mrs. Gandhi while she was prime minister. But within a year of her victory, the relationship between Devaraj Urs and Mrs. Gandhi had soured, primarily, it is said, because of the tension between Devaraj and Sanjay Gandhi but also, said some observers, because Mrs. Gandhi wanted to undermine a leader who had a popular base of his own.

In early 1979, following months of conflict, Mrs. Gandhi and her supporters expelled Devaraj from the party. He then joined the

[43] Mrs. Gandhi was elected from Chikmagalur on November 8, 1979. On December 19 the Lok Sabha passed a resolution expelling Mrs. Gandhi from the House on a charge of breach of privilege and sentencing her to imprisonment till the end of the winter session of Parliament. Mrs. Gandhi was then arrested and kept in jail in Delhi for a week.

Congress party that had broken from Mrs. Gandhi after the 1977 electoral defeat, and shortly thereafter Urs was elected president of the party, which became known as Congress (U). The party split in Karnataka, one section remaining with Devaraj and the other joining Mrs. Gandhi.

Within Karnataka, Devaraj's position appeared secure. He had built a popular base among the backward castes in the state and had wrested political power from the Lingayats and Vakkaligas, two castes who had earlier controlled the state government and administration. He had created institutional support for Congress in the *taluka* development boards and in thousands of village *panchayats*.

During the 1980 campign, Mrs. Gandhi came to the state three times and visited all twenty-eight constituencies. One reporter, after noting how large the crowds were for Mrs. Gandhi, wrote "Mr. Urs has assiduously sold Mrs. Gandhi for years, and now the same Mr. Urs is called upon to run down Mrs. Gandhi and to get all the credit for the good work done for the state's millions of have-nots transferred from her to himself." [44] After the elections, another correspondent wrote: "During the campaign one minister had the experience of being confronted with uncanny questions from a village audience. He was asked: 'All of these years you have asked us to vote for Mrs. Gandhi and now you want our votes for Mr. Urs. Is this *dharma* (correct behavior)?'" The reporter went on:

> Many knew that there had been a quarrel between Mrs. Gandhi and Mr. Urs but they believed that she had been wronged. . . . When some villagers were told that the benefits of the government's development program were entirely due to Mr. Urs, back came the remark: "It is like the pharmacist claiming to cure a disease. How can he do that unless the doctors give a prescription first?" In their minds, the doctor was Mrs. Gandhi and the pharmacist Mr. Urs.[45]

Mrs. Gandhi's Congress won over 56 percent of the vote, about the same as in 1977, and twenty-seven out of twenty-eight seats (compared with twenty-five out of twenty-eight in 1977). She not only won most of the scheduled-caste and Muslim votes but, according to observers, even won the support of most of the backward classes, who had been regarded as personally loyal to Devaraj Urs. The Congress party led by Urs won only 16 percent of the vote, falling behind Janata, which won 23 percent. Rather than taking votes from

[44] *Indian Express*, December 26, 1979.
[45] *Times of India*, January 17, 1980.

Mrs. Gandhi's Congress, Urs seems to have taken votes from the Janata party, since Janata dropped seventeen percentage points.

Immediately after his electoral defeat, Devaraj resigned as chief minister of Karnataka and as president of the Congress (U). The leader of the Congress (I) in the state legislative assembly and a close supporter of Sanjay Gandhi, Gundu Rao, was appointed chief minister by the governor.

Mrs. Gandhi's Congress did equally well in the neighboring state of Andhra Pradesh, winning forty-one out of forty-two seats, also with an absolute majority of votes. Though Mrs. Gandhi ran for Parliament in her traditional constituency in Uttar Pradesh, she also decided to stand in a "safe" constituency in Andhra. She chose Medak and won easily, with 301,000 votes against her opponent's 82,000.[46] In a constituency with many orthodox Hindus and a substantial number of Christians (5 percent of the population), Mrs. Gandhi made a point of offering prayers at the Rajaraswara temple at Vemulawada and visiting a nearby church. Asked by reporters why she was standing in a second constituency, she replied, "I have always felt myself at home in every part of the country since childhood." A party supporter added that "she wanted to assert her national stature which straddled the Vindhyas [the mountain range dividing the South from the North]."[47]

A four-party alliance of the Congress (U), Lok Dal, CPI, and CPI(M) did poorly, and the vote for Janata plunged from 32.7 percent to 15.3 percent. The split in the Congress party had a negligible impact, for the vote for Congress (I) declined only slightly over the Congress vote in 1977. In contrast to Karnataka, in Andhra the chief minister, Chenna Reddi, and the bulk of the Congress organization supported Mrs. Gandhi. But her victory in Karnataka reminded her backers in Andhra that it was she, not the party organization, that had once again won the electorate's support for Congress.

The Lower South. In both states in the lower South, Tamil Nadu and Kerala, the only hope of the national parties for winning a substantial number of parliamentary seats lay in an electoral arrangement with regional parties. In Tamil Nadu two regional parties, the DMK and the AIADMK, dominate electoral politics. The DMK governed the state until 1976, and the following year it was replaced by the

---

[46] Candidates for Parliament (and for state legislative assemblies as well) may run in more than one constituency. After her victory in both constituencies, Mrs. Gandhi chose to resign from her Uttar Pradesh seat and remain an M.P. from Andhra.

[47] *Times of India*, December 10, 1979.

AIADMK. In the 1977 elections the Janata party had allied itself with the DMK, while Mrs. Gandhi's Congress allied itself with the AIADMK. Now, less than three years later, the alliances were reversed as the DMK joined with the Congress party, while the governing AIADMK formed an electoral coalition with Janata. Once again, it was the coalition around Mrs. Gandhi's Congress that won. Indeed, in this election Congress (I) emerged with the largest number of votes, 4.8 million (out of 18.4 million), with the AIADMK winning 4.7 million and the DMK 4.2 million. Congress (I) won twenty seats and its ally, the DMK, sixteen (see table 27).

For both parties the electoral alliances of 1980 were quite cynically based upon strategic considerations. The DMK hoped to unseat the AIADMK state government by allying itself with what it perceived as the winning national party. Shifting from its anti-Congess stand of 1977, the DMK election manifesto described the emergency as a "temporary phenomenon" and denounced "fanatic communalism," that is, the Jana Sangh.[48] Karunanidhi, the president of the DMK, once an ardent federalist, called for "a strong edifice of Union government built on solid foundations of equally strong federated states," a clear bow toward Mrs. Gandhi.[49]

Mrs. Gandhi made a whirlwind tour of Tamil Nadu and was greeted by large and enthusiastic crowds. Reporters noted that her personal popularity, combined with the organizational strength of the DMK, was more than a match for the AIADMK chief minister, M. G. Ramachandran (known as MGR), a popular film actor.[50] Though MGR has a mass following, his party does not have as effective a local organization as the DMK. But a few months later the electorate voted quite differently in the state assembly elections. MGR's party, the AIADMK, was reelected with a majority of seats (129 out of 234) and 38.7 percent of the vote, well ahead of the 25.4 percent the party received in the parliamentary elections. And the DMK barely held its own, dropping from 23 percent to 22.5 percent. Clearly, a substantial portion of the supporters of the AIADMK switched to Mrs. Gandhi for the parliamentary elections, then returned "home" for the state assembly elections.

Similar electoral maneuvering took place in the neighboring state of Kerala, where the parliamentary elections were seen as a

---

[48] Ibid., December 2, 1979.

[49] Ibid., December 2, 1979.

[50] MGR has acted in over a hundred films that are still widely viewed in the rural areas of Tamil Nadu. In these films, MGR generally plays the role of a good Samaritan who wants to rid society of its evils.

prelude to the state's assembly elections a few weeks later. In Kerala, the main cleavage has been between the Communist and non-Communist parties. The struggle between pro- and anti-Communist forces has raged since the first Communist ministry was installed in 1957. In 1964 the Communist movement split between the CPI and the CPI(M). In the 1967 elections, the CPI(M) brought together the non-Congress forces in the state to win power. Then in 1970 the non-CPI(M) parties joined together in a coalition to defeat the CPI(M). The pattern was repeated in 1977: In the parliamentary elections a Congress-led front supporting a CPI-led government won all twenty seats. The CPI-led government fell in October 1979, and elections for the state assembly were scheduled for two weeks after the 1980 parliamentary elections.

Following weeks and months of political haggling, two coalitions were put together for both the parliamentary and the state assembly elections. The local unit of the Janata party joined with Mrs. Gandhi's Congress, the Muslim League, and a local party known as the Kerala Congress (Jacob Group) to form the United Democratic Front (UDF). The CPI(M), the CPI, the Congress (U), the All India Muslim League, the Revolutionary Socialist party, and a faction of the Kerala Congress—a mélange of leftist, centrist, and communal parties—formed the Left Democratic Front (LDF). Both coalitions were held together by electoral rather than ideological considerations. The local Janata party, the press reported, decided to support the Congress (I) front because the local Janata leadership wanted to settle scores with the CPI(M) for having "betrayed" it.[51] Congress (U), eager to weaken Mrs. Gandhi's Congress, chose to join with the Communists and bring its middle-class supporters to the Left Democratic Front. The CPI(M), in an effort to accommodate Congress (U) in the front, gave up some of its safe constituencies. "Gone are the days," wrote the reporter for the *Hindustan Times*, "when any individual party, whether national or regional, has the courage to face the electorate on its own. For the last two decades, it has been combinations of parties that have been contesting the polls."[52] The LDF had seven parties, the UDF six.

The elections were close. The Left Democratic Front won 51.6 percent of the vote and twelve out of the twenty seats, while the United Democratic Front won 48.4 percent and eight seats. The vote for Mrs. Gandhi's Congress party candidates declined from 29.1 percent to 26.3 percent, making Kerala the only state in which her party did significantly worse in 1980 than in 1977 (see table 28).

[51] *Times of India*, December 19, 1979.
[52] *Hindustan Times*, January 3, 1980.

The importance of the state assembly elections a few weeks later was highlighted by Mrs. Gandhi's decision, as prime minister, to tour the state to support the Congress (I)–led United Democratic Front. The correspondent for the *Statesman* described the opening of the tour:

> With an uncanny knack of touching the right chord, Mrs. Gandhi began her campaign by driving straight from the Trivandrum airport to Sri Padmanabhaswami temple, the State shrine of erstwhile rulers of Travancore. Breaking the long-established temple traditions, which even her father as Prime Minister was not allowed to do, she prostrated before the reclining idol of Vishnu, known as Anandasayanam . . . a privilege allowed only to the Travancore Maharajas even to this day. Tradition has it that Martanda Verma, founder of the Travancore State, dedicated his domain to Padmanabhaswami temple and he and his successors ruled the State as vassals of the Lord. . . . By this single act of seeming piety, Mrs. Gandhi endeared herself to the tradition-bound Travancore society, especially the upper caste Hindus, who came to look upon her worship at the temple as her desire to dedicate the entire nation to the benevolent guidance of Anandasayanam, and rule the country as his regent, the same way Travancore Maharajas did in the past.[53]

In spite of Mrs. Gandhi's personal efforts, the CPI(M)–led Left Democratic Front won a major victory in the state assembly elections. The LDF won 92 out of 140 assembly seats with 50.4 percent of the vote. The CPI(M) won thirty-five seats, double its strength in the previous assembly. The Congress (I)–led United Democratic Front and its Janata allies won forty-six seats. For the electorate, the state assembly elections were evidently more important than those for Parliament. The turnout was 72.3 percent, ten percentage points more than in the parliamentary elections. With the formation of a CPI(M)–led ministry, Kerala joined West Bengal and Tripura as states with CPI(M)–led governments. The victory of the Congress (I) in eight of the nine state assembly elections held in June brought an end to the non-Congress governments in all the remaining larger states except Jammu and Kashmir and Tamil Nadu. By mid-1980 the CPI(M) was the only national non-Congress party in India in control of a state government.

[53] *Statesman*, January 20, 1980.

India's cities voted much like the states in which they were located. Cities in the Hindi region—Lucknow, Agra, Varanasi, Indore, Jabalpur, Delhi, Kanpur, Allahabad—elected Congress M.P.s. Calcutta elected four CPI(M) M.P.s in its five constituencies, and Madras chose two DMK candidates and gave its third seat to Janata. Bombay was the one major exception: It elected four Janata candidates in its six constituencies, though the state gave a majority of its seats to Congress (I). In all, Congress won twenty-five out of thirty-nine seats in India's nineteen largest cities, well above its seven seats in 1977, and almost matching the twenty-six seats the party had won in 1971.

There was, however, a greater decline in voter turnout in urban than in rural constituencies all over the country. Thus, the turnout percentages for four major cities and for the states in which they are located were:

Calcutta	62.2
West Bengal	70.9
Bombay	52.7
Maharashtra	56.8
Hyderabad	53.5
Andhra Pradesh	57.0
Bangalore	51.8
Karnataka	57.9

And the pattern was the same (though the size of the gap varied) in Kanpur, Poona, Lucknow, Jaipur, Agra, Indore, and Jabalpur and their states. The decline in turnout in Delhi was also much greater than the national average. The cities in Tamil Nadu were noticeable exceptions: Turnouts in Madras, Coimbatore, and Madurai were above the state turnout.

In the 1950s turnout in rural areas had been lower than in the cities, but by the late 1960s the differences had more or less disappeared, and in the 1977 elections voter turnout in urban and rural constituencies was similar in most states. The very substantial decline in voter participation in many Indian cities in the 1980 elections (especially in the North) helps to explain why journalists, academics, and other observers described voters as apathetic and expected a far greater decline in voter turnout than actually occurred. They were apparently reacting to the decline in voter interest in the cities (see table 29), which proved to be greater than the decline (as measured by turnout) in the countryside.

The greater decline in urban turnout did not seem to make any noticeable difference in the vote for Congress. In the 49 urban constituencies contested by Congress, the vote for that party was 43.3 percent, slightly above the national figure (see table 30). In Gujarat, Madhya Pradesh, Punjab, Rajasthan, Uttar Pradesh, and West Bengal, Congress did better in the urban than in the rural areas, while in Andhra, Bihar, Karnataka, Maharashtra, and Tamil Nadu, Congress did worse.

In spite of the lower urban vote, however, Janata did substantially better in the urban than in the rural constituencies (see table 31). In Bombay, Delhi, Hyderabad, Ahmadabad, Bangalore, Poona, Lucknow, Jaipur, and Indore, the vote for Janata was higher than in the states. In thirty-six urban constituencies contested by Janata, the vote was 29.9 percent, well above their 18.9 percent national vote. The left parties did no better in the urban than in the rural areas: in West Bengal, as we noted earlier, the Communists actually did better in the countryside than in Calcutta.

Far from being radicalized and politicized, India's cities were centrist and less politically active than the countryside. They were, however, more polarized. The candidates of the two leading parties won 80 percent or more of the vote in a very large proportion of India's cities, including Calcutta, Bombay, Delhi, Hyderabad, Ahmadabad, Bangalore, Poona, Nagpur, Lucknow, Coimbatore, Madurai, Jaipur, Jabalpur, and Indore. In ten of these fourteen cities, Janata and Congress were the major contenders. It is interesting to note, however, that there is considerable diversity in India's four metropolitan cities. The majority of the parliamentary delegation from Delhi is Congress (I); from Bombay, it is Janata; from Calcutta, it is CPI(M); and from Madras, it is DMK. In these cities Congress won less than half the seats (ten out of twenty-one), though it took two-thirds of the seats in India as a whole (see table 32).

A victorious Congress was thus faced with a polarized urban electorate, particularly strong opposition in the major metropolitan areas, and, for the moment at least, a less interested (and perhaps dispirited) urban electorate.[54]

---

[54] For a review of the voting patterns in urban India in the 1977 elections, see Weiner, *India at the Polls, 1977*, pp. 74-82. For a study of how urban constituencies have voted in state assembly elections since 1952, see Myron Weiner and John Osgood Field, "India's Urban Constituencies," *Comparative Politics*, vol. 8, no. 2 (January 1976), pp. 183-222.

5

Minorities and the Congress Party

India's three largest minorities—the scheduled tribes, the scheduled castes, and the Muslims—constitute 32.7 percent of the Indian population. For historical and political reasons, they are viewed in India as "minorities" in relation to the caste Hindu majority. Before independence, these groups (along with several religious minorities, including Christians and Sikhs) were given reserved constituencies in which only members of these communities could stand as candidates for legislative bodies. After independence, the government of India ended reserved constituencies for religious communities, while continuing them for the scheduled tribes and castes. But the term "minorities" continued to be used to refer to all non-Hindus, the tribals (some of whom are Hindus), and the lowest-caste group in the Hindu social order, the ex-untouchables, or scheduled castes.

Partly because of the system of reserved seats in Parliament and in legislative assemblies in the states, the scheduled castes and scheduled tribes are a major target of the political parties. The scheduled castes have seventy-nine reserved constituencies, and the scheduled tribes another thirty-five. The scheduled tribes form a majority or near majority in most of their reserved constituencies, while the scheduled castes are a minority (averaging about 23 percent) in all of their reserved constituencies. Muslims have no reserved constituencies, but they form a majority in ten, and have 20 to 50 percent of the population in another sixty-four constituencies.

Altogether, then, the minorities occupy an important place in 192, or slightly more than a third, of the parliamentary constituencies. But since Muslims and the scheduled castes are dispersed, how they vote can have a considerable impact on many other constituencies as well. More than three-quarters of India's scheduled castes live in nonreserved constituencies, and there are few constituencies in northern India where Muslims are not at least 5 percent of the voting population.

The Congress party has always made a major effort to win the support of minorities. Even apart from needing their votes, Congress has had ideological reasons for seeking their support. To confirm its commitment to "secularism," Congress has needed the support of Muslims. And to emphasize its commitment to the poor and to "socialism," the party has needed the votes of the scheduled castes and the scheduled tribes. Indeed, any political party in India which wants to demonstrate the legitimacy of its claim to the symbols of "secularism" and "socialism" must explicitly appeal to minorities, by choosing minorities as candidates and by making promises to these communities.

In the battle for these groups, the Congress party has clearly been the winner—at least until the elections of 1977. In that election there was a massive desertion of Congress by the minorities. It was clear that what are called in India the "excesses" of the emergency had alienated the minorities—particularly the compulsory sterilization and slum clearance programs in northern India. Many local government officials and school teachers had filled their quotas for sterilization by forcing poor and vulnerable individuals—usually members of minorities—into the surgical rooms. And most of the people displaced by slum clearance, particularly in Delhi, were members of minorities. In some areas the minorities, especially the Muslims, fought back—so that the police and the state itself, once the protectors of Muslims, now became their antagonists.

In the 1977 elections, Congress candidates were overwhelmingly defeated in the scheduled-caste and scheduled-tribe constituencies in northern India, and in constituencies with large Muslim populations. The Janata party was the primary beneficiary. It was inconceivable to Mrs. Gandhi and her supporters that they could ever return to power without winning back a very sizable portion of the minority vote, or that the Janata party could win without minority support. The battle for these groups, therefore, was a central political concern of every major party.

The Campaign for Muslim Votes

The "Muslim issue" was as central in the 1980 parliamentary elections as the question of "stability," food prices, or "authoritarianism." It became a central issue a year before the fall of the Janata government, when Charan Singh, Morarji Desai's chief competitor for the office of prime minister, attacked his own party for falling under the influence of the Jana Sangh and the RSS, the voluntary youth group with which many Jana Sangh supporters were associated. Charan Singh insisted that membership in the RSS was incompatible with membership in the Janata party, arguing that the RSS was a communal, anti-Muslim organization and that membership in it implied a lack of devotion to the principles of a "secular state."

Critics of Charan Singh insisted that he was using the RSS issue to erode Morarji Desai's position, since Desai had been elected prime minister with the support of Jana Sangh members. Moreover, the Jana Sangh had extended its influence in many areas in which the Lok Dal segment of the party had its strength, and Charan Singh and his supporters feared that their own position was being weakened by the growing strength of the Jana Sangh.

Ironically, the Jana Sangh had become less of an anti-Muslim party since it had joined Janata and many of its leaders had entered the national government. A Jana Sangh minister of external affairs had led the move toward conciliation with Pakistan and pursued a pro-Arab policy in the Middle East. At home, Jana Sangh consciously sought to woo Muslim support, recognizing that the Janata victory in 1977 was partly the result of the disaffection of many Muslims from the Congress party.

In the language of Indian politics, the word "secularism" means the willingness of Hindus to accept the right of Muslims to maintain their personal community law, to use the Urdu language, and to preserve Islamic institutions; that is, the right of Muslims to maintain their cultural and religious identity. As used by Congressmen, secularism also refers to the willingness of the government to be the "protector" of Muslims against hostility and violence on the part of Hindus. Secularism also distinguishes India from Pakistan, a country formed by Muslims who not only wanted a state of their own but argued that Hindus were committed to the creation of a Hindu-dominated state in India. Jawaharlal Nehru and most Indian nationalists rejected the efforts of the Muslim League to characterize their movement as Hindu, insisting that the great debate was not between Hinduism and Islam, but between those who believed in secularism and those who did not. For Nehru, therefore, Hindus who advocated a Hindu state that denied rights to Muslims were as threatening as Muslims who wanted a separate state of their own.

The Indian National Congress not only opposed the Muslim League but distanced itself from the Hindu Mahasabha and other Hindu political organizations that took anti-Muslim positions. The hostility of Indian nationalists to "communal" Hindus became even more acute when Mahatma Gandhi was assassinated by Hindu nationalists associated with the RSS.

The opposition of the Congress party to Hindu-minded political forces attracted a large part of the Muslim electorate, for the Congress emphasis on secularism and its concern for the protection of Muslims was needed by a community that felt insecure, leaderless (its leaders had largely migrated to Pakistan), and dangerously vulnerable to Hindu militants. From the first parliamentary election of 1952 on, therefore, a large proportion of India's Muslims voted for the Congress party.

By the late 1960s, however, many Muslims had left Congress. As the threat to their security declined, Muslims felt free to support other political parties; the virtual disappearance of anti-Muslim parties in India was a liberation for them. (The Hindu Mahasabha was no longer an electoral force and the Jana Sangh had become less anti-Muslim.) Moreover, the emerging middle class within the Muslim community felt it had won less from the Congress government than some other communities. More and more Muslims drifted to other political parties as Muslim organizations became more assertive.

As we have seen, the Muslims were particularly hostile to the emergency.[1] When the emergency was suspended and elections were held in early 1977, the Muslim community in northern India exploded in anger at the Congress government. Muslims flocked to the polls to vote against Congress and for Janata party candidates. They did so in spite of the fact that Jana Sangh was an important constituent of the Janata party. In a mood of communal harmony, many Muslim leaders praised the RSS and the Jana Sangh for the role they had played in opposing the emergency and for their opposition to compulsory sterilization, slum clearance, and attacks against minorities and other vulnerable groups by government officials.

But for many Muslims it was an uncomfortable alliance. Their discomfort grew in 1978, when there was an upsurge in communal (Hindu-Muslim) disturbances in the country. The number of communal incidents was 190 in 1977, and 230 in 1978. Uttar Pradesh and Bihar topped the list with 46 and 34 incidents respectively. In 1978, 110 people were killed in communal riots; only 36 in 1977. In the first five months of 1979 the situation deteriorated still further:

---

[1] Muslims showed a greater willingness to fight against the government—and the police—during the emergency than did other communities. The domination of the police in Uttar Pradesh and Bihar by the Rajputs, traditionally an anti-Muslim caste, was a significant factor in the violent confrontations between Muslims and the police.

141 persons killed, 824 injured, and property losses of tens of millions of rupees.[2] Major well-publicized communal disturbances took place in Jamshedpur and Aligarh.

Why there were more Hindu-Muslim clashes than usual was itself a matter of political dispute. After the Janata victory, there was an increase in caste and communal clashes of all sorts—between Harijans and caste Hindus, forward and backward castes, Hindus and Muslims. Some observers attributed the increase to political factions who saw disturbances as a way of mobilizing supporters around caste or religion. Some attributed the growing tension to the increasing dissatisfaction of the Muslim community, now stirred by the militancy of Muslims in Iran, Pakistan, and Turkey. Some suggested that Indian Muslims returning from the Gulf were the sources of new Islamic ideas and that Arab funding for mosques, schools, and other Muslim institutions strengthened community consciousness. Still others suggested that a variety of local factors were at work, but that the Janata state governments were reluctant to exercise the force necessary to keep conflicts under control.

Whatever the reason, disturbances increased and critics of the Janata government blamed Jana Sangh. With each violent outburst between Hindus and Muslims, Mrs. Gandhi reasserted her claim as protector of the Muslims and denounced the Janata government as ineffectual. In the same vein, Charan Singh used the Muslim issue as a means of whipping the Jana Sangh group within Janata in his battle to win control of the party and become prime minister.

Charan Singh led the fight against "dual" membership, that is, membership in the RSS of Jana Sangh members of the Janata party. Jana Sangh members refused to dissociate themselves from the RSS, and they viewed Charan Singh's demand as a mischievous attempt to detach the Jana Sangh from its most active party cadres.

When Charan Singh and Raj Narain split from the Janata party in mid-1979 to form a party of their own, they made the "communalism" of the Janata party the focus of their attack and the justification for their withdrawal. Indeed, Charan Singh called his party the Janata (Secular) party to distinguish it from what he regarded as the communalist Janata party. Charan Singh's withdrawal from Janata not only split the party, it also broke the thin bonds created between Janata and the Muslim electorate in 1977. The remaining Janata leadership sought to reach out to India's Muslims in the 1980 elections by nominating Muslim candidates and by

[2] Data from N. L. Chowla, "Muslims Did Not Vote en Bloc," *Times of India,* January 26, 1980.

*Anti-RSS poster photographed by the author
in Delhi during the 1980 campaign.*

adding reassuring provisions to its electoral platform; but it now suffered a double handicap, being labeled anti-Muslim both by Mrs. Gandhi's Congress and by many of its own former supporters, the Lok Dal, and socialists in the Janata (Secular) party.

Mrs. Gandhi made a major effort to win the Muslims, for she recognized that their defection from the Congress party in the 1977 elections had played a major role in her defeat. A key target for Mrs. Gandhi was the shahi imam of Jama Masjid, Syed Abdullah Shah Bukhari, a prominent Muslim leader who had toured the country in the 1977 elections to oppose her. Following several meetings and a public exchange of correspondence, the imam endorsed Mrs. Gandhi. In a public letter, she alluded to "some incidents, including the 1975 Jama Masjid incident" (when the police had fired on a crowd), and she regretted that these had left an atmosphere of "misunderstanding and bitterness." "Let this past be forgotten," she wrote, "so that we can begin on a note of harmony and cooperation." She promised that the Congress party would "not interfere in Muslim personal law," and that her government would also "assure the minority character of Aligarh University." She promised the "protection, preservation and promotion of Urdu by providing all facilities for the teaching of Urdu at all levels." And without promising reservations in government appointments, she wrote that "equitable employment opportunities to minorities, including Muslims and Christians, will be ensured in government service, including the law and order and security personnel." [3]

Mrs. Gandhi also welcomed back to the Congress party H. N. Bahuguna, a prominent Uttar Pradesh politician, who had resigned from the Congress on the eve of the 1977 elections to oppose Mrs. Gandhi. Bahuguna had been regarded as a friend by the Muslim population of Uttar Pradesh when he was Congress chief minister in the state. He was also a close associate of the imam. Now, on the eve of the 1980 elections, Bahuguna returned to Mrs. Gandhi's Congress and was appointed secretary general of the party.

The imam's endorsement of Mrs. Gandhi was not universally acclaimed in the Muslim community. There was conflict in Muslim organizations over what position they should take during the elections. Many Muslims were dismayed by the imam's endorsement and booed him when he appeared at Delhi's Jama Masjid. Posters appeared on the walls of the mosque attacking the imam. "Mrs. Gandhi's alliance is with the Imam, not with the people," said graffiti

[3] *Correspondence between Indira Gandhi and Syed Abdullah Bukhari, Imam of Jama Masjid* (New Delhi: Indian National Congress, 1979).

on the walls of Jama Masjid. For a brief period the imam wavered in his support, expressing his disappointment at her unwillingness to promise to reserve 20 percent of the jobs in government service, the police, and the armed forces for Muslims. But by the end of December he had become her outspoken supporter.

Competition by the major political parties for the Muslim vote was more acute in 1980 than in other elections. The Congress (I) manifesto promised a special peacekeeping force composed of "people drawn from the minority communities, scheduled castes and scheduled tribes" to prevent and control communal riots. Mrs. Gandhi, in several speeches, alluded to the possibility of reserving jobs for Muslims, though she was careful to avoid any specific commitment. All major political parties promised to respect Muslim personal law, maintain the Muslim character of Aligarh University, encourage the development of Urdu, and prevent Hindu-Muslim riots. Arab diplomats in Delhi were sought out by party leaders, and the Arabs in turn attempted to extend their influence. A dinner was given by Arab ambassadors in New Delhi in honor of Mrs. Gandhi, and receptions were held by Jagjivan Ram (on behalf of the Janata party) and by Raj Narain (on behalf of the Lok Dal) for Arab diplomats.[4]

Both Mrs. Gandhi and Sanjay blamed the Janata party for the increase in Hindu-Muslim riots and sought to allay the fears of Muslims that the "excesses" of the emergency might be repeated if Congress (I) were returned to power. Sanjay Gandhi, speaking to Muslims in Lucknow, reminded his audience that "under the Islamic law no guilty person is punished twice for the same offence. . . . You have punished me more than necessary."[5] He apologized for the treatment of Muslims during the emergency, but blamed the former Union health minister, Karan Singh, and the former state health minister in Uttar Pradesh, Prabhu Narain Singh, for the forcible vasectomy operations. Mrs. Gandhi avoided discussions of the emergency, but she reminded Muslims of the historic role of the Congress party as the "protector" of minorities.

The Soviet intervention in Afghanistan at the end of December had surprisingly little impact. The imam condemned the Soviets, asking Indian Muslims to "lend full support to the Afghan *mujahuddin* ["freedom fighters"] who are fighting against communism in Afghanistan."[6] A few Janata and Lok Dal leaders spoke out against the Soviet actions, but their criticisms were muted when the United

[4] *The Hindu*, December 29, 1979.
[5] *Times of India*, December 18, 1979.
[6] *Statesman*, January 17, 1980.

States offered $400 million in arms and economic assistance to Pakistan. Anxieties over a Soviet presence in Afghanistan were soon transformed into anxieties over a potential U.S.–Chinese–Arab buildup of Pakistan. Mrs. Gandhi's initial statement on Afghanistan, while critical of the Soviet intervention, alluded to the presence of other foreign powers in the region, implying that the Soviets were simply reacting to the behavior of others. Once United States support for Pakistan was declared, Mrs. Gandhi's opponents seemed unwilling to get engaged in a foreign policy debate; none of the election speeches heard by this observer in either Patna or Lucknow during the last week of the campaign referred to Afghanistan. Nor was it an issue in Calcutta, although the CPI(M) actually endorsed the Soviet mission as an appropriate response to the "counterrevolutionary armed activities against the new regime with the full backing mainly of U.S. imperialists and the military dictatorship in Pakistan."[7] There was a similar endorsement from the CPI.

For many Indians the Soviet invasion raised complex questions, not only about its implications for Pakistan but also over the issue of Islamic fundamentalism. Many who were critical of Soviet intervention were at the same time fearful of Islamic resurgence in Western Asia, with its implications for India's Muslims. Some Indians privately expressed the opinion to this writer that the Soviets seemed to be the only force capable of halting the spread of Islamic fundamentalism.

While Afghanistan did not loom large in the campaign, Mrs. Gandhi's supporters emphasized that in this moment of international crisis in the region, a strong stable government was essential and that Mrs. Gandhi had the kind of international stature and expertise that neither Charan Singh nor Jagjivan Ram possessed.

How Muslim Constituencies Voted

Muslims constitute 11.2 percent of the Indian population or (in 1971) 61.4 million out of a population of 581 million. The largest concentrations of Muslims are in the states of Uttar Pradesh (13.6 million), West Bengal (9.1 million), Bihar (7.6 million), Maharashtra (4.2 million), Kerala (4.2 million), Assam (3.6 million), Jammu and Kashmir (3 million), and Karnataka (3.1 million), with approximately 2 million more each in Gujarat, Madhya Pradesh, Tamil Nadu, and Rajasthan. (Given the population increase from 1971 to 1980, the

[7] *The Hindu*, January 12, 1980.

Muslim population in each of these states is now approximately 24 percent higher).[8]

In most constituencies Muslims are a minority of the electorate. In the absence of survey data, estimates of how India's Muslims voted are based upon reports from journalists and politicians or on inferences from electoral data. The latter, of course, are not foolproof. The outcome in a constituency with a large Muslim population may or may not have been produced by a united Muslim vote. Before they can be considered reliable, inferences about the voting patterns of a particular group from aggregate electoral results must be corroborated by other evidence, such as the observations of journalists and politicians.

There are ten constituencies in which Muslims form a majority (in Jammu and Kashmir, Kerala, West Bengal, and Assam) and another sixty-four in which Muslims constitute 20 to 50 percent of the population. The largest blocs of "Muslim" constituencies are in West Bengal (twenty-four), Uttar Pradesh (twenty-three), Kerala (eight), Andhra (five), Bihar (four), and Jammu and Kashmir (four). Observers of the 1977 elections reported that Muslims had broken from their traditional partisan support for the Congress party.[9] This had clearly been so in north India. In Uttar Pradesh, for example, only 25.9 percent of the vote in Muslim constituencies had been cast for Congress, 29.1 percent in West Bengal, and 30.5 percent in Bihar. Except for Bihar, where the vote in Muslim constituencies exceeded that of the rest of the state, Muslim constituencies in the North generally had given a smaller vote to Congress than non-

[8] In any discussion of the Muslim vote in India it is important to note how heterogeneous Muslims are in their religious, social, economic, and political affiliations, and their demographic position. While a large part of the Muslim middle classes assert a pan-Islamic identity and are particularly concerned with the preservation of Muslim personal law and the minority character of Aligarh University, Muslims are pulled in innumerable directions politically. In some states (for example, Kashmir and Kerala) there are explicitly Muslim parties, while in Bihar, Uttar Pradesh, and West Bengal, Muslims support existing national or regional parties. One should also note that there are Shi'ite-Sunni differences, particularly in Lucknow and Hyderabad, that affect relations among Muslims as well as their attitudes toward non-Muslim political parties.

[9] For a particularly penetrating analysis of the role of Muslims in the 1977 elections see Theodore P. Wright, Jr., "Muslims and the 1977 Indian Elections: A Watershed?" *Asian Survey*, vol. 17, no. 12 (December 1977), pp. 1207-20. Wright argues that the "incongruous coalition of traditionalists, secularists and repentant former Muslim League modernists" who had supported Congress in previous elections was broken up by four features of the emergency: *nasbandi*, slum removal, police firing on Muslims, and the suspension of civil liberties, which included the banning of a number of Muslim organizations (p. 1208).

Muslim constituencies. This had also been the pattern in the Muslim constituencies in Andhra.[10]

There was a swing back to the Congress party in Muslim constituencies in 1980. Congress won twenty-nine out of seventy-four Muslim constituencies, compared with twenty out of eighty-one in 1977. In West Bengal the vote for Congress in Muslim constituencies rose to 37.6 percent, in Uttar Pradesh to 34.4 percent, in Bihar to 48.7 percent (see table 35).

Were Muslims more pro-Congress than the remainder of the population? Here the evidence is murky. In Uttar Pradesh, the Congress vote in the Muslim constituencies was slightly less than in the state as a whole. The same pattern held in Kerala, while in Andhra the vote for the Congress party was substantially lower in the five Muslim constituencies (52.4 percent as against 56.2 percent in the state as a whole). In the three Muslim majority constituencies of West Bengal, Congress won 3 percent more than in the state, not a significant difference. Only in the four Muslim constituencies of Bihar was the vote for Congress significantly higher than elsewhere— 48.7 percent as against 36.4 percent for the state as a whole. (It is interesting to note that even in 1977 the Congress vote was higher in Muslim constituencies in Bihar, 30.5 percent, than in the state as a whole, 22.9 percent.)

Except for Bihar, then, there is no evidence from electoral data that constituencies with a large Muslim population behaved very differently from other constituencies, or that Muslims voted in greater numbers for Congress candidates. In the four states with the largest number of Muslim constituencies contested by Congress (Andhra, Bihar, Uttar Pradesh, and West Bengal), Congress averaged 38 percent of the vote in the Muslim constituencies in 1980, up from 29.1 percent in 1977. Statewide in these states Congress won 40 percent in 1980, 31.4 percent in 1977. In both elections, therefore, the Muslim constituencies gave a slightly smaller vote (two points smaller in both) to Congress than their states. Did Muslims in these constituencies actually vote less for Congress than other groups, or was a Hindu backlash at work in the form of increased voting for non-Congress parties? We cannot say. We can only note that in 1977 constituencies with a large Muslim population had voted more or less as heavily against Congress and for Janata as other constituencies, while in 1980 the swing back to Congress was as great in Muslim as in non-Muslim constituencies.

[10] It is difficult to draw any conclusions from Kerala or Jammu and Kashmir, where Congress ran in only a few constituencies and electoral arrangements were made with other parties.

How did the Janata and Lok Dal parties fare in Muslim constituencies? In 1977 Janata won overwhelming victories in the Muslim constituencies of Uttar Pradesh and Bihar, more or less comparable to its victories in non-Muslim constituencies. Janata did badly in the same constituencies in 1980; again, its performance was comparable to its performance in non-Muslim constituencies.

The surprise in 1980 was how well the Lok Dal performed in Muslim constituencies. Both in Bihar and in Uttar Pradesh the Lok Dal vote in Muslim constituencies was significantly above its vote elsewhere in the state. In fact, Lok Dal won twelve out of the twenty-three Muslim constituencies in Uttar Pradesh.[11] Lok Dal won 35.3 percent of the vote in twenty-three Muslim constituencies, which gave 34.4 percent to the Congress party and 22.1 percent to the Janata party (see tables 35 and 36). In the remaining sixty-two constituencies in Uttar Pradesh where Muslims constituted less than 20 percent of the population, Lok Dal won only 26.7 percent of the vote, Congress 36.5 percent.

Even in Bihar, where Congress did exceptionally well in Muslim constituencies, the Lok Dal did better (23.4 percent) in the Muslim constituencies than in the state as a whole (16.6 percent), while Janata did worse (21.6 percent and 23.6 percent). One can hesitatingly conclude that, while the Congress party won back a considerable portion of the Muslim vote, a large proportion of the Muslims in Uttar Pradesh and Bihar must have voted for the Lok Dal.

In West Bengal there are twenty-four constituencies where Muslims constitute more than 20 percent of the electorate. Most were carried by the CPI(M), the CPI, and other left parties, and only three by Congress. Congress did slightly better in Muslim than in non-Muslim constituencies, with 37.6 percent in the former and 36.5 percent in the state as a whole. In none of the other states with several Muslim constituencies did Congress do better in Muslim than in non-Muslim constituencies.

One final statistic reveals the diversity of India's Muslim constituencies. Among India's seventy-four constituencies in which Muslims constituted more than 20 percent of the electorate, Congress

[11] In a detailed report from Muzaffarnagar constituency in Uttar Pradesh, the *Times of India* correspondent, J. D. Singh noted that among many Muslims the emergency continued to be an issue since there had been police firing and compulsory *nasbandi* in this constituency. He concluded that Muslims were disaffected from Janata but were unwilling to return to Congress, and he estimated that 45 percent of the 110,000 Muslim voters would support Lok Dal, 40 percent would vote Congress, and the remainder would go to Janata. Lok Dal actually won the Muzaffarnagar constituency with 41.5 percent of the vote, while Congress took 30 percent and Janata 18.9 percent. (*Times of India*, December 19, 1979)

won twenty-nine (39 percent), the CPI(M) nineteen (26 percent), Lok Dal twelve (16 percent), and independents and other political parties fourteen (19 percent). There is no evidence from the electoral data to support the assertions of journalists that India's Muslims voted Congress, either in a higher vote for Congress in constituencies with large numbers of Muslims or in a greater number of seats won there than elsewhere. It would appear that a substantial number of Muslims who had voted for other parties in 1977 voted for Congress in 1980, but in no greater proportion than other communities (and except for Bihar and West Bengal, possibly even less).

How Scheduled-Caste Constituencies Voted

India's ex-untouchables or, as they are officially called, scheduled castes, are as traditionally associated with India's Congress party as American blacks are with the Democratic party. The association with Congress goes back to the preindependence era, when Mahatma Gandhi won their support, and it has been nurtured by successive Congress leaders, including Jawaharlal Nehru and Indira Gandhi. Congress leaders explicitly appeal to India's poor, and through its commitment to reservations in education and employment and a variety of special programs, the party has sought the support of the scheduled castes. While critics of Congress have argued that the party's commitment is one of rhetoric, not performance, even the critics note (and lament) the electoral support given to Congress by a majority of the scheduled-caste voters in most elections.

Scheduled castes form a significant portion of the electorate. They constitute 14.6 percent of the Indian population, but in some states they are more numerous: 21 percent in Uttar Pradesh, 20 percent in West Bengal, 18 percent in Tamil Nadu, 19 percent in Haryana, 24 percent in Punjab, 22 percent in Himachal Pradesh, 16 percent in Rajasthan, 15 percent in Orissa. They are also 14 percent of the population in Bihar and 13 percent in Madhya Pradesh, two large states with many reserved constituencies.

The Indian constitution assures proportional representation for scheduled castes in Parliament and in the state assemblies. Constituencies are reserved for scheduled-caste candidates, although all electors in the constituency, irrespective of caste, can vote. In 1980, seventy-nine parliamentary constituencies were reserved for scheduled-caste candidates. The Election Commission chooses these constituencies from those in each state with the largest number of scheduled-caste inhabitants; but since these castes are widely dispersed, there are not many reserved constituencies where the scheduled castes form more than a fourth of the constituency, and in most they are a fifth or less. To infer how the scheduled castes voted on the basis of the election results in these constituencies is, therefore, difficult, but we can draw on the reports of journalists, politicians, and scholars as well as from the election data, as we did for the Muslims.

Before we discuss the 1980 elections in reserved constituencies, two points should be made about the 1977 election. The first is that there was an exceptionally high turnout in the reserved constituencies in northern India in that year. In earlier elections reserved constituencies typically had had a substantially lower turnout than other constituencies—as much as 7 percentage points on the average for the eighteen reserved constituencies in Uttar Pradesh, and 5.6 points for the eight reserved constituencies in Bihar. The national turnout increased from 55.3 percent in 1971 to 60.5 percent in the 1977 elections, but the increases were even greater in the reserved constituencies. In Uttar Pradesh the statewide turnout increased by 10.4 points, while for the reserved constituencies it increased by 15.4 points; in Bihar the statewide turnout increased by 11.1 points, turnout in the reserved constituencies by 20.2 points. There were also substantial increases in the turnout in the reserved constituencies of Haryana, Himachal Pradesh, Punjab, and Madhya Pradesh.

The second feature of the 1977 elections is that this increased politicization was accompanied by a sharp decline in the vote for Congress. While Congress had won fifty of the reserved seats in 1971, it won only sixteen in 1977, none of them in northern India. Moreover, in the popular vote Congress fared badly in reserved constituencies throughout the North, with a below-average vote in Bihar, Himachal Pradesh, Punjab, and Uttar Pradesh. The election data supported the reports of observers that India's scheduled castes, once the mainstay of the Congress party, had turned against the government as a result of what had been done to them during the emergency.

Following her defeat in 1977, Mrs. Gandhi made a major effort to win back the support of the scheduled castes, just as she sought to win back the Muslims. Moreover, just as the Muslims felt uncomfortable in their association with Janata because of the Jana Sangh, so too the scheduled castes were ill at ease in their association with Janata because of the Lok Dal. The Lok Dal was widely regarded as the party of the middle peasantry, the backward-caste small-property owners who cultivate their own land and employ scheduled castes as agricultural laborers. The growing economic assertiveness of the middle peasantry has often been at the expense of agricultural laborers. The traditional ties between agriculturalists and attached laborers, who receive daily wages when there is work and food when there is not, have been eroded in many areas by the green revolution. Many agriculturalists now prefer unattached or free laborers, to whom they pay daily wages without further financial obligations for the rest of the year. As the old ties have broken, some of the agricultural laborers have become more militant in their demand for higher wages, while some of the agriculturalists have become more ruthless in their efforts to keep scheduled castes in their "place," both economically and socially. The Jat caste in western Uttar Pradesh is particularly repressive in its efforts to prevent the scheduled castes from organizing. And since the Jats supported Janata, it seemed unlikely that the ex-untouchables could long remain with the Janata party in Uttar Pradesh.

The campaign by the governments of Bihar and Uttar Pradesh for reservations for the backward castes in education and employment further eroded the relationship between the scheduled castes and the Janata party. Many scheduled castes viewed the extension of reservations to other communities as an inroad into their own benefits. Violent clashes between scheduled castes and caste Hindus in northern India in 1978 and early 1979 provided Mrs. Gandhi with an opportunity to identify herself with their cause once again. She frequently visited the site of clashes, and articulated the plight of the scheduled castes, particularly when atrocities had been committed.

When Jagjivan Ram was chosen as the party's new leader after the resignation of Morarji Desai, Janata leaders anticipated that the party would be in a good position to win the vote of the scheduled castes. In his campaign, Jagjivan Ram appealed to the pride and interests of his fellow caste-men, holding out the promise that, as India's first ex-untouchable prime minister, he would be in a position to provide them with greater benefits than previous governments.

When the results came in, it was clear that Mrs. Gandhi's Congress had successfully wooed back the vote in the reserved constituencies. Congress won fifty out of the seventy-nine reserved constituencies (63 percent), Janata took four (5 percent), and the Lok Dal ten (13 percent). In contrast, Congress had won only sixteen seats (20 percent) in 1977, and Janata had won forty-five (58 percent). In the 1971 elections Congress had won fifty reserved seats. In short, Congress had totally restored its position in the reserved constituencies (see tables 39 and 40).

Though led by an ex-untouchable, the Janata party did not do well in the reserved constituencies. It had polled a massive vote in these constituencies in 1977, particularly in Bihar (76 percent) and Uttar Pradesh (74 percent). Janata dropped to barely a quarter of the vote in these states in 1980. While Janata had won an over-whelming forty-five reserved seats in 1977, it now won only four. Even in Bihar, Jagjivan Ram's home state, the party did poorly in the reserved constituencies (see table 41). What was surprising was how well the Lok Dal did. Lok Dal won ten reserved seats, nine in Uttar Pradesh and one in Bihar. Moreover, Lok Dal often won a higher vote in reserved than in nonreserved constituencies. It con-tested forty-six reserved seats and in thirty-three of them it did better than in the state as a whole.

It seems difficult to believe that a substantial proportion of the scheduled castes gave their vote to Lok Dal, a party traditionally viewed as antagonistic to their interests. An alternative explanation for the substantial Lok Dal vote in the reserved constituencies is that a larger proportion of the nonscheduled castes voted for Lok Dal than in other constituencies—that is, there was a polarization between the scheduled castes and caste Hindus in constituencies with Lok Dal candidates. One piece of supporting evidence for this hypothesis is that the turnout in the reserved constituencies of Uttar Pradesh won by the Lok Dal was far higher than in constituencies won by Congress candidates; the figures were 52 percent and 38 percent. Similarly, the tournout in the one reserved constituency won by the Lok Dal in Bihar was 61 percent, well above the turnout for the nonreserved constituencies of the state (53 percent). In all four states where Lok Dal candidates contested reserved constituencies, the party won a larger vote in the reserved than in the nonreserved constituencies. Some journalists also reported that scheduled castes were intimidated in some of the reserved constituencies contested by Lok Dal candidates and that there was a substantial amount of bogus voting and booth capturing.

Turnout declined in the reserved constituencies in Delhi, Haryana, Maharashtra, and Uttar Pradesh, where it had been very high in 1977, but the decline was less than in the nonreserved constituencies (see table 37). In West Bengal and Orissa, the turnout actually increased in both reserved and nonreserved constituencies. And in the remaining states of Andhra, Bihar, Gujarat, Himachal Pra-desh, Karnataka, Kerala, Madhya Pradesh, Punjab, and Rajasthan, the turnout declined more in the reserved constituencies. However, in a majority of the reserved constituencies throughout the country, turnout was still substantially higher than in 1971. Moreover, the difference in turnout between the reserved and nonreserved con-stituencies was smaller in 1980 than in the election of 1971 and all earlier elections. The political mobilization of the reserved con-stituencies brought about by the emergency clearly persisted into 1980.

127

In 1980 Congress generally fared better in reserved than in nonreserved constituencies (see table 40). This was the pattern in Andhra, Bihar, Delhi, Karnataka, Rajasthan, West Bengal, Himachal Pradesh, Kerala, Tamil Nadu, Orissa, Gujarat, Maharashtra, and Haryana. The spread was as great as ten percentage points in the case of Andhra, with lower but still substantial spreads elsewhere. There were only three states—Madhya Pradesh, Uttar Pradesh, and Punjab—where the vote for Congress was lower in reserved than in nonreserved constituencies. In the country as a whole, Congress did better in forty-three of the seventy-three reserved constituencies it contested than in the states in which those constituencies were located.

Can we conclude that the scheduled castes gave a larger proportion of their vote to the Congress party than the rest of the country? Between 1977 and 1980 the vote for Congress leaped by as much as twenty percentage points in the reserved constituencies in Bihar, eighteen points in Rajasthan, eleven in Uttar Pradesh, nearly seven in West Bengal, and five in Madhya Pradesh. These results are consistent with journalists' reports that the scheduled castes were returning to the Congress party. In 1977 Congress won 33.3 percent of the vote in reserved constituencies, and in 1980, 44 percent.

But since the vote for Congress increased in nonreserved constituencies as well, what indication is there that scheduled castes gave a larger proportion of their vote to Congress than nonscheduled castes? One indication—though by no means proof—is that the vote for Congress was higher in reserved than in nonreserved constituencies in almost all of the states. As we have noted, only in Madhya Pradesh, Punjab, and Uttar Pradesh was the vote for Congress on the average lower in the reserved constituencies. In the reserved constituencies in India as a whole, the average vote for Congress was 44.7 percent, while in the remaining constituencies it was 42.3 percent.

This margin (2.4 percentage points) would appear insignificant except that the difference between the number of scheduled-caste voters in reserved and in nonreserved constituencies is by no means overwhelming. It should be recalled that only 15 percent of India's constituencies are reserved and that most of the ex-untouchables live and vote in nonreserved constituencies. The Election Commission chooses as reserved constituencies those areas with a higher proportion of scheduled castes. On average, scheduled castes cast 22.6 percent of the valid votes in reserved constituencies and 13.2 percent in nonreserved constituencies (see table 38).

The Congress party won 13.1 million votes in the reserved constituencies and another 70.8 million votes in the nonreserved constituencies. What would the vote for Congress have to be among the scheduled castes in reserved constituencies to account for a 2.4 percentage point difference between reserved and nonreserved constituencies? One would first have to assume that scheduled-caste voters and others voted no differently in reserved and in nonreserved constituencies, and one would also have to assume that the turnouts of the two groups were the same. If these assumptions are correct then the vote for Congress among the scheduled castes in reserved constituencies was 60.4 percent and among others 39.6 percent.[12]

This estimate of the scheduled-caste vote would not be inconsistent with the results in the scheduled-caste constituencies of Andhra, Karnataka, Maharashtra, Orissa, and Rajasthan, which Congress won with a clear majority, and perhaps even the Punjab, Kerala, and Madhya Pradesh, but it seems implausibly high for Bihar, Haryana, Uttar Pradesh, and West Bengal. However, it should be noted that the Congress vote in the reserved constituencies of Bihar, Haryana, and West Bengal was above that in the nonreserved constituencies, which could be accounted for by a high scheduled-caste vote for Congress. In Uttar Pradesh, though, where the vote for Congress was lower in the reserved constituencies (and the vote for Lok Dal correspondingly higher), the vote for Congress among scheduled castes was probably smaller and may have been lower than that of others in the state.[13]

---

[12] The formula for deriving these percentages is:

$$6.7X + 22.9Y = 13.1$$
$$22.1X + 145.3Y = 70.8$$

X = percentage of Congress vote among scheduled castes.
Y = percentage of Congress vote among others.

[13] Two recent studies available to me after this chapter was written raise questions about the magnitude of the scheduled-caste vote for Congress (I). Lloyd and Suzanne Rudolph ("Transformation of Congress Party: Why 1980 Was Not a Restoration," *Economic and Political Weekly*, vol. 16, no. 18, May 2, 1981, pp. 811-18) note that Congress(I) did not regain the position in the reserved constituencies in the northern states that it had had in 1971, but in contrast did as well in the South. Barbara R. Joshi in an unpublished paper she sent me ("Scheduled Caste Voters: New Data, New Questions") analyzes the voting patterns in both nonreserved and reserved constituencies and reports no significant correlation between the scheduled-caste proportion of the population and the level of Congress(I) support. She does, however, note high positive correlations in some states (e.g. Andhra and Maharashtra). Her data are also consistent with mine on the difference between the proportion of scheduled-caste voters in reserved and nonreserved constituencies. Why an analysis of reserved constituencies alone and an analysis of all constituencies with scheduled-caste voters bring different statistical results is unclear. These studies do, however,

If the national vote for Congress among the scheduled castes really was as high as this, then as much as a fifth of the national vote for Congress must have come from the scheduled castes.

How Tribal Constituencies Voted

India's tribal population numbered 38 million in 1971, or 6.9 percent of the population. The tribal communities generally speak non-Indo-Aryan languages, are territorially more concentrated than castes, and are less stratified than caste Hindu society. Though they are a national minority, tribals constitute a majority of the population in Nagaland (89 percent), Meghalaya (80 percent), and Arunachal Pradesh (79 percent) in India's Northeast; and they are a fifth or more of the population in Manipur (31 percent), Tripura (29 percent), Orissa (23 percent), and Madhya Pradesh (20 percent). They are also a substantial minority in Gujarat (14 percent) and Assam (13 percent). Moreover, outside the Northeast, the tribes form a majority in nine-teen administrative districts—three in Orissa, six in Madhya Pradesh, two each in Rajasthan, Himachal Pradesh, Assam, and Gujarat, and one each in Bihar and the Laccadive Islands. In another nineteen districts they constitute more than 30 percent of the population.

India's tribals are located in three principal regions. One is the Northeast, including Assam and its neighboring states. The second is in middle India and includes southern Bihar, the hill areas of inland Orissa, southeastern Madhya Pradesh, and a portion of northern Andhra. The third is in India's West, and includes parts of eastern Gujarat, western Madhya Pradesh, and southern Rajasthan. There is also a small tribal area in the mountain regions of Himachal Pradesh and another in the Nilgiri mountains in south India. Coinciding with these territorial divisions are three distinct political tendencies. In the Northeast, some of the tribals have been secessionist and have even supported armed insurrections. In southern Bihar, Orissa, and Madhya Pradesh, many of the tribals have supported the separatist Jharkhand party, which has called for the creation of a tribal state in the region. And in Rajasthan, Madhya Pradesh, and Orissa, many of the tribals were loyal to the former maharajas and supported political parties with which they were

agree on two points: that the scheduled-caste vote for Congress was considerably higher in 1980 than in 1977, and that Congress did significantly better among scheduled-caste voters than among the general population in some states. What is uncertain is the magnitude of the shift toward Congress(I) in the North and whether in these constituencies the scheduled-caste vote for Congress was higher than among the general population.

affiliated. In recent years, tribals in each of these regions have supported Congress candidates, or at least given as many votes to Congress as have other constituencies in the states in which they were located. In each election the vote for Congress in tribal areas has been similar to the vote of the nontribal constituencies in the same states.

Like the scheduled castes, the scheduled tribes have reserved constituencies. In these constituencies only members of scheduled tribes can stand as candidates, though every citizen in the constituency can vote. But unlike the scheduled-caste constituencies, where only a minority of the voters belong to scheduled castes, the constituencies reserved for tribal voters tend to be predominantly tribal. Tribals are a majority in seven of the eight reserved constituencies in Madhya Pradesh, four of the five in Bihar, all the reserved constituencies of Orissa and Gujarat, and two of the three in Maharashtra. They form a majority in the constituencies of the small states in the Northeast.

In 1980 Congress won twenty-nine out of the thirty-seven reserved scheduled-tribe constituencies; it had taken thirteen in 1977 and twenty-six in 1971 (see table 43). In 1977, the majority of these constituencies, twenty, voted for Janata, while in 1980 only one returned a Janata candidate. The vote for the Congress candidates in the reserved constituencies by state in 1977 and in 1980 and the statewide vote are shown in table 44.

Once again, the most significant feature of the vote is that in both elections the scheduled-tribe constituencies were similar to the other constituencies. In the 1977 elections Congress did only slightly better in the tribal than in the nontribal constituencies; in 1980 Congress performed somewhat better in the tribal than in the nontribal constituencies in Madhya Pradesh, Maharashtra, Rajasthan, and Gujarat, and less well elsewhere. In two-thirds of the reserved tribal constituencies the Congress vote equaled or exceeded the statewide results.

The overwhelming tendency of the reserved tribal constituencies in 1980 was to vote for Congress. Congress won an absolute majority of the vote in nineteen out of the thirty-five reserved constituencies it contested, or 54 percent, while it only won a clear majority of the vote in 41.5 percent of the constituencies in the country as a whole. In all of the reserved tribal constituencies Congress won 49 percent of the vote in 1980, well over its 38.1 percent in 1977.

In West Bengal, the two reserved constituencies elected candidates from the CPI(M) and the Revolutionary Socialist party, reflecting the general left tendency in the state. And in Nagaland and Mizoram, the tribals elected independents in preference to voting for any national party. But these were exceptions to the general swing toward Congress.

Scheduled-tribe constituencies have typically had a smaller turnout than other constituencies. This was the case even in the highly politicized election of 1977, though in that year their turnout also increased. In the 1980 elections, these constituencies followed the national pattern, although in most constituencies the decline in turnout was below the state average (see table 42). In the 1980 elections, the turnout in the reserved tribal constituencies was 46.7 percent, while the national turnout was 57.0 percent. The figures in 1977 were 47.6 percent and 60.5 percent.

Conclusion

"The electorate treats us like chapatis," said an Indian politician, referring to the way Indians make the pancake-like bread that is the mainstay of the north Indian diet. "First you slap one side, next you slap the other. In the process, hopefully, one will knock Indian politics into a shape suitable to the plate and the palate." [14]

This homespun metaphor seems particularly apt to describe the electoral swing of India's minorities. To recapitulate our findings:

- In constituencies with substantial Muslim populations, the Congress vote increased from 29.1 percent in 1977 to 38 percent in 1980.
- In scheduled-caste reserved constituencies, the Congress vote increased from 33.3 percent in 1977 to 44.7 percent in 1980.
- In scheduled-tribe reserved constituencies, the Congress vote increased from 38.1 percent to 49 percent.

These constituencies gave Congress 30.3 million votes in 1980, 22 million votes in 1977. These figures, of course, do not tell us how many votes minorities gave to Congress, but only the vote in constituencies in which greater than average numbers of minorities live. It would appear however that scheduled tribes gave a substantially larger proportion of their votes to Congress than did other communities and that scheduled castes gave Congress a larger proportion of their votes (with the notable exception of scheduled-caste voters in

[14] The statement by Krishan Kant, an M.P., is quoted in Somdeb Das Gupta, "Fallen by the Wayside: Some Comments of the Defeated," *Statesman*, January 16, 1980.

Uttar Pradesh, Madhya Pradesh, and Punjab), while Muslims seem to have given a smaller proportion of their votes to Congress than other voters in their states.

From a study of these constituencies, I have made some crude inferences as to how many votes minorities gave to Congress throughout the country. I would estimate that in 1980 Congress won 32.4 million of its 83.9 million votes from among the minorities, or 38.6 percent of its vote. In 1977, the minorities had probably given Congress about 17 million of its 64.7 million votes, or 26.3 percent. As ballpark estimates, these numbers convey the substantial extent to which the Congress victory in 1980 depended on a shift in the vote of the minorities. Without their support Congress could not have won in 1980, and with their support Congress probably would have won in 1977.

6

Conclusion: A Reinstating Election

Why was Mrs. Gandhi's Congress returned to power? Did the electorate vote for Congress to elect "a government that works"? Was the country simply voting for a popular leader? Were voters disillusioned with the government because of high food prices and shortages? Was the country indifferent to the dangers of authoritarianism and more concerned with the price of onions? Were the 1980 elections an example of the triumph of personality and the greater importance Indians give to economic issues than to civil liberties? Was the country sick of political squabbles and searching for strong authority?

It is tempting to draw such conclusions from the 1980 elections. But one must not reify India when Indians, like voters elsewhere, voted in different ways for many different reasons. High prices and shortages may have affected some voters, but they evidently did not turn the middle peasants in northern India against Prime Minister Charan Singh and his party. Mrs. Gandhi's personality may have attracted support from some voters, but then why were there substantial variations in voting from one state and one constituency to another?

In any event only a small fraction of the electorate switched to the Congress party in 1980. The election outcome, it should again be emphasized, was the result of an increase of 8.2 points in the national vote for the Congress party. While there were increases in many areas of the country, in urban no less than in rural areas, the greatest increases were in the Hindi belt and in western India. The evidence we have suggests that the largest swings to Congress were among the scheduled tribes and scheduled castes and, to a lesser extent, the Muslims. These minorities are numerous and dispersed, but they are more heavily concentrated in central and northern India.

It is also important to note that while these and other voters turned back to Congress after turning against the party in 1977, Congress still did not do as well as it had done in the 1971 elections. Had Janata not split, Congress probably would not have won a majority of seats in the Hindi-speaking states, and its parliamentary majority, if any, would have been precarious.

This is not to say that the rise in the price of food, the decline in industrial production and employment, the power shortages, and the stagnation in per capita income—economic facts for the last six months before the elections—did not affect the behavior of voters. But economic changes are mediated by social structures and political organizations in such complex ways that any projection from economic facts to political behavior is bound to oversimplify the Indian political scene. It is true that Charan Singh's government was defeated during a period of inflation and recession, but the Congress government had been defeated in 1977 when inflation was not as high and the economy was doing better. Moreover, the Janata government lost its vote of confidence in Parliament in July 1979, and much of the economic decline took place after its defeat, and perhaps because of it.

Then too, some groups that were badly affected by the poor performance of the economy supported Charan Singh's party during the elections; and as we have seen, the vote for Mrs. Gandhi's party by scheduled castes, tribals, and Muslims had as much to do with the state of politics as with the state of the economy. One need not dismiss the impact of economic changes on voters to argue that voters are not only wage earners and job seekers, producers and consumers, employers and employees, but also members of social and religious groups, with political attachments that are not simply the reflection of economic and class interests. Furthermore, as Max Weber pointed out, interests are in any event defined by beliefs.

In any analysis of voting behavior in India, the central analytical issues are: What are the major social cleavages? How do they overlap? How and by whom are groups politically mobilized? What political coalitions are formed? and What is the political logic of factional and leadership conflicts that make or break political coalitions capable of winning elections and governing the country? Central to any analysis of Indian parties and elections is one fundamental principle: The political necessity of coalition building transcends program, ideology, and class interests.

None of this is by way of deprecating Mrs. Gandhi's extraordinary political comeback. On the contrary, she did, after all, regain the support of many voters who had been embittered by the emergency.

She proved remarkably adept at projecting herself as the undisputed leader of the Congress party in spite of efforts by her own party members, as well as Janata, to discredit her. And if Janata fell apart on its own, she and her son get considerable "credit" for the political skill with which they helped to maneuver the fall of the Morarji Desai and Charan Singh governments.

But the central feature of Mrs. Gandhi's victory was the breakup of the Janata party. Had Janata remained intact there would have been no elections in 1980. Moreover, in parliamentary by-elections held between March 1977 and June 1979, when the government fell, Janata won most of the seats, though often by a reduced margin.[1] The real disintegration of Janata support came with the disintegration of the party. It was in this atmosphere that Congress was able to win back many of the voters it had lost in 1977.

Personality played an important role in the success of Mrs. Gandhi's Congress over the Congress party of Y. B. Chavan and Devaraj Urs in assuming the status of the former Congress and attracting the support of traditional partisan Congress voters. There is little doubt that Mrs. Gandhi, and no one else, personifies Congress. In her person she represents both authority and a concern for the underdog. It is these perceived attitudes that enabled her and her party to win support from the very rich and from the very poor, from Brahmins and ex-untouchables, from well-to-do businessmen and government bureaucrats, from tribal agricultural laborers and Muslim weavers. A centrist program won for Mrs. Gandhi and her party not the support of the center, that is, the middle classes and the middle peasantry, who were either divided or opposed to Congress, but the extremes of the class structure.[2]

The Congress party that won the 1980 parliamentary elections was the party of a single personality (or one and a half personalities, as one wit put it). Virtually none of the country's national or regional leaders remained with Mrs. Gandhi. Those who had been in the cabinet during the emergency either left when the 1977 elections were called (like Jagjivan Ram and H. N. Bahuguna) or split with Mrs. Gandhi after her defeat (like Y. B. Chavan). Though a few prominent politicians returned to support her when she seemed likely to return to power (Bahuguna, for example), others were leaving (like Devaraj Urs). Even after her election the process of consolidation did not bring in many former national leaders, and in at least one instance

---

[1] For an analysis of the by-elections, see G. G. Mirchandani, *The People's Verdict* (New Delhi: Vikas Publishing House, 1980), pp. 53-56.

[2] I am grateful to Paul Brass for his articulation of this paradox.

(the resignation of Bahuguna as general secretary and then as a member of Congress) the defections continued.

Mrs. Gandhi's need for subordination and loyalty on the part of her supporters and her growing dependence upon Sanjay and his associates precluded the emergence at the state or national level of Congress politicians with significant local followings. When candidates were to be chosen for the June 1980 state assembly elections, there was a great rush to Delhi by thousands who hoped to be selected by Mrs. Gandhi, Sanjay, and their associates. Hardly anywhere could one find local or regional leaders who commanded authority independent of the authority bestowed on them by Delhi. And when Congress won a majority in eight of the nine state elections by a handsome margin, the elected Congress members of state assemblies turned to Delhi for guidance as to who should be the chief ministers of their states.

The country's national leadership was a major casualty of the 1980 elections. Morarji Desai, never a popular leader, was politically destroyed by the split in the Janata party and did not stand for Parliament. Charan Singh demonstrated his continued capacity to elicit support from the middle peasantry and the backward castes in portions of northern India, but the elections confirmed the impression that he was a regional, not a national, leader. Jagjivan Ram failed to win the support of ex-untouchables and thereby lost whatever standing he had had as a credible national figure. The elections may have ended the political career of all these elders, while the younger leaders within Janata continued to fight one another after the elections. Janata split once again as the Jana Sangh group withdrew to form the Bharatiya Janata party. And the Lok Dal split as Raj Narain broke with Charan Singh to form his own party.

All of this confirmed Mrs. Gandhi's position as the undisputed national leader. She showed no signs of permitting, much less encouraging, regional leaders to emerge within Congress. With few exceptions, her appointments to the cabinet and the new state chief ministers were not well-known public figures. The new head of the planning commission was a politician from Uttar Pradesh with no expertise in national planning; the foreign minister had little experience in foreign affairs and was little known outside his home province; and the defense portfolio remained in Mrs. Gandhi's own hands. In Uttar Pradesh Congress members of the legislative assembly unanimously petitioned Mrs. Gandhi to appoint Sanjay chief minister, though he was only thirty-three, had never held public office, and was not even a member of the Uttar Pradesh legislative assembly. The Congress party had become a patrimony of Mrs. Gandhi, an estate inherited from her father, in time to be conferred upon her son.

In what direction does Mrs. Gandhi want to lead her party and her government? She is, as several observers have noted, a leader with attitudes rather than policies, with a point of view rather than a coherent ideology. She is, first of all, a centralizer. She believes that central government ought to have overriding authority over the Indian states. Within government, power should be concentrated in the office of the prime minister. Federalism and democracy, the two institutional pillars of the Indian political system, should be pushed in the direction of greater central authority. She and her supporters have hinted that a presidential system may be preferable to India's parliamentary framework.

The drive for private gain, Mrs. Gandhi apparently believes, is rarely in the public interest. Inflation, hoarding, and corruption result, in her judgment, largely from venal behavior by selfish individuals, not from public policies. Strikes, communal clashes, and public demonstrations are in her eyes more often the result of provocations by politicians seeking political gain than the result of broader social and economic forces. To restrain the disruptive and selfish behavior of those who seek to maximize their wealth and power is a major goal of the state, which, she believes, can best be achieved through a strong center and firm authority.

Mrs. Gandhi believes that the state ought to play a large role in improving the well-being of the populace through the regulation of the economy; her ideal is that of a maximalist, not a minimalist state. She believes that individuals are more likely to comply with authority if they are required rather than rewarded to do so; thus, authority rests on the capacity to command compliance rather than on the ability to induce behavioral change by providing rewards. She sees political competition and multiple power centers as potentially disruptive of the social and political order in a society with weak civil loyalties and fragile group relationships. She sees the state as an instrument for reform, but not as an instrument for social transformation. The state should strive to maintain a stable social order and can best do so if it is more centralized, protective, and regulatory.

As we noted earlier, Mrs. Gandhi's election slogan, "Elect a government that works," was a conservative, not a radical message. The masses were not urged to rush to the barricades against the rich, nor did she promise, as she had earlier, that if elected she would make ending poverty her priority. Instead she promised to restore law and order—to bring an end to strikes, to restore electric power, to get the trains moving, to end hoarding, to bring prices down, to protect Muslims and ex-untouchables against violence—in short, to make the existing social, economic, and political order work by exercising governmental authority.

To what extent Mrs. Gandhi has been guided by the conviction that India needs a stronger center to be governed effectively, or by her own fear that she needs such authority to protect herself against her political enemies, is a matter on which her supporters and critics disagree. No doubt both elements are at work. Mrs. Gandhi is not the first or the last political leader to believe that what is good for the country is good for herself or vice versa.

How has she behaved as prime minister? To many critics, her actions during her first months in office were indicative of an inclination to move in an authoritarian direction: she restored her loyal followers to authority in the Delhi Municipal Corporation and in the Delhi police; she terminated the special courts established to review cases against her and her supporters; she appointed subservient loyal politicians to the cabinet and kept politicians with a local political base out of power; she brought down the state governments controlled by the opposition and, when Congress won the elections, she appointed chief ministers of her own choice rather than permit local organizations to choose their leaders; and—most ominous of all in the eyes of her critics—she began to move Sanjay into positions of enormous political authority.

Sanjay's death in an air crash in June 1980 was not only a personal tragedy for Mrs. Gandhi but an extraordinary shock to her as prime minister, to the party, to the state governments, and to his associates in the Youth Congress, who were beginning to move into important positions in the party and in the state governments. His death was widely described as "destabilizing," an odd word to use for the death of a man in his thirties who held no official position other than a seat in Parliament and at a time when the governing party so securely dominated the country's legislative bodies. But in truth his death *was* destabilizing, for the key political institution, the Congress party, had become organizationally so fragile, so devoid of organizational roots in the countryside and of state and national leaders, that the entire political system seemed to rest upon a single personality.[3] Sanjay's death revealed how dynastic the system had

[3] Reflecting upon the hope that Sanjay might have rebuilt the party organization, the *Hindustan Times* editorial (Overseas Edition, July 10, 1980, "A Party without Sanjay," p. 6) had this to say: "The Congress has been for many years now an almost moribund organization. Successive secretaries have taken up the chal-

become, a point further emphasized when many of Mrs. Gandhi's supporters publicly expressed the hope that her elder son, Rajiv, might be persuaded to enter politics to assume the mantle once worn by Sanjay. Rajiv, a professional pilot for Indian Airlines, successfully ran for Sanjay's vacant parliamentary seat in June 1981 and soon was widely regarded as the most likely successor to Mrs. Gandhi as the leader of the Congress party.

The 1980 general election was a reinstating election. The older electoral coalition was reassembled by the Congress party. Congress rule, both at the center and in most of the states, was restored. Mrs. Gandhi was again prime minister, and, as before, she led an organizationally weak political party. And once again, the party system was fragmented. Janata remained the most national of the opposition parties, but in terms of votes polled, it was the second largest party in only nine states. Lok Dal and the CPI(M) were each the second largest party in three states, and elsewhere single-state parties were the closest competitors (see table 46).

The fragmentation of the party system was further demonstrated in the state assembly elections in June. As in the parliamentary elections, the non-Congress vote was split among a variety of parties. In fact, in almost each state, a different party was Congress's major competitor. In Bihar, Uttar Pradesh, and Orissa it was Charan Singh's Lok Dal; in Rajasthan and Madhya Pradesh, the Bharatiya Janata party, the old Jana Sangh in new garb; in Gujarat, the Janata party, reduced to what had once been the Congress (O); in Maharashtra, the Congress (U); and in Tamil Nadu, the AIADMK was reelected. In the state assembly elections the fragmentation was so great that the combined vote won by the two leading parties in any state was rarely above 70 percent. In Bihar the combined vote for

---

lenge of reactivating the party, but it has continued to be no more than a conglomerate of flabby political busybodies. It failed to become an organisation that reached out to the people or might serve as a conveyer belt for important decisions between the Government and the grass roots. There was hardly any sign of coherent activity in any of its offices or branches. There was not even an awareness of the need for its systematic or efficient functioning. And except at election time when it came alive for a few weeks, there was evidence only of a sporadic and largely desultory activity at its headquarters and branches in the States. Sanjay Gandhi's importance as the new General Secretary lay in his promise of not only attracting youth back to its rank and file but also of making the organisation tick more efficiently and effectively. . . . In Gandhiji's time, the Congress party was as loosely structured as it is now. What gave it an edge was the fact that there was hardly any taluka, tehsil, mohala or locality in the country in which the party did not have a small group of loyal followers. . . . With his well-known pragmatism, Mr. Sanjay Gandhi would have no doubt given a new reorientation to the Congress. That unfortunately was not to be."

Congress and the second largest party was under 50 percent (see table 48).

The Janata realignment had failed. For a brief moment in post-independence India a new national party, forged in the wake of a period of authoritarian rule, governed India. Though the realignment was largely of political groups in northern and western India, it was large enough to command a majority in Parliament and to control most of the states. Its disintegration hardly two years later brought India politically to where it had been in the early 1970s, when the combination of a popular prime minister, an institutionally weak governing party, a fragmented opposition, and a deteriorating economy had set authoritarian forces in motion.

India's Political Economy in the 1980s

The immediate problems facing Mrs. Gandhi's government were formidable: agitation in Assam that affected the country's supply of oil, high inflation that had generated strikes among industrial workers, a deteriorating situation in electric power, coal, railways, and steel that had held back industrial growth. Added to these problems was another increase in the price of oil.

Many of the immediate problems were also indications of long-term economic problems that are likely to have further political repercussions. First is the growing balance-of-payments deficit, the result of rising oil prices, a slow growth in trade, a halt in the growth of remittances from Indians abroad, and growing dependence upon imports not only for petroleum and petroleum products, but for iron and steel, aluminum, fertilizers, man-made fibers and yarn, paper, and even edible oils. Domestic oil production, though rising, has been able to meet only 40 percent of the country's requirements.

The deficit in the balance of payments in 1979–1980 was approximately $3 billion, and with the 1980 rise in the price of oil, it is expected to increase. If the deficit persists and the country's exchange reserves are drawn down, then India may experience a foreign exchange deficit as it did in the 1960s. Under these circumstances policy makers will try to reduce imports through import substitution and encourage exports. Dependence on external agencies for funding—the World Bank for long-term loans, the IMF for short-term relief—will grow. Inevitably there will be disputes, particularly if the foreign exchange situation becomes serious enough for international donors to press for devaluation and the end of subsidies. The question of private foreign investment, more or less dormant for some time, has already been raised by a government decision to encourage investment by OPEC countries on more favorable terms. India's policies in West Asia will of necessity be affected by its need for an assured oil supply, for concessional payment terms, and for barter agreements (such as oil from the Soviet Union in return for grain).

The second problem is the disparity between the price of agricultural commodities and the soaring cost of agricultural production. As we saw earlier, the middle peasantry is concerned with the price and availability of agricultural inputs: commercial fertilizers, fuel for pump sets and tractors, electric power, warehouses and marketing facilities, irrigation, and credit. Farmers want prices for their produce that will cover the cost of their inputs and provide them with a profitable return on their investment. As a class, they want better terms of trade with the city—cotton prices commensurate with the cost of finished textiles, sugarcane prices commensurate with the cost of refined sugar, and so on. The Lok Dal has been the spokesman for this class in Uttar Pradesh, Bihar, and Haryana. But since the elections the middle peasants have become politically articulate elsewhere. In late 1980 there were peasant demonstrations in Maharashtra, Tamil Nadu, and Karnataka. One interesting feature of these agitations is that they were not organized by political parties, but had their own leaders.

Higher procurement prices are not easily provided by the government, since they result in higher food prices, which generate protests from industrial labor, the urban middle class, and the urban and rural poor. Leftist supporters (and critics) of the government are divided, some discrediting the middle peasantry by labeling them "kulaks" and "capitalist farmers," whereas others see in their protest a revolutionary potential. For the government, all the solutions are politically painful. The country needs the energies of the middle peasantry, whose productivity is essential if the economy is to expand and exports to grow, but the government finds it politically difficult to pass on the higher costs of production to consumers.

A third set of issues has to do with the growth of middle-class employment. Unemployment is linked to the high birth rates and declining mortality rates of the 1960s and the slow industrial growth of the 1970s and early 1980s. But the problem of unemployment should also be seen in the context of expanding enrollments in secondary schools and colleges. The result is a higher educational level among the unemployed. The combined effect of rapid population growth and expanding education has been to create not a middle class, but middle-class aspirants in search of white-collar jobs.

One safety valve has been the export of educated manpower. Nearly a million Indians have emigrated to advanced industrial countries, particularly to Britain, the United States, Canada, and the Netherlands. Since 1973 another half-million Indians, many of them unskilled construction workers, but also clerks, typists, nurses, doctors, managers, shopkeepers, foremen, accountants, skilled machine operators, technicians, and engineers have found employment in the Middle East, particularly in the Gulf states. Most of the emigrants have come from Kerala, Tamil Nadu, Punjab, Goa, Gujarat, and Bombay, where education levels are high and there are traditions of emigration.

But for those from social classes that have not previously been educated, opportunities for overseas employment are more limited, while the competition for employment within India is more acute. The problem, therefore, of educated unemployment is particularly severe in some of the less developed regions—in Assam, Orissa, the Telangana region of Andhra, and backward regions of Maharashtra, Madhya Pradesh, and Bihar. An unemployment problem has also developed among the scheduled castes and scheduled tribes as their educational level has increased, although they are partially helped by the system of job reservations. And there is now a growing demand for nonagricultural white-collar employment from the sons and daughters of the backward castes, many belonging to the middle peasantry, who have graduated from secondary schools and colleges.

The employment demands of the newly educated take a variety of forms: for regional development, for industries located in rural areas, and for job reservations that can assure their social group a share of positions. The educated unemployed do not, of course, form a single class. As members of particular linguistic communities, castes, and tribes, they turn to their community for political support, with the result that demands often take an ethnic form. Demands for reservations from the backward castes in Uttar Pradesh and Bihar are the most recent manifestation of this phenomenon. But there are also signs of growing politicization in the emerging Muslim middle classes, whose demand for the adoption of Urdu as an official language in various states has implications for employment as well as culture.

In human terms the problem of unemployment among the recently educated is probably less acute than the larger problem of unemployment among the rural poor, but in political terms it is often more serious, since the middle classes are politically more articulate and are able to rally large numbers of people to their cause by appeals to ethnic solidarity.

Mrs. Gandhi's government is thus faced with a series of gaps—between imports and exports, between agricultural prices and the cost of agricultural inputs, and between the rapid expansion of education

143

and the slow growth of employment. Each of these economic issues creates political challenges for the government, particularly since policies to deal with the political problems arising from these gaps often have political costs. To give job reservations to one community, for example, is to generate political hostility in another. To help peasants is to hurt consumers. To invite more foreign investment is to evoke the anger of left nationalists.

The Indian government may, of course, muddle through, as governments often do. Several good monsoons that increase agricultural productivity would slow the inflation rate and might stimulate the demand for and the production of consumer goods. A more rapid development of offshore oil and an improvement in coal production would ease the energy and foreign exchange situations. If the agitations are confined to a few areas, then ad hoc political solutions may be possible. With the expansion of a market economy in agriculture and the growing trade linkages between India and the outside world, however, the economic problems and the policies the government adopts are often international or national, not regional or local.

If these economic problems grow, if they are accompanied by an increase in agitation, if neither the national government nor the states can find political ways of managing these demands, if the level of violence increases, then, in the bureaucracy, the government, and the Congress party, there will be many who will call for authoritarian measures. In the mid-1970s a government led by Mrs. Gandhi failed to muddle through and had recourse instead to authoritarianism. The reinstating election of 1980 produced an even more fragile system of authority than was produced by the elections of 1971 and 1972. It is this combination—intractable economic problems and a fragile institutional structure for the management of political conflict—that makes the Indian system vulnerable to authoritarianism.

Tables

ABBREVIATIONS

CPI   Communist party of India
CPI(M)   Communist party of India (Marxist)
DMK   Dravida Munnetra Kazhagam
AIADMK   All India Anna Dravida Munnetra Kazhagam

TABLE 1

PARTY MEMBERSHIP IN THE LOK SABHA, 1977 AND AUGUST 22,1979

Party	Lok Sabha Elected in 1977	Lok Sabha Dissolved August 22, 1979
Congress	153	—
Congress(I)	—	80
Congress(U)	—	56
Janata	298	203
Janata(S) [a]	—	77
CPI	7	7
CPI(M)	21	22
AIADMK	18	17
Akali Dal	8	8
Independents	14	33
Other	20	32
Total [b]	539	535

Dash (—): Not applicable.

[a] Lok Dal.

[b] There are 542 elective seats in Parliament, but the actual number of M.P.s varies as a result of deaths and postponed elections.

SOURCE: Government of India, Press Information Bureau, New Delhi, December 1979.

TABLE 2

Election Data, Indian Parliamentary Elections, 1952–1980

Year	Seats	Candidates	Electorate (millions)	Polling Stations	Votes Polled (millions)	Turnout (percent)
1952	489	1,864	173.2	132,560	80.7	46.6
1957	494	1,519	193.7	220,478	91.3	47.1
1962	494	1,985	217.7	238,355	119.9	55.1
1967	520	2,369	250.1	267,555	152.7	61.1
1971	518	2,784	274.1	342,944	151.5	55.3
1977	542	2,439	321.2	373,908	194.3	60.5
1980	525	4,611	354.0	437,166	201.7	57.0

SOURCE: Press Information Bureau, *General Election 1980, Reference Hand Book*, New Delhi, 1979; 1980 data from G. G. Mirchandani, *The People's Verdict: DCM Computer-based Study* (New Delhi: Vikas Publishing House, 1980).

TABLE 3

Growth of the Indian Electorate, 1952–1980

Year	Population (millions)	Electorate Number (millions)	Electorate Percent of population
1952	368.9	173.2	47.0
1957	407.9	193.7	47.5
1962	449.3	217.7	48.4
1967	502.1	250.1	49.8
1971	548.2	274.1	50.0
1977	625.8	321.2	51.3
1980	668.8	354.0	52.9

SOURCE: "Population, Decadal Growth Rates and Density, 1951-81, Census of India 1981," in *Economic and Political Weekly*, vol. 16, no. 15 (April 11, 1981), p. 643, and Press Information Bureau, *General Election 1980, Reference Hand Book*, New Delhi, 1979.

TABLE 4
VOTER TURNOUT, BY STATE, 1971, 1977, AND 1980
(percent)

State	1971	1977	1980	Change, 1977–1980
Andhra Pradesh	59.1	62.5	57.0	−5.5
Arunachal Pradesh	a	56.3	68.6	+12.3
Assam	50.7	54.9	53.4[b]	−1.5
Bihar	49.0	60.8	51.7	−9.1
Gujarat	55.5	59.2	55.4	−3.8
Haryana	64.4	73.3	64.8	−8.5
Himachal Pradesh	41.2	59.2	59.7	+0.5
Jammu and Kashmir	58.1	57.9	47.6	−10.3
Karnataka	57.4	63.2	57.9	−5.3
Kerala	64.5	79.2	62.2	−17.0
Madhya Pradesh	48.0	54.9	51.8	−3.1
Meghalaya	a	49.9	51.0	+1.1
Maharashtra	59.9	60.3	56.8	−3.5
Manipur	48.9	60.2	81.9	+21.7
Mizoram	a	49.9	56.1	+6.2
Nagaland	53.8	52.8	64.4	+11.6
Orissa	43.2	44.3	47.2	+2.9
Punjab	59.9	70.1	62.7	−7.4
Rajasthan	54.0	56.9	54.7	−2.2
Tamil Nadu	71.8	67.1	66.8	−0.3
Tripura	60.8	70.1	80.0	+9.9
Uttar Pradesh	46.1	56.4	50.0	−6.4
West Bengal	61.9	60.2	70.9	+10.7
Delhi	65.2	71.3	64.9	−6.4
India	55.3	60.5	57.0	−3.5

[a] Arunachal Pradesh, Meghalaya, and Mizoram did not participate in the parliamentary elections in 1971.

[b] Two constituencies only. Elections were not held in the remaining twelve constituencies.

SOURCE: *Report on the Fifth General Election to the House of the People of India, 1971*, vol. 2 (statistical), Election Commission of India, New Delhi, 1973; *Report on the Sixth General Election to the House of the People of India, 1977*, vol. 2 (statistical), Election Commission of India, New Delhi, 1978. Figures for 1980 based on materials made available by the Election Commission, the Press Information Bureau of the Ministry of Information and Broadcasting, and by DCM Data Products, New Delhi.

TABLE 5

Change in Turnout and in Janata and Congress Vote, by State, 1977–1980

(percentage points)

State	Turnout	Congress	Janata plus Lok Dal[a]
Andhra Pradesh	−5.5	−1.2	−10.6
Bihar	−9.1	+13.5	−24.8
Gujarat	−3.8	+7.9	−9.7
Haryana	−8.5	+11.3	−8.8
Himachal Pradesh	+0.5	+12.1	−15.4
Jammu and Kashmir	−10.3	+4.1	+0.8
Karnataka	−5.3	−0.6	−15.7
Kerala	−17.0	−2.8	−0.5
Madhya Pradesh	−3.1	+14.0	−23.3
Maharashtra	+3.5	+6.3	−9.8
Manipur	+21.8	−22.3	+9.0
Nagaland	+11.6	a	a
Orissa	+2.9	+17.5	−17.9
Punjab	−7.4	+17.6	−0.3
Rajasthan	−2.2	+12.1	−22.7
Tamil Nadu	−0.3	+9.3	−7.3
Tripura[b]	+9.9	−17.1	b
Uttar Pradesh	−6.4	+10.9	−16.5
West Bengal	+10.7	+7.1	−16.4
Delhi	−6.4	+20.2	−23.4
India	−3.5	+8.2	−14.9

[a] Neither Congress nor Janata ran in Nagaland in 1980.

[b] Janata did not run in Tripura in 1980.

SOURCE: See table 4.

TABLE 6

PARLIAMENTARY ELECTION RESULTS, 1971, 1977, AND 1980

	1971		1977		1980	
Party	Seats won	Percent of valid votes	Seats won	Percent of valid votes	Seats won	Percent of valid votes
Congress(I)	352	43.7	153	34.5	351	42.7
Congress(U)	—	—	—	—	13	5.3
Janata	—	—	298	43.2	31	18.9
Congress(O)	16	10.4	—	—	—	—
Jana Sangh	22	7.4	—	—	—	—
Swatantra[a]	8	53 3.1 27.6	—	—	—	—
Socialists	5	3.5	—	—	—	—
Bharatiya Lok Dal[b]	2	3.2	—	—	41	9.4
CPI	23	4.7	7	2.8	11	2.6
CPI(M)	25	5.1	21	4.3	35	6.0
DMK	23	3.8	1	1.7	16	2.1
AIADMK	—	—	18	3.0	2	2.4
Akali Dal	—	—	8	1.3	1	0.7
Independents	14	8.3	9	5.7	8	6.5
Other parties	28	6.8	24	3.5	16	3.4
Total	518	100.0	539	100.0	525	100.0

Dash (—): Not applicable.

[a] Merged with the Bharatiya Lok Dal in 1974.

[b] Includes the Bharatiya Kranti Dal, the Utkal Congress, and the Bangla Congress, although they did not actually unite to form the Bharatiya Lok Dal (along with a few smaller parties) until after the 1971 elections.

SOURCE: See table 4.

TABLE 7
SEATS WON AND VOTES POLLED, BY PARTY, 1977 AND 1980

Party	Year	Seats Won		Votes Polled					
				Total		Winning candidates		Losing candidates	
		Number	Percent	Number	Percent	Number	Percent	Number	Percent
Congress(I)	1980	351	66.86	83,938,634	42.7	65,172,500	77.6	18,766,134	22.4
	1977	153	28.60	64,750,243	34.5	30,362,536	46.9	34,387,707	53.1
Congress(U)	1980	13	2.48	10,453,549	5.3	2,431,715	23.3	8,021,834	76.7
Janata[a]	1980	31	5.90	37,259,854	18.9	4,920,478	13.2	32,339,376	86.8
	1977	297	54.80	81,177,093	43.2	64,393,848	79.3	16,783,245	20.7
Lok Dal	1980	41	7.81	18,560,976	9.4	6,711,544	36.2	11,849,432	63.8
CPI	1980	11	2.10	5,122,172	2.6	2,059,729	40.2	3,062,443	59.8
	1977	7	1.29	5,201,832	2.8	1,741,592	33.5	3,460,240	66.5
CPI(M)	1980	35	6.67	11,867,796	6.0	9,072,210	76.4	2,795,586	23.6
	1977	22	4.06	8,113,659	4.3	4,410,558	54.4	3,703,101	45.6
Other[b]	1980	35	6.67	16,691,782	8.5	8,117,997	48.6	8,573,785	51.4
	1977	52	9.59	18,557,612	9.5	12,289,539	66.2	6,268,073	33.8
Independents	1980	8	1.52	12,866,145	6.5	1,120,211	8.7	11,745,934	91.3
	1977	9	1.66	10,714,144	5.7	1,159,592	10.8	9,554,552	89.2

[a] In 1977 Janata included Lok Dal.
[b] Akali, DMK, AIADMK and other.
SOURCE: See table 4.

TABLE 8
Seats Contested, Won, and Lost, by Party, 1977 and 1980

Party	Seats Contested		Seats Won				Share of Seats in Lok Sabha		Seats Lost			
			Number		Percent				Number		Percent	
	1977	1980	1977	1980	1977	1980	1977	1980	1977	1980	1977	1980
Congress(I)	490	489	155	351	31.6	71.8	28.6	66.9	335	138	68.4	28.2
Congress(U)	—	212	—	13	—	6.1	—	2.5	—	199	—	93.9
Janata	424	431	298	31	70.1	7.2	54.8	5.9	127	400	30.0	92.8
Lok Dal	—	292	—	41	—	14.0	—	7.8	—	251	—	86.0
CPI	90	48	7	11	7.8	22.9	1.3	2.1	83	37	92.2	77.1
CPI(M)	53	62	22	35	41.5	56.5	4.1	6.7	31	27	58.5	43.6
Akali Dal	9	7	9	1	100.0	14.3	1.7	0.2	0	6	0.0	85.7
DMK	19	16	1	16	5.3	100.0	0.2	3.1	18	0	94.7	0.0
AIADMK	21	24	19	2	90.5	8.3	3.5	0.4	2	22	9.5	91.7
Independents	1,228	2,830	9	8	0.3	0.7	1.7	1.5	1,219	2,822	99.3	99.7
Others	105	200	23	16	21.9	8.0	4.2	3.1	82	184	78.1	92.0
India	2,439	4,611	542	525[a]	22.2	11.4	100.0	100.0	1,897	4,086	77.8	88.6

NOTE: Percentages may not add to totals because of rounding.

Dash (—): Not applicable.

[a] Elections not held in twelve of the fourteen constituencies in Assam.

SOURCE: See table 4.

TABLE 9

Distribution of Seats by State, Parliamentary Elections of 1980

State	Seats	Congress (I)	Janata	Lok Dal	Congress (U)	CPI	CPI (M)	Others	Independent
Andhra Pradesh	42	41	0	0	1	0	0	0	0
Assam[a]	2	2	0	0	0	0	0	0	0
Bihar	54	30	8	5	4	4	0	0	3
Gujarat	26	25	1	0	0	0	0	0	0
Haryana	10	5	1	4	0	0	0	0	0
Himachal Pradesh	3	3	0	0	0	0	0	0	0
Jammu and Kashmir	5	1	0	0	1	0	0	3	0
Karnataka	28	27	1	0	0	0	0	0	0
Kerala	20	5	0	0	3	2	6	3	1
Madhya Pradesh	40	35	4	0	0	0	0	0	1
Maharashtra	48	39	8	0	1	0	0	0	0
Manipur	2	1	0	0	0	1	0	0	0
Meghalaya	1	1	0	0	0	0	0	0	0
Nagaland	1	0	0	0	0	0	0	0	1
Orissa	20	19	0	1	0	0	0	0	0
Punjab	13	12	0	0	0	0	0	1	0
Rajasthan	25	18	4	2	1	0	0	0	0
Sikkim	1	0	0	0	0	0	0	1	0
Tamil Nadu	39	20	0	0	0	0	0	19	0
Tripura	2	0	0	0	0	0	2	0	0
Uttar Pradesh	85	51	3	29	0	1	0	0	1
West Bengal	41	4	0	0	0	3	27	7	0
Andaman and Nicobar Islands	1	1	0	0	0	0	0	0	0
Arunachal Pradesh	2	2	0	0	0	0	0	0	0
Chandigarh	1	1	0	0	0	0	0	0	0
Dadra and Nagar Haveli	1	1	0	0	0	0	0	0	0
Delhi	7	6	1	0	1	0	0	0	0
Goa, Daman, and Diu	2	0	0	0	0	0	0	1	0
Lakshadweep	1	0	0	0	1	0	0	0	0
Mizoram	1	0	0	0	0	0	0	0	1
Pondicherry	1	1	0	0	0	0	0	0	0
Total	525	351	31	41	13	11	35	35	8

[a] Elections not held in twelve of the fourteen constituencies in Assam.

Source: See table 4.

TABLE 10
Votes Polled by the Major Parties, 1967–1980

Year	Congress	Janata[a]	CPI and CPI(M)	DMK and AIADMK	Total Valid Votes
1967	59,400,000	38,001,000	13,700,000	5,524,000	145,860,000
1971	64,040,000	40,650,000	14,445,000	5,622,000	146,602,000
1977	64,750,000	81,177,000	13,314,000	8,803,000	188,514,000
1980	83,938,000	55,819,000	16,989,000	8,910,000	196,760,000

[a] Including Lok Dal in 1980 and its constituent elements for elections before 1977.
SOURCE: See tables 4 and 18.

TABLE 11
Congress Party Vote, by State, 1962–1980
(percent)

State	1962	1967	1971	1977	1980
Andhra Pradesh	48.0	46.9	55.8	57.4	56.2
Assam	45.2	45.8	57.0	50.6	[a]
Bihar	43.9	34.8	40.1	22.9	36.4
Gujarat	49.5	46.9	45.3	46.9	54.8
Haryana	40.3	44.1	52.6	18.0	29.3
Himachal Pradesh	56.7	48.3	77.0	38.6	50.7
Jammu and Kashmir	—	50.5	53.9	16.4	19.3
Karnataka	52.7	49.0	70.8	56.8	56.3
Kerala	34.3	36.2	19.8	29.1	26.3
Madhya Pradesh	39.6	40.8	45.5	32.5	46.5
Maharashtra	30.3	48.3	63.5	47.0	53.3
Manipur	26.0	32.7	30.1	45.3	23.0
Nagaland	—	—	39.5	48.3	—
Orissa	55.5	33.3	38.4	38.2	55.7
Punjab	41.9	37.3	45.9	34.9	52.5
Rajasthan	37.6	39.9	50.3	30.6	42.7
Tamil Nadu	47.4	41.7	12.5	22.3	31.6
Tripura	31.9	58.3	36.3	39.7	22.6
Uttar Pradesh	38.2	33.7	48.0	25.0	35.9
West Bengal	46.8	39.8	27.7	29.4	36.5
Delhi	40.0	38.8	64.5	30.2	50.4
India	44.7	40.7	43.6	34.5	42.7

Dash (—): Congress did not run.
[a] Elections were not held in twelve of the fourteen constituencies.
SOURCE: See tables 4 and 18.

153

TABLE 12

SHIFT IN CONGRESS VOTE, BY STATE, 1967–1980
(percentage points)

State	1967–1971	1971–1977	1977–1980
Andhra Pradesh	+8.9	+1.6	−1.2
Assam	+11.2	−6.4	[a]
Bihar	+5.3	−17.2	+13.5
Gujarat	−1.6	+1.6	+7.9
Haryana	+8.5	−34.6	+11.3
Himachal Pradesh	+28.7	−38.7	+12.1
Jammu and Kashmir	+3.4	−37.5	+2.9
Karnataka	+21.8	−14.0	−0.6
Kerala	−16.4	+9.3	−2.8
Madhya Pradesh	+4.7	−13.0	+14.0
Maharashtra	+15.2	−16.5	+6.3
Manipur	−2.6	+15.2	−22.3
Nagaland	—	+8.8	—
Orissa	+5.1	−0.2	+17.5
Punjab	+8.6	−11.0	+17.6
Rajasthan	+10.4	−19.7	+12.1
Tamil Nadu	−29.2	+9.8	+9.3
Tripura	−22.0	+3.4	−17.1
Uttar Pradesh	+14.3	−23.0	+10.9
West Bengal	−12.1	+1.7	+7.1
Delhi	+25.7	−34.3	+20.2
India	+2.9	−9.1	+8.2

Dash (—): Not contested by Congress.

[a] Elections not held in twelve of the fourteen constituencies.

SOURCE: See table 4.

TABLE 13
"Janata Party" Vote, by State, 1971, 1977, and 1980
(percent)

State	1971[a]	1977[b]	1980 Janata	1980 Lok Dal	1980 Total
Andhra Pradesh	12.1	32.3	15.3	6.4	21.7
Assam	11.6	35.8	c	c	c
Bihar	34.0	65.0	23.6	16.6	40.2
Gujarat	48.6	49.5	36.9	2.9	39.8
Haryana	25.6	70.4	28.1	33.5	61.6
Himachal Pradesh	17.7	57.2	36.2	5.6	41.8
Jammu and Kashmir	13.1	8.2	9.0	—	9.0
Karnataka	24.2	39.8	22.9	1.2	24.1
Kerala	6.1	7.2	6.7	—	6.7
Madhya Pradesh	38.7	57.9	31.7	7.9	34.6
Maharashtra	12.5	31.4	20.6	1.1	21.6
Manipur	14.2	8.6	17.6	—	17.6
Nagaland	—	—	—	—	—
Orissa	50.6	51.8	14.4	19.5	33.9
Punjab	9.9	12.5	10.0	2.2	12.2
Rajasthan	31.3	65.2	30.4	12.1	42.5
Tamil Nadu	40.7	16.1	8.0	0.5	8.5
Tripura	0.5	17.8	—	—	—
Uttar Pradesh	38.0	68.1	22.6	29.0	51.6
West Bengal	12.9	21.5	4.6	0.5	5.1
Delhi	31.4	68.2	37.9	6.9	44.8
India	27.7	43.2	18.9	9.4	28.3

Dash (—): Janata did not run.

[a] Combined vote for Congress (0), Jana Sangh, the Samyutka Socialist party, Bharatiya Kranti Dal, the Praja Socialist party, the Utkal Congress, the Swatantra party, and the Bangla Congress.

[b] Combined vote for Janata party, Congress for Democracy, and in Tamil Nadu the Congress (0).

[c] Elections not held in twelve of the fourteen constituencies.

Source: See table 4.

TABLE 14

COMMUNIST PARTY OF INDIA (MARXIST) VOTE, BY STATE,
1971, 1977, AND 1980
(percent)

State	1971	1977	1980
Andhra Pradesh	2.8	4.7	3.6
Assam	1.4	2.9	a
Kerala	26.2	20.3	19.1
Maharashtra	0.5	3.6	1.4
Orissa	1.1	2.0	0.9
Punjab	2.2	4.9	2.5
Tamil Nadu	1.6	1.6	3.2
Tripura	43.5	34.1	47.5
West Bengal	34.5	26.2	39.4
India	5.2	4.3	6.0

NOTE: All the states where the Communist party of India (Marxist) ran candidates in 1971 and 1977 are shown. In 1980 the CPI(M) also put up three candidates in Bihar (winning 0.9 percent) and one candidate in each of the following states: Karnataka, Madhya Pradesh, Rajasthan, and Uttar Pradesh. Tripura, where the CPI(M) won its highest percentage in all three elections, has only two seats in Parliament. For distribution of CPI(M) seats in Parliament in 1980, see table 9.

a Elections not held in twelve of the fourteen constituencies.

SOURCE: See table 4.

TABLE 15

COMMUNIST PARTY OF INDIA VOTE, BY STATE, 1971, 1977, AND 1980
(percent)

State	1971	1977	1980
Andhra Pradesh	5.9	2.7	3.7
Assam	5.6	1.4	a
Bihar	9.9	5.6	7.3
Himachal Pradesh	1.7	1.4	2.5
Kerala	9.1	10.4	6.5
Madhya Pradesh	1.1	0.5	0.6
Maharashtra	1.7	0.7	0.5
Manipur	15.0	11.5	9.7
Orissa	4.3	3.2	0.9
Punjab	6.2	1.7	1.3
Tamil Nadu	5.4	4.6	3.6
Tripura	6.8	2.2	0.0
Uttar Pradesh	4.4	1.1	1.6
West Bengal	10.3	6.5	4.4
India	4.8	2.8	2.6

NOTE: All of the states in which the Communist party of India ran candidates in 1971 or 1977 are shown. In 1980, the CPI also put up one candidate in each of the following states: Karnataka, Rajasthan, Gujarat, and Delhi. For the distribution of CPI seats in Parliament in 1980, see table 9.

a Elections not held in twelve of the fourteen constituencies.

SOURCE: See table 4.

TABLE 16

CONGRESS PARTY RESULTS IN SIX PARLIAMENTARY ELECTIONS, 1952–1980

Election	Percent of Vote	Seats	
		Number	Percent
1952	45.0	357	73
1957	47.8	359	73
1962	44.7	358	73
1967	40.7	283	54
1971	43.7	352	68
1977	34.5	153	28
1980	42.7	351	67

SOURCE: See tables 4 and 18.

TABLE 17

Congress Vote, 1971, 1977, and 1980, in States Where Congress Won a Majority in 1980
(percent)

State	1971	1977	1980
Andhra Pradesh	55.8	57.4	56.2
Gujarat	45.3	46.9	54.8
Himachal Pradesh	77.0	38.6	50.7
Karnataka	70.8	56.8	56.3
Maharashtra	63.5	47.0	53.3
Orissa	38.4	38.2	55.7
Punjab	45.9	35.9	52.5
Delhi	64.5	30.2	50.4

Source: See table 4.

TABLE 18

Congress Vote and Voter Turnout in Uttar Pradesh, 1957–1980
(percent and percentage points)

	1957	1962	1971	1977	1980
Congress vote	46.3	38.2	48.0	25.0	35.9
Turnout	47.8	51.8	46.1	56.5	50.0
Change in Congress vote	—	−4.5	+14.3	−23.0	+10.9
Change in Turnout	—	+3.4	−5.7	+10.4	−6.5

Source: Same as table 4 plus *Report on the Second General Election to the House of the People in India, 1957*, 2 vols., Election Commission of India, New Delhi, 1958; *Report on the Third General Election to the House of the People in India, 1962*, 2 vols., Election Commission of India, New Delhi, 1966; and *Report of the Fourth General Election to the House of the People in India, 1967*, 2 vols., Election Commission of India, New Delhi, 1968.

TABLE 19

PERFORMANCE OF MRS. GANDHI'S CONGRESS PARTY, BY REGION, 1967–1980

(percent)

	1967	1971	1977	1980
Hindi belt				
Bihar	34.8	40.1	22.9	36.4
Delhi	38.8	64.5	30.2	50.4
Haryana	44.1	52.6	18.0	29.3
Himachal Pradesh	48.3	77.0	38.6	50.7
Jammu and Kashmir	50.5	53.9	16.4	19.3
Madhya Pradesh	40.8	45.5	32.5	46.5
Punjab	37.3	45.9	34.9	52.5
Rajasthan	39.9	50.3	30.6	42.7
Uttar Pradesh	33.7	48.0	25.0	35.9
Western India				
Gujarat	46.9	45.3	46.9	54.8
Maharashtra	48.3	63.5	47.0	53.3
Northeast and Eastern India				
Assam	45.8	57.0	50.6	[a]
Manipur	32.7	30.1	45.3	23.0
Orissa	33.3	38.4	38.2	55.7
Tripura	58.3	36.3	39.7	22.6
West Bengal	39.8	27.7	29.4	36.5
South India				
Andhra Pradesh	46.9	55.8	57.4	56.2
Karnataka	49.0	70.8	56.8	56.3
Tamil Nadu	41.7	12.5	22.3	31.6
Kerala	36.2	19.8	29.1	26.3

[a] Elections not held in twelve of fourteen constituencies.

SOURCE: See tables 4 and 18.

TABLE 20

Effects of the Janata Split in the Hindi-Speaking States, 1980

State	Congress			Janata		Total Seats in State
	Seats won	Seats won by more votes than Janata & Lok Dal	Seats Congress would have lost without split	Seats won	Seats Janata would have won without split	
Bihar	30	23	7	13	20	54
Haryana	5	4	1	5	6	10
Madhya Pradesh	35	29	6	4	10	40
Rajasthan	18	14	4	6	10	25
Uttar Pradesh	51	16	35	32	67	85
Delhi	6	5	1	1	2	7
Total	145	91	54	61	115	221

Source: See table 4.

TABLE 21

Distribution of the Vote in the Hindi-Speaking States, 1971–1980
(percent)

State	Congress			Janata[a]			Lok Dal 1980	Lok Dal and Janata 1980
	1971	1977	1980	1971	1977	1980		
Bihar	40.1	22.9	36.4	34.0	64.0	23.6	16.6	40.2
Haryana	52.6	18.0	29.3	25.6	70.4	28.14	33.5	61.6
Madhya Pradesh	45.6	32.5	46.5	38.7	57.9	31.7	7.9	39.8
Rajasthan	50.4	30.6	42.7	31.3	65.2	30.4	12.1	42.5
Uttar Pradesh	48.6	25.0	35.9	38.0	68.1	22.6	29.0	51.7
Delhi	64.4	30.2	50.4	31.4	68.2	37.9	6.9	44.8
All Hindi states	46.4	25.9	39.1	35.4	65.4	25.9	20.1	46.0

[a] For the parties included under Janata in 1971, see table 6.
SOURCE: See table 4.

TABLE 22

Distribution of Seats in the Hindi-Speaking States, 1971–1980

State	Congress			Janata[a]			Lok Dal 1980
	1971	1977	1980	1971	1977	1980	
Bihar (54)	39	0	30	7	52	8	5
Haryana (10)	7	0	5	1	10	1	4
Madhya Pradesh (40)	21	1	35	12	37	4	0
Rajasthan (25)	14	1	18	7	24	4	2
Uttar Pradesh (85)	73	0	51	6	85	3	29
Delhi (7)	7	0	6	0	7	1	0
Total	161	2	145	33	215	21	40

NOTE: Number of constituencies in state in parentheses.
[a] For list of parties included under Janata for 1971, see table 6.
SOURCE: See table 4.

TABLE 23

Voter Turnout in Northeastern India, 1971–1980

(percent)

State	1971	1977	1980
Assam	50.7	54.9	53.4[a]
West Bengal	61.9	60.2	70.9
Meghalaya	[b]	49.9	51.0
Tripura	60.8	70.1	80.0
Mizoram	[b]	49.9	56.1
Arunachal Pradesh	[b]	56.3	68.6
Nagaland	53.8	52.8	64.4
Manipur	48.9	60.2	81.9

[a] Two constituencies only.

[b] No parliamentary elections in 1971.

SOURCE: See table 4.

TABLE 24

Vote for Regional Parties and Independents in Northeastern India, 1971–1980

(percent)

State	1971		1977		1980	
	Vote	Party	Vote	Party	Vote	Party
Meghalaya	—	—	64.1	Ind.	7.1	Ind.
					11.8	HLC
Nagaland	60.5	UFN	51.7	UDF	100.0	Ind.
	39.5	NNO				
Tripura	12.9	Ind.	6.1	TUS	14.9	Ind.
					13.5	TUS
Manipur	29.0	Ind.	11.2	Ind.	19.5	Ind.
	12.0	MPP	23.5	MPP	6.9	MPP
Arunachal Pradesh	—	—	43.7	Ind.	4.8	Ind.
					40.2	PPA
Mizoram	—	—	62.9	Ind.	100.0	Ind.

Dash (—): No parliamentary elections in 1971.

NOTE: Ind. = Independent; HLC = All Party Hill Leaders' Conference; UFN = United Front of Nagaland; NNO = Nagaland Nationalist Organization; UDF = United Democratic Front; TUS = Tripura Upajati Juba Samiti; MPP = Manipur People's party; PPA = People's party of Arunachal Pradesh.

SOURCE: See table 4.

TABLE 25

Vote for Congress, CPI(M), and Janata in Northeastern India, 1971–1980

(percent)

State	Congress 1971	Congress 1977	Congress 1980	CPI(M) 1971	CPI(M) 1977	CPI(M) 1980	Janata 1971	Janata 1977	Janata 1980
Assam	57.0	50.6	[a]	1.4	2.9	[a]	11.6[b]	35.8[c]	[a]
West Bengal	27.7	29.4	36.5	34.5	26.2	39.4[d]	12.9	21.5	4.6
Meghalaya	—	57.6	74.3	—	—	—	—	—	—
Tripura	36.3	39.7	22.6	43.5	34.1	47.5	0.5	17.8	—
Mizoram	—	37.1	—	—	—	—	—	—	—
Arunachal Pradesh	—	41.3	41.9	—	—	—	—	—	—
Nagaland	39.5	48.3	—	—	—	—	—	—	—
Manipur	30.1	45.3	23.0	—	—	—	14.2	8.6	17.6

Dash (—): Party did not run.

[a] No election in twelve of fourteen constituencies.

[b] For the parties included under Janata in 1971, see table 6.

[c] Janata plus Congress for Democracy.

[d] The CPI(M) was part of the left front, which won a total of 53.7 percent in 1980.

Source: See table 4.

TABLE 26

Election Results in West Bengal, 1977 and 1980

Party	Percent of Votes 1977	Percent of Votes 1980	Seats 1977	Seats 1980
Congress	29.4	36.5	3	4
Janata	21.5	4.6	15	0
CPI	6.5	4.4	0	3
CPI(M)[a]	26.2	39.4	16	27
Other parties	9.8	13.5[b]	6	7
Independents	6.8	1.6	1	0
Total	100.0	100.0	41	41

Note: Percentages may not add to totals because of rounding.

[a] The CPI(M) led a Left Front in both 1977 and 1980. In 1977 the Left Front won 23 seats; in 1980, when it included the CPI and several other small parties as well as the CPI(M), it won 37 seats with 53.7 percent of the vote.

[b] Includes Congress (U), 1.2 percent; Lok Dal, 0.5 percent; and members of the Left Front, 9.9 percent.

Source: See table 4.

TABLE 27
Election Results in Tamil Nadu, 1977 and 1980

Party	Percent of Votes		Seats	
	1977	1980	1977	1980
Congress (I)	22.3	31.6	14	20
Janata	17.7	8.0	3	0
DMK	18.1	23.0	1	16
AIADMK	30.6	25.4	18	2
CPI	4.6	3.6	3	0
CPI(M)	1.6	3.2	0	0
Other parties and independents	5.2	5.2	0	1
Total	100.0	100.0	39	39

Source: See table 4.

TABLE 28

ELECTION RESULTS IN KERALA, 1977 AND 1980

Party	Percent of Votes	Seats
1977		
United Front		
Congress	29.1	11
CPI	10.4	4
Kerala Congress	5.4	2
Muslim League	5.9	2
Revolutionary Socialist party	3.0	1
Total	53.8	20
Opposition Front		
CPI(M)	20.3	0
Kerala Congress (Pillai Group)	5.8	0
Janata	7.2	0
Opposition Muslim League	3.5	0
Total	36.8	0
Other parties and independents	9.4	0
1980		
United Democratic Front		
Congress (I)	26.3	5
Janata	6.7	0
Other parties[a]	15.4	3
Total	48.4	8
Left Front		
CPI(M)	19.1	6
CPI	6.5	2
Congress (U)	15.8	3
Other parties[b]	10.2	1
Total	51.6	12

[a] Muslim League (2 seats), Kerala Congress Joseph Group (1 seat), National Democratic party.

[b] Kerala Congress Mani Group (1 seat), Revolutionary Socialist party, Muslim League.

SOURCE: See table 4.

TABLE 29

Voter Turnout and Major Party Vote in Large Urban Constituencies, 1977 and 1980
(percent)

City[a]	Turnout		Congress (I)		Janata		Other[b]		Party
	1977	1980	1977	1980	1977	1980	1977	1980	
Calcutta (5)	58.9	62.2	28.9	41.3	35.9	6.5	25.7	43.7	CPI(M)
Bombay (6)	61.2	52.7	36.5	39.2	49.9	40.2	—	—	—
Madras (3)	56.0	69.1	17.3	21.2	18.6	11.9	34.2	37.9	DMK
							28.1	26.2	AIADMK
Delhi (7)	71.3	64.9	30.2	50.4	68.2	37.9	—	—	—
Hyderabad (2)	57.3	53.5	47.3	46.8	36.3	38.8	—	—	—
Ahmadabad (2)	64.8	58.4	46.1	57.6	52.8	39.1	—	—	—
Bangalore (2)	62.3	51.8	48.3	49.5	48.5	36.2	—	—	—
Kanpur	58.4	51.3	25.1	45.5	71.0	24.5	—	—	—

Poona	63.0	58.0	42.9	50.8	55.7	44.0	—	—	—
Nagpur	64.4	61.7	44.6	54.1	—	—	33.8	26.3	RPK[c]
Lucknow	54.2	38.2	23.2	47.7	73.0	35.9	—	43.3	CPI
Coimbatore	62.0	66.1	—	—	47.9	—	52.1	54.3	DMK
Madurai	64.3	67.7	62.1	55.6	—	44.6	34.2	42.4	CPI(M)
Jaipur	60.0	53.1	17.0	43.4	70.9	30.0	—	29.6	Lok Dal
Agra	65.8	54.0	26.5	34.9	70.3	23.5	—	29.8	Lok Dal
Varanasi	55.8	53.7	17.4	36.9	66.2	35.9	—	—	—
Indore	64.7	61.0	39.1	51.8	49.6	35.9	—	—	—
Jabalpur	58.1	49.6	36.0	53.0	59.1	29.2	—	—	—
Allahabad	54.2	48.1	30.5	45.8	57.7	17.2	—	23.9	Lok Dal

Dash (—): Not applicable.

a Number of constituencies in parentheses.

b Parties receiving more than 20 percent of the state vote.

c Republican party.

SOURCE: See table 4.

TABLE 30

Congress Vote in Urban Constituencies and Surrounding States, 1980
(percent)

| State[a] | Congress Vote | | |
	Average in urban constituencies	Statewide	Difference
Andhra Pradesh (3)	46.7	56.2	−9.5
Bihar (2)	22.4	36.4	−14.0
Gujarat (4)	56.0	54.8	+1.2
Karnataka (3)	49.7	56.3	−6.6
Madhya Pradesh (3)	47.3	46.5	+0.8
Maharashtra (9)	43.7	53.3	−9.6
Punjab (3)	54.8	52.5	+2.3
Rajasthan (3)	47.5	42.7	+4.8
Tamil Nadu (4)	29.8	31.6	−1.8
Uttar Pradesh (9)	39.5	35.9	+3.6
West Bengal (6)	41.3	36.5	+4.8
India (49)	43.3	42.7 (national)	+0.6

[a] Includes states where Congress contested two or more urban constituencies. Number of urban constituencies in parentheses.

Source: See table 4.

TABLE 31

Janata Vote in Urban Constituencies and Surrounding States, 1980

(percent)

| | Janata Vote | | |
State[a]	Average in urban constituencies	Statewide	Difference
Andhra Pradesh (3)	35.0	15.3	+19.7
Bihar (2)	32.1	23.6	+8.5
Gujarat (4)	29.1	36.9	−7.8
Karnataka (3)	36.4	22.9	+13.5
Madhya Pradesh (3)	36.7	31.7	+5.0
Maharashtra (9)	38.9	20.6	+18.3
Punjab (3)	23.5	10.0	+13.5
Uttar Pradesh (6)	24.7	22.6	+2.1
Rajasthan (3)	36.7	30.4	+6.3
India (36)	29.9	18.9 (national)	+11.0

[a] Includes states where Janata contested two or more urban constituencies and its vote was not negligible. Number of urban constituencies in parentheses.
SOURCE: See table 4.

TABLE 32
Distribution of Seats in India's Largest Cities, 1967–1980

Party	Calcutta '67	'71	'77	'80	Bombay '67	'71	'77	'80	Madras '67	'71	'77	'80
Congress	2	2	0	1	4	6	0	2	0	0	1	1
"Janata party"[a]	0	0	3	0	1	0	4	4	0	0	1	0
CPI	1	1	0	0	1	0	0	0	0	0	0	0
CPI(M)	2	2	2	4	0	0	1	0	0	0	0	0
Other parties	0	0	0	0	0	0	1	0	2	2	1	2
Independents	0	0	0	0	0	0	0	0	0	0	0	0

Party	Delhi '67	'71	'77	'80	Hyderabad '67	'71	'77	'80	Ahmadabad '67	'71	'77	'80
Congress	1	7	0	6	2	0	2	2	1	1	1	2
"Janata party"	6	0	7	1	0	0	0	0	0	1	1	0
CPI	0	0	0	0	0	0	0	0	0	0	0	0
CPI(M)	0	0	0	0	0	0	0	0	0	0	0	0
Other parties	0	0	0	0	0	2	0	0	0	0	0	0
Independents	0	0	0	0	0	0	0	0	1	0	0	0

Party	Bangalore '67	'71	'77	'80	Kanpur '67	'71	'77	'80	Poona '67	'71	'77	'80
Congress	2	2	1	1	0	0	0	1	0	1	0	1
"Janata party"	0	0	1	1	0	0	1	0	1	0	1	0
CPI	0	0	0	0	0	0	0	0	0	0	0	0
CPI(M)	0	0	0	0	0	0	0	0	0	0	0	0
Other parties	0	0	0	0	0	0	0	0	0	0	0	0
Independents	0	0	0	0	1	1	0	0	0	0	0	0

Party	Nagpur '67	'71	'77	'80	Lucknow '67	'71	'77	'80	Coimbatore '67	'71	'77	'80
Congress	1	0	1	1	0	1	0	1	0	0	0	0
"Janata party"	0	0	0	0	0	0	1	0	0	0	0	0
CPI	0	0	0	0	0	0	0	0	1	1	1	0
CPI(M)	0	0	0	0	0	0	0	0	0	0	0	0
Other parties	0	1	0	0	0	0	0	0	0	0	0	1
Independents	0	0	0	0	1	0	0	0	0	0	0	0

(Table continues)

TABLE 32 (continued)

	Madurai				Jaipur				Agra			
	'67	'71	'77	'80	'67	'71	'77	'80	'67	'71	'77	'80
Congress	0	1	1	1	0	0	0	0	1	1	0	1
"Janata party"	0	0	0	0	1	1	1	1	0	0	1	0
CPI	1	0	0	0	0	0	0	0	0	0	0	0
CPI(M)	0	0	0	0	0	0	0	0	0	0	0	0
Other parties	0	0	0	0	0	0	0	0	0	0	0	0
Independents	0	0	0	0	0	0	0	0	0	0	0	0

	Varanasi				Indore				Jabalpur			
	'67	'71	'77	'80	'67	'71	'77	'80	'67	'71	'77	'80
Congress	0	1	0	1	1	1	0	1	1	1	0	1
"Janata party"	0	0	1	0	0	0	1	0	0	0	1	0
CPI	1	0	0	0	0	0	0	0	0	0	0	0
CPI(M)	0	0	0	0	0	0	0	0	0	0	0	0
Other parties	0	0	0	0	0	0	0	0	0	0	0	0
Independents	0	0	0	0	0	0	0	0	0	0	0	0

	Allahabad				Total, All Nineteen Cities			
	'67	'71	'77	'80	'67	'71	'77	'80
Congress	1	1	0	1	17	26	7	25
"Janata party"	0	0	1	0	9	2	25	7
CPI	0	0	0	0	5	2	1	0
CPI(M)	0	0	0	0	2	2	3	4
Other parties	0	0	0	0	2	5	2	3
Independents	0	0	0	0	3	1	1	0
					38	38	39	39

NOTE: Included are cities with populations exceeding half a million at the 1971 census.

[a] For a list of parties included under Janata for 1967 and 1971, see table 6.

SOURCE: See tables 4 and 18.

TABLE 33
Voter Turnout in Muslim Constituencies, 1977 and 1980

State	1977	1980
Andhra Pradesh (5)	57.2	55.2
Bihar (4)	56.8	51.3
Jammu and Kashmir (4)	54.9	59.1
Kerala (8)	79.0	64.3
Uttar Pradesh (23)	61.0	52.6
West Bengal (24)	62.0	71.2

NOTE: Muslim constituencies are those whose populations are 20 percent or more Muslim. The number of Muslim constituencies is indicated in parentheses.
SOURCE: See table 4.

TABLE 34
Seats Won in Muslim Constituencies, 1977 and 1980

Party	1977	1980
Congress	20	29
Janata	39	0
Lok Dal	—	12
Congress(U)	—	4
CPI	1	1
CPI(M)	11	19
Independent	3	0
Other parties	7	9
Total	81	74[a]

Dash (—): Not applicable.
NOTE: Muslim constituencies are those whose populations are 20 percent or more Muslim.

[a] Elections were not held in twelve of the fourteen constituencies in Assam, where there are substantial numbers of Muslims. The exclusion of these constituencies is one reason for the lower total in 1980.
SOURCE: See table 4.

TABLE 35
Congress Vote in Muslim Constituencies, 1977 and 1980
(percent)

State	Congress Vote in "Muslim" Constituencies		Congress Vote in State		Difference	
	1977	1980	1977	1980	1977	1980
Andhra Pradesh (5)	55.8	52.4	57.4	56.2	−1.6	−3.8
Bihar (4)	30.5	48.7	22.9	36.4	+7.6	+12.3
Uttar Pradesh (23)	25.9	34.4	25.0	35.9	+0.9	−1.5
West Bengal (24)	29.1	37.6	29.4	36.5	−0.3	+1.1

NOTE: Muslim constituencies are those whose populations are 20 percent or more Muslim. The number of Muslim constituencies is indicated in parentheses. There are eight Muslim constituencies in Kerala, but comparisons from one election to another are precluded because Congress candidates did not stand in all the constituencies or in the same constituencies in each election. Jammu and Kashmir are not included because Congress ran in only one Muslim constituency in 1980.
SOURCE: See table 4.

TABLE 36
Janata and Lok Dal Vote in Muslim Constituencies, 1977 and 1980
(percent)

State	Janata		Lok Dal 1980
	1977	1980	
Andhra Pradesh			
State	32.3	15.3	6.4
Muslim constituencies (2)	33.1	20.8	0
Bihar			
State	65.0	23.6	16.6
Muslim constituencies (4)	62.3	21.6	23.4
Uttar Pradesh			
State	68.1	22.6	29.0
Muslim constituencies (23)	66.2	22.1	35.3

NOTE: Muslim constituencies are those whose populations are 20 percent or more Muslim. The number of Muslim constituencies contested by Janata and Lok Dal is indicated in parentheses.
SOURCE: See table 4.

TABLE 37

VOTER TURNOUT IN SCHEDULED-CASTE CONSTITUENCIES AND STATES,
1977 AND 1980
(percent)

State	1977		1980	
	Scheduled-caste constituencies	State	Scheduled-caste constituencies	State
Andhra Pradesh (6)	59.9	62.5	50.6	57.0
Bihar (8)	63.3	60.8	53.0	51.7
Delhi (1)	69.0	71.3	65.7	64.9
Gujarat (2)	52.3	59.2	44.9	55.4
Haryana (2)	72.9	73.3	64.6	64.8
Himachal Pradesh (1)	58.7	59.2	51.9	59.7
Karnataka (4)	59.1	63.2	53.3	57.9
Kerala (2)	79.1	79.2	55.9	62.2
Madhya Pradesh (5)	55.6	54.9	46.5	51.8
Maharashtra (3)	54.0	60.3	53.0	56.8
Orissa (3)	46.4	44.3	50.1	47.2
Punjab (3)	73.4	70.1	63.2	62.7
Rajasthan (4)	55.1	56.9	50.5	54.7
Uttar Pradesh (18)	52.8	56.4	47.1	50.0
West Bengal (8)	60.3	60.2	73.0	70.9

NOTE: The number of scheduled-caste constituencies is indicated in parentheses.
SOURCE: See table 4.

TABLE 38

Valid Votes Cast in Scheduled-Caste and Nonreserved Constituencies, 1980

	Scheduled-Caste Votes		Other Votes		Total Valid Votes	
	Millions	Percent	Millions	Percent	Millions	Percent
Reserved constituencies	6.7	22.6	22.9	77.4	29.6	100.0
Nonreserved constituencies	22.1	13.2	145.3	86.8	167.4	100.0
India	28.8	14.6	168.2	85.4	196.8	100.0

Note: Numbers and percentages of scheduled-caste votes are based on a sample of constituencies in each of the states.
Source: See table 4.

TABLE 39

Seats Won in Scheduled-Caste Constituencies, 1971, 1977, and 1980

	1971		1977		1980	
Party	Seats won	Percent of scheduled-caste seats	Seats won	Percent of scheduled-caste seats	Seats won	Percent of scheduled-caste seats
Congress	50	64	16	20	50	63
Janata party	8	10	45	58	4	5
Lok Dal					10	13
CPI	3	4	2	3	1	1
CPI(M)	6	8	6	8	6	8
Other parties	10	13	7	9	7	9
Independents	1	1	2	3	1	1
Total[a]	78	100	78	100	79	100

Dash (—): Party did not run.
Note: Columns may not add to totals because of rounding.

[a] Congress contested 70 scheduled-caste constituencies in 1980, 71 in 1977, and 66 in 1971; Janata contested 64 in 1980, 59 in 1977, and 109 in 1971; Lok Dal contested 43 in 1980.
Source: See table 4.

TABLE 40

CONGRESS VOTE IN SCHEDULED-CASTE CONSTITUENCIES, 1977 AND 1980
(percent)

State	1977		1980	
	Scheduled-caste constituencies	State	Scheduled-caste constituencies	State
Andhra Pradesh (6)	63.4	57.4	66.5	56.2
Bihar (8)	20.4	22.9	40.3	36.4
Delhi (1)	34.2	30.2	55.4	50.4
Gujarat (2)	37.8	46.9	55.7	37.8
Haryana (2)	27.7	18.0	35.9	29.3
Himachal Pradesh (1)	32.0	38.6	51.0	50.7
Karnataka (4)	55.3	56.8	57.4	56.3
Kerala (2)	27.3	29.1	45.9	26.3
Madhya Pradesh (5)	38.4	32.5	43.4	46.5
Maharashtra (3)	39.7	47.0	54.4	53.3
Orissa (3)	41.1	38.2	56.6	55.7
Punjab (3)	30.1	34.9	47.2	52.5
Rajasthan (4)	32.7	30.6	50.5	42.7
Uttar Pradesh (18)	22.5	25.0	33.8	35.9
West Bengal (8)	31.6	29.4	38.2	36.5
Tamil Nadu[a]	65.7	22.3	58.6	31.6

NOTE: The number of scheduled-caste constituencies is indicated in parentheses.

[a] In 1977 the Congress party contested two out of seven reserved constituencies; in 1980 it contested three out of seven.

SOURCE: See table 4.

TABLE 41
Janata and Lok Dal Vote in Scheduled-Caste Constituencies, 1977 and 1980
(percent)

| State | Janata | | Lok Dal |
	1977	1980	1980
Andhra Pradesh (6)	26.7(5)	17.1	5.1(3)
Bihar (8)	76.1	24.3	26.4(6)
Delhi (1)	64.4	39.8	2.9
Gujarat (2)	55.5	39.3	—
Haryana (2)	68.4	29.3	28.2
Himachal Pradesh (1)	64.7	37.9	10.6
Karnataka (4)	37.6	17.2	1.2
Madhya Pradesh (5)	59.1	42.0	8.2(4)
Maharashtra (3)	11.0(1)	4.7(1)	neg.(1)
Orissa (3)	55.9	9.5	27.9
Rajasthan (4)	63.3	14.9	18.8
Uttar Pradesh (18)	73.6	24.3	33.9

Dash (—): Party did not run.
neg.: Negligible.
NOTE: The number of scheduled-caste constituencies is indicated in parentheses. Except where another number is given in the body of the table, the party ran in all scheduled-caste constituencies. The table only includes states where the number of votes for Janata and Lok Dal in scheduled-caste constituencies was significant.
SOURCE: See table 4.

TABLE 42
Voter Turnout in Scheduled-Tribe Constituencies, 1977 and 1980
(percent)

State	1977	1980
Andhra Pradesh (2)	47.9	51.2
Bihar (5)	39.2	38.4
Gujarat (4)	54.9	53.7
Madhya Pradesh (8)	47.8	45.0
Maharashtra (3)	54.1	46.8
Orissa (4)	33.1	33.7
Rajasthan (3)	54.9	53.9
West Bengal (2)	61.1	70.3

NOTE: The number of scheduled-tribe constituencies is indicated in parentheses.
SOURCE: See table 4.

TABLE 43

SEATS WON IN SCHEDULED-TRIBE CONSTITUENCIES, 1971, 1977, AND 1980

Party	1971		1977		1980	
	Number	Percent	Number	Percent	Number	Percent
Congress	26	70	13	34	29	78
Janata party	5	14	20	53	1	3
Congress(U)	—	—	—	—	2	5
CPI(M)	1	3	3	8	2	5
Other parties	2	5	1	3	1	3
Independents	3	8	1	3	2	5
Total[a]	37	100	38	100	37	100

Dash (—): Not applicable.

NOTE: Percentages may not add to totals because of rounding.

[a] Congress contested thirty-five scheduled-tribe constituencies in 1980, thirty-eight in 1977, and thirty-three in 1971; Janata contested thirty-three in 1980, thirty in 1977, and forty-five in 1971; Lok Dal contested seventeen in 1980.

SOURCE: See table 4.

TABLE 44

CONGRESS VOTE IN SCHEDULED-TRIBE CONSTITUENCIES AND STATES, 1977 AND 1980
(percent)

State	1977		1980	
	Scheduled-tribe constituencies	State	Scheduled-tribe constituencies	State
Andhra Pradesh (2)	57.2	57.4	47.8	56.2
Bihar (5)	23.7	22.9	35.6	36.4
Gujarat (4)	52.0	46.9	55.5	54.8
Madhya Pradesh (8)	34.6	32.5	52.3	46.5
Maharashtra (3)	49.7	47.0	57.8	53.3
Orissa (4)	43.6	38.2	53.6	55.7
Rajasthan (3)	21.6	30.6	51.0	42.7
West Bengal (2)	37.4	31.7	32.1	36.5

NOTE: The number of scheduled-tribe constituencies is indicated in parentheses.

SOURCE: See table 4.

TABLE 45

JANATA AND LOK DAL VOTE IN SCHEDULED-TRIBE CONSTITUENCIES,
1977 AND 1980
(percent)

State	Janata		Lok Dal 1980
	1977	1980	
Andhra Pradesh (2)	35.1	5.8	—
Bihar (5)	47.1	22.3	7.2(4)
Gujarat (4)	46.1	38.8	—
Madhya Pradesh (8)	61.3	28.1	9.3(6)
Maharashtra (3)	29.2(2)	31.5	neg.(1)
Orissa (4)[a]	49.1	18.1	19.3
Rajasthan (3)	66.4	30.3	10.4(2)

Dash (—): Party did not run.

neg.: negligible.

NOTE: The number of scheduled-tribe constituencies is indicated in parentheses. Except where another number is given in the body of the table, the party ran in all scheduled-tribe constituencies. The table includes only states where the number of votes for Janata and Lok Dal in tribal constituencies was significant.

[a] The scheduled-tribe constituency Keonjhar is excluded because no elections were held there in 1980.

SOURCE: See table 4.

TABLE 46

Congress and Its Closest Competitor, by State, Parliamentary Elections, 1980

(percent)

State	Congress(I)	Closest Competitor	
Andhra Pradesh	56.2	15.3	Janata
Bihar	36.4	23.6	Janata
Gujarat	54.8	36.9	Janata
Haryana	29.3	33.5	Lok Dal
Himachal Pradesh	50.7	36.2	Janata
Jammu and Kashmir[a]	19.3	37.1	JKNC
Karnataka	56.3	22.9	Janata
Kerala	26.3	19.1	CPI(M)
Madhya Pradesh	46.5	31.7	Janata
Maharashtra	53.3	20.6	Janata
Manipur	23.0	17.6	Janata
Orissa	55.7	19.5	Lok Dal
Punjab	52.5	23.4	Akali Dal
Rajasthan	42.7	30.4	Janata
Tamil Nadu	31.6	25.4	AIADMK
Tripura	22.6	47.5	CPI(M)
Uttar Pradesh	35.9	29.0	Lok Dal
West Bengal	36.5	39.4	CPI(M)

[a] Srinigar and Ladakh are not included because the Jammu and Kashmir National Conference (JKNC) stood uncontested in Srinigar and elections were not held in Ladakh during January 1980.

SOURCE: See table 4.

TABLE 47

STATE ASSEMBLY ELECTION RESULTS, JUNE 1980
(seats)

State	Total	Con-gress (I)	Janata	Bharatiya Janata	Lok Dal	Con-gress (U)	CPI	CPI (M)	Other
Bihar	321	167	13	21	42	14	23	6	35
Gujarat	181	140	21	9	1	0	0	0	10
Kerala[a]	140	18	5	0	0	20	17	35	45[b]
Madhya Pradesh	320	246	2	60	1	0	2	0	9
Maharashtra	288	186	17	14	0	47	2	2	20
Orissa	146	117	3	0	13	2	4	0	7
Punjab	117	63	0	1	0	0	9	5	39[c]
Rajasthan	200	133	8	32	7	6	1	1	12
Tamil Nadu	234	30	2	0	0	0	10	11	181[d]
Uttar Pradesh	421	306	4	11	59	13	7	0	21

[a] Elections held in January 1980.

[b] Muslim League, 14 seats; All India Muslim League, 5 seats; Kerala Congress (Jacob Group), 6 seats; Kerala Congress (Manli Group), 8 seats; Revolutionary Socialist party, 6 seats.

[c] Akali Dal, 37 seats.

[d] AIADMK, 129 seats; DMK, 38 seats.

SOURCE: Figures provided by the Election Commission, Government of India, New Delhi.

TABLE 48

Congress and Its Closest Competitor, State Assembly Elections, 1980

(percent)

State	Congress(I)	Closest Competitor
Bihar	32.4	15.7 Lok Dal
Gujarat	51.1	22.6 Janata
Kerala	17.7	19.4 CPI(M)
Madhya Pradesh	47.5	30.3 Bharatiya Janata party
Maharashtra	44.5	20.8 Congress(U)
Orissa	47.9	19.6 Lok Dal
Punjab	45.2	26.9 Shrimoni Akali Dal
Rajasthan	43.0	18.6 Bharatiya Janata party
Tamil Nadu	20.5	38.7 AIADMK
Uttar Pradesh	37.6	21.6 Lok Dal

SOURCE: See table 47.

Appendix A

Bengali Election Art

During election campaigns, slogans and cartoons are drawn on walls all over India, but nowhere are they more ubiquitous or elaborate than in Calcutta. Here, political art is a business. Parties pay rent for the use of spaces, which they often reserve from one election to the next, and at the height of the campaign virtually every accessible surface in the city is covered. Most of the paintings are the work of professional artists and sign painters, who can earn several hundred rupees for a large cartoon or a fine piece of calligraphy, one of the traditional arts of Bengal.

The paintings reproduced here were photographed by the author during the 1980 campaign—although one of them, the CPI(M)'s picture marking the centennial of Stalin's birth in 1979, was not directly related to the election. Some are designed to show the voter how to cast his vote for a particular party by stamping the party's symbol on the ballot; the small crossed circle visible in some of the pictures is a simplified representation of the stamp voters use to mark their ballots. The large number of CPI(M) advertisements reflects the fact that the CPI(M) is the predominant party in West Bengal.

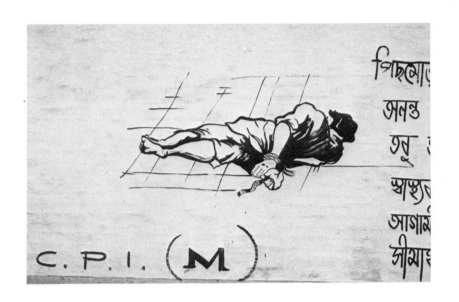

188

Appendix B

Indian Ballots, 1980

The ballots used in India's 542 single-member parliamentary constituencies differ in the number of candidates listed and the languages used, but everywhere they show the candidates' names and party symbols. The procedure is also uniform: The voter signs or places his thumb impression on the stub of the ballot. The ballot is separated from the stub and given to the voter, who goes behind a curtain to mark it with an inked rubber stamp provided by a polling officer. The voter then folds the ballot and places it in the ballot box in the presence of polling officials.

Ballots are usually printed in the regional language and English, though for state assembly elections sometimes only the regional language is used. Election symbols are allocated by the Election Commission in New Delhi.

Reproduced here are two ballots used in the 1980 parliamentary elections—one from the Andaman and Nicobar Islands, printed in Hindi and English, and one from Tura, in Meghalaya, printed in English only—and a 1980 state assembly ballot from Usilampatti, in Tamil Nadu, printed in Tamil.

मतदाता सूची भाग नं०
Electoral Roll Part No.........................

मतदाता का क्रम संख्या
Serial No. of Elector...............................

N⁰ 101752

Signature/Thumb Impression

के॰ कंठास्वामी 1. K. Kanda Swamy		रमेश मजूमदार 6. Ramesh Mazumder	
23—A & N I/HP/80/Genl.			
कन्नु चार्मी 2. Kannu Chemy		के॰ एन॰ राज 7. K. N. Raju	
N⁰ 101752 करपू स्वामी 3. Karpu Swamy		राजेन्द्र लाल साहा 8. Rajender Lall Saha	
पी॰ के॰ एस॰ प्रसाद 4. P. K. S. Prasad		सामार चौदरी 9. Samar Choudhury	
मनोरंजन भक्ता 5. Manoranjan Bhakta		अलगानि स्वामी 10. Abagiri Swamy	

191

2-Tura H.P./80-Genl.

Electoral Roll Part No......................

Serial No. of Elector......................

№ 234753

Signature/Thumb impressi

GROHONSING MARAK

№ 234753

№ 2-TURA H.P./80-GENL.

PURNO A. SANGMA

ROBIN REMA

SIBENDRA NARAYAN KOCH

138. USILAMPATTI—L.A./80-BYE

வாக்காளர் படடியல்
      பாகம் எண்..........

வாக்காளரின்
      தொடர் எண் ....

கையொப்பம்/கைப்பெருவிரல் அடையாளம்.

ஆண்டித்தேவர், எஸ்.

138. USILAMPATTI
L.A./80-BYE

கருத்தபாண்டியன், த. க.

முத்துராமலிங்கம்,
பா. க. மூ.

மொக்கமாயத்தேவர்,
எஸ்.

Index

197

AEI's *At the Polls* Studies

Australia at the Polls: The National Elections of 1975, Howard R. Penniman, ed. Chapters by Leon D. Epstein, Patrick Weller, R. F. I. Smith, D. W. Rawson, Michelle Grattan, Margaret Bridson Cribb, Paul Reynolds, C. J. Lloyd, Terence W. Beed, Owen Harries, and Colin A. Hughes. Appendixes by David Butler and Richard M. Scammon. (373 pp., $5)

The Australian National Elections of 1977, Howard R. Penniman, ed. Chapters by David Butler, David A. Kemp, Patrick Weller, Jean Holmes, Paul Reynolds, Murray Goot, Terence W. Beed, C. J. Lloyd, Ainsley Jolley, Duncan Ironmonger, and Colin A. Hughes. Appendix by Richard M. Scammon. (367 pp., $8.25)

Britain at the Polls: The Parliamentary Elections of 1974, Howard R. Penniman, ed. Chapters by Anthony King, Austin Ranney, Dick Leonard, Michael Pinto-Duschinsky, Richard Rose, and Jay G. Blumler. Appendix by Richard M. Scammon. (256 pp., $3)

Britain Says Yes: The 1975 Referendum on the Common Market, Anthony King. (153 pp., $3.75)

Britain at the Polls, 1979: A Study of the General Election, Howard R. Penniman, ed. Chapters by Austin Ranney, Anthony King, Dick Leonard, William B. Livingston, Jorgen Rasmussen, Richard Rose, Michael Pinto-Duschinsky, Monica Charlot, and Ivor Crewe. Appendixes by Shelley Pinto-Duschinsky and Richard M. Scammon. (345 pp., cloth $16.25, paper $8.25)

British Political Finance, 1830–1980, Michael Pinto-Duschinsky. (339 pp., cloth $17.95, paper $10.50)

Canada at the Polls: The General Election of 1974, Howard R. Penniman, ed. Chapters by John Meisel, William P. Irvine, Stephen Clarkson, George Perlin, Jo Surich, Michael B. Stein, Khayyam Z. Paltiel, Lawrence LeDuc, and Frederick J. Fletcher. Appendix by Richard M. Scammon. (310 pp., $4.50)

Canada at the Polls, 1979 and 1980: A Study of the General Elections, Howard R. Penniman, ed. Chapters by Alan C. Cairns, John Meisel, William P. Irvine, Robert J. Williams, John C. Courtney, Stephen Clarkson, Walter D. Young, Vincent Lemieux and Jean Crete, F. Leslie Seidle and Khayyam Zev Paltiel, Frederick J. Fletcher, and M. Janine Brodie and Jill Vickers. Appendix by Richard M. Scammon. (426 pp., cloth $17.25, paper $9.25)

France at the Polls: The Presidential Election of 1974, Howard R. Penniman, ed. Chapters by Roy Pierce, J. Blondel, Jean Charlot, Serge Hurtig, Marie-Thérèse Lancelot, Alain Lancelot, Alfred Grosser, and Monica Charlot. Appendix by Richard M. Scammon. (324 pp., $4.50)

The French National Assembly Elections of 1978, Howard R. Penniman, ed. Chapters by Roy Pierce, Jérôme Jaffré, Jean Charlot, Georges Lavau, Roland Cayrol, Monica Charlot, and Jeane J. Kirkpatrick. Appendix by Richard M. Scammon. (255 pp., $7.25)

Germany at the Polls: The Bundestag Election of 1976, Karl H. Cerny, ed. Chapters by Gerhard Loewenberg, David P. Conradt, Kurt Sontheimer, Heino Kaack, Werner Kaltefleiter, Paul Noack, Klaus Schönbach and Rudolf Wildenmann, and Max Kaase. Appendix by Richard M. Scammon. (251 pp., $7.25)

Greece at the Polls: The National Elections of 1974 and 1977, Howard R. Penniman, ed. Chapters by Roy C. Macridis, Phaedo Vegleris, J. C. Loulis, Thanos Veremis, Angelos Elephantis, Michalis Papayannakis, and Theodore Couloumbis. Appendix by Richard M. Scammon. (220 pp., $15.25 cloth, $7.25 paper)

India at the Polls: The Parliamentary Elections of 1977, Myron Weiner. (150 pp., $6.25)

Ireland at the Polls: The Dáil Elections of 1977, Howard R. Penniman, ed. Chapters by Basil Chubb, Richard Sinnott, Maurice Manning, and Brian Farrell. Appendixes by Basil Chubb and Richard M. Scammon. (199 pp., $6.25)

Israel at the Polls: The Knesset Election of 1977, Howard R. Penniman, ed. Chapters by Daniel J. Elazar, Avraham Brichta, Asher Arian, Benjamin Akzin, Myron J. Aronoff, Efraim Torgovnik, Elyakim Rubinstein, Leon Boim, Judith Elizur, Elihu Katz, and Bernard Reich. Appendix by Richard M. Scammon. (333 pp., $8.25)

Italy at the Polls: The Parliamentary Elections of 1976, Howard R. Penniman, ed. Chapters by Joseph LaPalombara, Douglas Wertman, Giacomo Sani, Giuseppe Di Palma, Stephen Hellman, Gianfranco Pasquino, Robert Leonardi, William E. Porter, Robert D. Putnam, and Samuel H. Barnes. Appendix by Richard M. Scammon. (386 pp., $5.75)

Italy at the Polls, 1979: A Study of the Parliamentary Elections, Howard R. Penniman, ed. Chapters by Sidney Tarrow, Giacomo

Sani, Douglas A. Wertman, Joseph LaPalombara, Gianfranco Pasquino, Robert Leonardi, Patrick McCarthy, Karen Beckwith, William E. Porter, and Samuel H. Barnes. Appendixes by Douglas A. Wertman and Richard M. Scammon. (335 pp., $16.25 cloth, $8.25 paper)

Japan at the Polls: The House of Councillors Election of 1974, Michael K. Blaker, ed. Chapters by Herbert Passin, Gerald L. Curtis, and Michael K. Blaker. (157 pp., $3)

A Season of Voting: The Japanese Elections of 1976 and 1977, Herbert Passin, ed. Chapters by Herbert Passin, Michael Blaker, Gerald L. Curtis, Nisihira Sigeki, and Kato Hirohisa. (199 pp., $6.25)

New Zealand at the Polls: The General Election of 1978, Howard R. Penniman, ed. Chapters by Stephen Levine, Keith Ovenden, Alan McRobie, Keith Jackson, Gilbert Antony Wood, Roderic Alley, Colin C. James, Brian Murphy, Les Cleveland, Judith Aitken, and Nigel S. Roberts. Appendix by Richard M. Scammon. (295 pp., $7.25)

Scandinavia at the Polls: Recent Political Trends in Denmark, Norway, and Sweden, Karl H. Cerny, ed. Chapters by Ole Borre, Henry Valen, Willy Martinussen, Bo Särlvik, Daniel Tarschys, Erik Allardt, Steen Sauerberg, Niels Thomsen, C. G. Uhr, Göran Ohlin, and Walter Galenson. (304 pp., $5.75)

Venezuela at the Polls: The National Elections of 1978, Howard R. Penniman, ed. Chapters by John D. Martz, Henry Wells, Robert E. O'Connor, David J. Myers, Donald Herman, and David Blank. Appendix by Richard M. Scammon. (287 pp., cloth $15.25, paper $7.25)

Democracy at the Polls: A Comparative Study of Competitive National Elections, David Butler, Howard R. Penniman, and Austin Ranney, eds. Chapters by David Butler, Arend Lijphart, Leon D. Epstein, Austin Ranney, Howard R. Penniman, Khayyam Zev Paltiel, Anthony Smith, Dennis Kavanagh, Ivor Crewe, Donald E. Stokes, Anthony King, and Jeane J. Kirkpatrick. (367 pp., $16.25 cloth, $8.25 paper)

Referendums: A Comparative Study of Practice and Theory, David Butler and Austin Ranney, eds. Chapters by Jean-François Aubert, Austin Ranney, Eugene C. Lee, Don Aitkin, Vincent Wright, Sten Sparre Nilson, Maurice Manning, and David Butler. (250 pp., $4.75)

At the Polls studies are forthcoming on the latest national elections in Australia, Belgium, Germany, Greece, Ireland, Israel, Jamaica, the Netherlands, New Zealand, Portugal, and Spain. In addition, cross-national volumes on the first elections to the European Parliament, women in electoral politics, and candidate selection are under way.

See also the first volume in a new series of studies of American elections:

The American Elections of 1980, Austin Ranney, ed. Chapters by Austin Ranney, Nelson W. Polsby, Charles O. Jones, Michael J. Malbin, Albert R. Hunt, Michael J. Robinson, William Schneider, Thomas E. Mann and Norman J. Ornstein, Anthony King, and Aaron Wildavsky. Statistical appendix. (391 pp., $16.25 cloth, $8.25 paper)

The second volume of the new series is forthcoming:

The American Elections of 1982, Norman J. Ornstein and Thomas E. Mann, eds. Chapters by Albert R. Hunt, Alan Ehrenhalt, Thomas E. Mann and Norman J. Ornstein, Larry J. Sabato, and John F. Bibby.

A NOTE ON THE BOOK

This book was edited by Katharine Tait, and Ann Gurian
and Donna Spitler of the Publications Staff
of the American Enterprise Institute.
The staff also designed the cover and format, with Pat Taylor.
The figures were drawn by Hördur Karlsson.
The text was set in Palatino, a typeface designed by Hermann Zapf.
Hendricks-Miller Typographic Company of Washington, D.C.,
set the type, and Thomson-Shore, Inc.,
of Dexter, Michigan, printed and bound the book,
using Warren's Olde Style paper.